# Money and Finance
# in Contemporary
# Yugoslavia

# Dimitrije Dimitrijevic
# George Macesich
foreword by
Milton Friedman

# Money and Finance in Contemporary Yugoslavia

PRAEGER SPECIAL STUDIES IN INTERNATIONAL ECONOMICS AND DEVELOPMENT

**Praeger Publishers**   New York   Washington   London

Library of Congress Cataloging in Publication Data

Dimitrijevic, Dimitrije.
    Money and finance in contemporary Yugoslavia.

    (Praeger special studies in international
economics and development)
    Bibliography: p.
    1. Finance—Yugoslavia.  2. Money—
Yugoslavia.  3. Monetary policy—Yugoslavia.
I. Macesich, George, 1927-     joint author.
II. Title.
HG186.Y8D55    1973      332.4'9497     72-92889

PRAEGER PUBLISHERS
111 Fourth Avenue, New York, N.Y. 10003, U.S.A.
5, Cromwell Place, London SW7 2JL, England

Published in the United States of America in 1973
by Praeger Publishers, Inc.

Printed in the United States of America

My first contact with Yugoslavia, and Dimitrije Dimitrijević, came more than a decade ago when I visited Yugoslavia to study monetary relations in a socialist country. Very shortly after landing at the Belgrade airport in the middle of the night on a plane from Moscow, we became aware that this was a socialist country in a rather special sense.

The initial pleasant shock was followed by many others. Here we found a society that was rediscovering the virtues of a market mechanism and that was exhibiting vigor, variety, and a healthy independence.

In my own special field, figures on the quantity of money, far from being a state secret, were published in full detail along with much other data in the National Bank's excellent monthly bulletin, available in English as well as Serbo-Croatian.

I was fortunate in having Dr. Dimitrijević, then as now at the Narodna Banka, the Central Bank of Yugoslavia, as a guide to the monetary data and financial system of Yugoslavia. With infinite goodwill, he explained to me out of his vast store of knowledge the novel elements of the system, answered numerous questions, and furnished the more elusive statistics I began to request.

On the monetary side, I quickly discovered that Yugoslavia fits into familiar molds, even with respect to quantitative magnitudes: for example, currency in public circulation amounted to the equivalent of about six weeks' personal income in Yugoslavia at the time, almost exactly the same as in neighboring capitalistic and at that time monarchist Greece. The concepts of demand and supply of money, and the elaborations of these concepts developed for advanced capitalistic countries, applied almost directly to socialist and underdeveloped Yugoslavia.

On the financial or credit side, the situation was very different. Many of the words were the same--banks, deposits, credits--but they corresponded to different substantive entities. The financial institutions had been constructed to serve as the controlling and monitoring elements of a highly centralized and collectivistic economic system. They were being reconstructed to serve the very different functions required by a decentralized system increasingly trying to combine market mechanisms with very different conceptions of property and property rights than we are accustomed to in the United States.

Ever since my first visit, I have followed the developments in Yugoslavia with great fascination, intrigued by the possibility of observing how its financial system would change under the pressures to adapt to the growing market orientation of the industrial structure.

The reader of this book could not have better teachers from whom to learn the present status of this still emerging financial structure than Dimitrije Dimitrijević and George Macesich.

Dr. Dimitrijević has been at the center of the developments, helping to guide them yet simultaneously observing them with the detached eye of the scholar. Thoroughly familiar with modern monetary theory and with financial institutions in the West, he has a solid basis for comparison. In charge of the compilation of the monetary statistics of Yugoslavia, he has been able to provide the basic material for the comprehensive and unique collection of data in the Appendixes. Dr. Macesich has specialized in money and banking since his days as a graduate student at the University of Chicago; he has done basic work on monetary developments in the United States before the Civil War, when it too was an underdeveloped country. In addition, he has long had a passionate interest in Yugoslavia, speaks, reads, and writes Serbo-Croatian fluently, is in charge of an exchange program between Florida State University and the University of Belgrade, and lectures on monetary theory and policy at the University of Belgrade where he is Professor of Economics with the Faculties of Political Science and Organizational Sciences.

You are in good hands.

The Yugoslav economic system and economic experience represent a stimulating challenge for both Western and Eastern economists. This is particularly true for economists working in the field of money and finance. There are at least two reasons: first, the specific institutional framework of the Yugoslav economic system; second, the frequent and significant institutional changes that have transformed the Yugoslav economic system from a centrally planned into a decentralized system based on individual decision-making and a market mechanism.

The Yugoslav economic system is unique when compared to both Western market and Eastern centrally planned economies. It represents a combination of socialist and market components: it combines the socialist principle of public ownership of means of production with the principles of individual decision-making and initiative, market valuation, and market integration of individual economic units. It is obvious that the role of money and finance, their working mechanisms and functional relationships, have necessarily been highly specific within this institutional environment. That is why the usual questions of monetary theory and monetary policy may have unusual answers under Yugoslav conditions. What is the role of money under these conditions? Does money matter in the Yugoslav economic system? What are the determinants of money supply and how stable is the demand function for money? How is money created? What is the mechanism and what are the effects of the adjustment processes of demand to supply of money? What is the role of monetary policy and how efficient is it within the Yugoslav framework? What is the role of financial intermediation and financial markets?

These and other related questions have had different answers in different times and from different schools of theory. Which of these answers fit the Yugoslav case? Does Yugoslav experience prove or disprove views presented by different monetary schools? Are the existing monetary theories at such a level of generality that they may cover the Yugoslav peculiarities, or does the specific Yugoslav experience require a specific monetary theory?

These are but a few of the many provocative questions Yugoslav experience provides for an expert in money and finance.  This study attempts to answer some of these questions.  Needless to say, not all questions will have complete answers.  Owing to the changing institutional structure and the difficulties created by significant and frequent changes in relevant functional relationships, some questions will be answered only in part and some will only be raised.

Our study of the problems of money and finance does not start from a _tabula rasa_.  It will be seen later that there already have been several investigations of the problems.  There has, moreover, been practical experience in the field of money and finance in Yugoslavia.  These investigations and experience have resulted in a consensus that a monetarist approach best fits the Yugoslav situation.  Indeed, the monetarist approach has always been dominant in the Yugoslav monetary field.  It was not superseded by Keynesian monetary theory before World War II.  After the war the dominant Marxist monetary theory, under conditions of paper money, in effect has meant acceptance of a strong monetarist approach--particularly since this approach is firmly supported by practical experience.

It is for that reason that this study accepts the monetarist approach as a starting hypothesis.  The study thus should be understood as the testing of a monetarist hypothesis under Yugoslav conditions.

The study is presented in four parts.  Part I is devoted to the institutional background and its changes, involving four stages of development:  perfect planning system, mixed central planning stage, first stage of decentralization, and advanced stage of decentralization.  Part II investigates the basic questions of monetary theory: definition of money, role of money, demand for money, creation of money, adjustment processes of demand to supply of money.  Part III deals with monetary policy:  role of monetary policy, problems of monetary policy goals, formation of monetary policy, instruments and efficiency of monetary policy.  Finally, Part IV presents a short summary of findings and prospects for future development of the Yugoslav financial system and changes in money and finance.

The Appendix presents extensive and comparative time-series data.  These data have not hitherto been available in one source.

# CONTENTS

LIST OF TABLES

xiv

LIST OF APPENDIX TABLES

# FINANCIAL SYSTEM

# 1

## DETERMINANTS OF
## THE FINANCIAL
## SYSTEM

### INTRODUCTION

For the purpose of this book the financial system is defined broadly. Three groups of closely related elements are considered: financial structure, fiscal system, and system of public debt management. The term "financial structure" includes financial institutions, financial instruments, and financial flows.

A broad definition of financial system is suitable for the interpretation of the Yugoslav experience because of the country's specific and frequently changing institutional structure. It is presumably easier to examine problems in the country's specific economic system if they are considered within the context of a broadly designed financial system than if they are interpreted partially and independently of such a system. The fact that these three groups of phenomena are dependent on nearly the same group of institutional determinants and that their development and changes in role, size, and pattern are closely interrelated and complementary requires their interpretation within a unit concept involving all of them.

Our presentation of the contemporary financial system of Yugoslavia will consider the existing financial system as the result of a continuous line of institutional development involving a series of successive interrelated changes in the real infrastructure* and financial suprastruc-

---

*Institutional structure as it is related to the organization of production, pricing, integration of the individual economic units, income distribution, saving, invest-

ture* of the economy.

Three reasons recommend this approach to the interpretation of the financial system of Yugoslavia. First, it will help to a better understanding of the forces that determined its development and of the nature and functioning of present institutions. Second, we may be able to draw general conclusions that are valid not only for Yugoslavia but for other countries as well. These general conclusions, for example, might be relevant to the "reform" processes in several socialist economies in Eastern Europe. Third, our approach will facilitate appraisal of the course future development of the Yugoslav financial system is likely to take.

This study provides an opportunity to examine several hypotheses dealing with financial structure and development in the case of a changing economy:

1. Economic growth requires adequate adjustment of a country's real infrastructure to the growing complexity of economic processes and changed determinants of functional relationships. Failure to adjust results in deterioration of efficiency in the economy and a slowing down in the rate of economic growth.

In the case of a central planning economic system as a starting point, these institutional changes are characterized by a process of decentralization of the central planning mechanism and the vesting of individual economic units (socialist enterprises particularly) with an increasing degree of decision-making power, which leads to an increase in the role and scope of the market mechanism.

2. Adjustments in the infrastructure require appropriate adjustments in the financial suprastructure. The infrastructure adaptations lead to an increase in the role of financial variables, induce autonomous financial processes (monetary processes, financial intermediation flows), and require appropriate financial mechanisms able to meet more sophisticated needs for financing and control of complex financial processes. This requires an increase in size and differentiation of financial institutions, financial instruments, and financial flows and organization of efficient financial markets (first money and then capital markets).

---

ment, foreign trade, and the ownership of the means of production.

*This includes the financial institutions, financial instruments, and financial interrelations.

3. Parallel to the increase in the role, size, and differentiation of financial structure, a complementary process of disintegration and decentralization of the all-inclusive fiscal system (in the case of a central planning system) should be involved, and adaptation of its pattern and targets to new requirements. At the same time, an increase in the size and differentiation of the public debt may be expected as the third parallel adjustment.

4. Adaptation of the financial system to changes in real infrastructure is an essential precondition for efficient functioning of real infrastructure and failure in this respect would require a backward readaptation to the level of efficiency of the financial system, e.g., recentralization of economic decision-making.

The general line of development indicated by the above hypotheses is not specific to the Yugoslav case. It is generally recognized that there is a close association between economic development and development of financial structure.[1] However, in the case of Yugoslavia the interrelationship is specific in many respects, primarily because of the specific starting point of the adjustment processes: the central planning system.

In the following four chapters we shall attempt to appraise the consistency of these hypotheses against Yugoslav experience. The empirical investigation will be based primarily on the Flow-of-Funds Accounts of the National Bank of Yugoslavia.[2] These accounts provide the most comprehensive and consistent body of information, involving both financial and nonfinancial transactions classified according to institutional sectors. These accounts are particularly useful in providing information about financial effects of infrainstitutional changes, particularly changes in sector distribution of saving and financial saving. The other basic sources of information are the Statisticki bilten Sluzbe drustvenog knjigovodsta (Statistical Bulletin of the Social Accounting Service)* and annual reports of the National Bank of Yugoslavia.


ECONOMIC GROWTH

To judge from the evidence presented in Table 1.1, a relatively high rate of economic growth has taken place in

---

*This monthly publication, issued by the Social Accounting Service, Belgrade, contains the most comprehensive and detailed data available in the financial field.

TABLE 1.1

Average Annual Rate of Increase in Gross National Product
at Constant Prices
(percentage)

| | Total | Per Capita |
|---|---|---|
| Central planning period (1947-52) | 4.8 | 3.3 |
| First stage of decentralization (1953-64) | 8.6 | 7.3 |
| Advanced stage of decentralization (1965-70) | 5.5 | 4.5 |

Source: Annual Report of the National Bank of Yugoslavia, 1962, 1971.

the Yugoslav economy, particularly in the period 1953-64.

The lower rate of increase in GNP[3] during the 1947-52 period reflects in part the decreasing efficiency of the economic system (a rigid central planning system) and in part the results of extraordinary difficulties brought about by the economic blockade of Yugoslavia by the Cominform countries in 1948 and later.[4] The lower rate of increase of GNP since 1964 can be explained mainly as a result of extensive stabilization measures taken as a part of the Economic Reform of 1965 and thereafter.*

Composition of the country's output has also changed. An increase in the share of industrial and nonagricultural production in total GNP has increased. At the same time the nonagricultural population rose from about 30 percent of total population in 1948 to 34 percent in 1953 and about 50 percent in 1968.**

---

*The Economic Reform measures and institutional changes are explained on pp. 42-49 of this study.

**Recent investigation shows that the percentage of nonagricultural population is even larger. If mixed households (at least one person working outside agriculture, e.g., in industry, mining, or transportation) are taken into account, nonagricultural population may reach more than two-thirds of total population. This is because the Yugoslav type of dispersed development of industry has given many members of farm families a chance to work outside agriculture.

6

These indicators suggest that the rate of economic growth of the Yugoslav economy has been sufficiently high to initiate significant institutional changes. This would be consistent with the above hypothesis. And, in fact, economic development was accompanied by fundamental institutional adjustments, as we shall now discuss.

## INSTITUTIONAL DEVELOPMENT UP TO 1964

This section examines the central planning stage and the first stage of decentralization. In order to facilitate understanding we shall present and discuss a hypothetical economic system with perfect central planning.

### Economic System with Perfect
### Central Planning

The term "central economic planning" is by no means as self-explanatory as it may seem. Economic systems that are usually called central planning systems (e.g., the Soviet Union) involve significant nonplanning components. Similarly, "market economies" comprise significant nonmarket, central planning components, including government intervention. It will help to clarify the issues we shall discuss in this section if the concept of a perfect economic central planning system is discussed first. This concept

TABLE 1.2

Gross National Product by Branches at Constant Prices,
1966
(percentage of total)

|  | 1952 | 1964 | 1968 | 1969 | 1970 |
|---|---|---|---|---|---|
| Industry and mining | 22 | 34 | 35 | 35 | 37 |
| Total nonagricultural production | 67 | 75 | 77 | 78 | 80 |
| Agriculture | 33 | 25 | 23 | 22 | 20 |

Source: Statisticki godisnjak Saveznog zavoda za statistiku, 1971.

7

is presented in the form of a hypothetical system, produced by extrapolating the basic components of existing central planning systems of the Soviet type. In a sense this system will be an antithesis of the perfect market system and will help to explain existing mixed central planning systems in the same way that a perfect market economy would serve to explain existing mixed market economic systems.

Accordingly, the concept of a perfect central economic planning system will be treated as the first link in the chain of institutional development of the contemporary Yugoslav economy. It will serve first to explain the central planning system that existed until 1952. Explanation of this system will facilitate understanding of the second stage of institutional developments during the period 1953-64, which we shall call the first stage of decentralization. This will provide a suitable basis for examination and analysis of the recent stage, which we shall call the advanced stage of decentralization.

## Infrainstitutional Structure

The basic feature of the institutional infrastructure of this system is social ownership of all means of production and centrally planned solutions to all basic economic problems (valuation, organization of production, income distribution, saving, investment), as opposed to the solution of these problems by the market mechanism in a perfect free-market economy. Prices are fixed by central planning authorities both for goods and services and for factors of production. They reflect neither consumer preferences nor producers' standards. They do not transmit these preferences and standards and do not influence allocation of inputs to competing areas. Wages are fixed and no differentials exist. Since all means of production are socialized, the interest rate does not exist as a price of capital. There is no consumer choice nor choice of education or occupation.

Organization of production (what to produce, how to produce, allocation of goods) is determined by central planners. Enterprises are only agents of central planners, obliged to fulfill detailed instructions concerning all elements of organization of production. They have no decision-making power. Allocation of goods and services involves all levels of the production-consumption-investment processes.

Saving is centrally determined and accumulated. Investment is completely planned by the central planning authorities. Foreign trade is fully centralized and regulated. The same is true for all foreign exchange transactions. There is no room for indirect economic policy measures.*

The use of the concept of financial system in this study requires an explanation of the financial structure, fiscal system, and debt management system. The definition of financial structure includes financial flows, financial institutions, financial instruments, financial markets, and monetary system.

Financial structure in the perfect central planning system is rather insignificant and undeveloped. The role of financial variables is reduced to the role of money, so that money is the only financial instrument (in addition to credits, if money is created by granting credits to enterprises rather than by issuing it). The structure of financial institutions involves only one bank, which is at the same time an agent of the central planning authorities, involved primarily in performing payment transactions, controlling legal conformity of money transactions, implementing plan targets, statistics, etc. Granting credits accounts for a minor part of its operations, and credits are granted in accordance with a detailed credit plan, which makes the bank nothing but an administrative agency of the central planning authority.

There is no need for financial intermediation and financial markets, in view of the fact that all saving and investment together with short-term credits, are centrally planned.

Thus, the monetary system is the only component of the financial structure that deserves attention. The monetary system in this study is defined to include functions of money, definition of money, monetary institutions, creation of money, demand function of money, adjustment processes of demand to supply of money, and payment mechanism.

The question of the functions of money in this type of economy first involves the question whether money is necessary at all. The fact that there are many economic

---

*Although our hypothetical system may look highly unrealistic, it has been argued that it approximates reality under conditions of extreme scarcity of capital and land and a very low level of production, where demand for goods has outpaced supply.

units that take part in production, income distribution, consumption, etc., and that there are many types of goods and services, necessarily leads to the conclusion that barter transactions cannot be used to organize solutions for problems of valuation, income distribution, exchange of goods and services, balancing of aggregate targets (e.g., consumption), and savings and that the economy is in need of monetary services.

However, this does not mean that monetary services in this economy are the same as in a market economy. Presumably the functions of money in this type of economic system are also specific. First, the unit-of-account function is specific in the sense that prices are centrally fixed, are arbitrary, and do not necessarily express scarcities, consumer preferences, or producers' standards. Thus, the unit-of-account function of money measures a quite different structure of values than in a market economy. Second, the medium-of-exchange function is specific because money is not used independently for buying goods and services. It follows planned transactions, e.g., allocation of goods and services, planned labor force, and wage rates. Thus, there is no room for the exchange function of money in a proper sense. The store-of-value function does not exist because there is no individual saving (except for short periods between two pay days). Finally, the function of deferred payments is negligible in this system of very poor financial flows.

The definition of money in this undifferentiated financial structure is very simple because there are no financial assets in the hands of the nonfinancial sector except money. The monetary institution is also very simple; it may be monobank or government. The process of the creation of money under these conditions is necessarily elementary. The supply function of money is reduced to bank credits if these are not created by government. The monobank system excludes problems of monetary multiplication and such relevant issues as public behavior and bank behavior. The creation of money is equal in effect to the creation of a monetary base of high-powered money that is equal to the money in circulation. Thus, money is created directly by monobank credits, without a time lag and multiplication and the concomitant uncertainty.

Demand for money under these conditions is necessarily confined to transaction purposes. However, it may be supposed that the monobank creates more money than is necessary for transaction purposes. Because of the impossibility of using this money for the purchase of additional goods or services, owing to their planned allocation, the holding of excess money may be called "quasi-demand for money." It is an important component of the demand function in this type of economic system, with very significant consequences. The existence of a quasi-demand for money (which should not be confused with a demand for quasi-money) means that all extra money is absorbed by moneyholders without any attempt to transform it into other types of asset and adjust their "portfolio" to the desired pattern. Thus, if the quantity of money is higher or equal to the transaction demand for money, there is monetary equilibrium.

It is obvious that the adjustment processes of demand to supply of money under these conditions are very simple. There are no adjustments in portfolio if the quantity of money is higher than the transaction demand for money. However, there are adjustment processes when the quantity of money is lower than the transaction demand. A shortage of money could presumably result in a delay of payments but not in portfolio adjustments or effects on demand for goods and services and financial assets. There is no room for wealth effects, substitution effects, or real balance effects in a perfect central planning system, because there is no room for free behavior on the part of individual economic units. The most likely reaction may be expected from central planners, who may quickly discover a shortage of money and, also very quickly, decide to create additional amounts of money.

The fiscal system in a perfect central planning system is far more comprehensive than in a market economy. If defined in a broad sense so as to include all government revenues and expenditures, it comprises all transactions related to savings, investment, and balance of payments, in addition to classic fiscal revenues and expenditures. Obviously, the pattern of these flows is necessarily different from that in a market economy. The fiscal system is part of a central planning mechanism, and fiscal flows are part of centrally planned flows. Thus, there is no need for a differentiated structure of taxes to be used for different purposes, and there is no need to have more than one source of revenue. The fiscal mechanism in a perfect central planning system involves all transactions performed by the financial structure except creation of money.

There is no need for debt management under perfect central planning. The system of comprehensive and detailed direct regulations leaves no room for indirect policy measures.

## Mixed Central Planning System

This is what is typically called a Soviet-type system. It is related to the economic system that existed in Yugoslavia in 1947-52 and that still exists, with some variations, in socialist countries of Eastern Europe. Unlike perfect central planning, it is not a hypothetical system.

The term "mixed centrally planned economic system" is to some extent self-explanatory. It indicates that the system is basically of the central planning type but that it includes nonplanning components. The mixed system will be interpreted by explaining its deviations from perfect central planning.

### Institutional Infrastructure

Departures from perfect central planning start with the basic components--social ownership of the means of production--although generally speaking the principle of social ownership was strictly implemented in manufacturing, mining, transportation, and communications. The greatest departure from the rule existed in agriculture, where nearly 90 percent of the land was in the hands of private producers.* In addition, a major part of the means of production in handicrafts was also in private hands. Thus, a significant part of the means of production escaped rigid central planning regulation and left room for free decision-making (although limited by extensive control measures**).

Another significant deviation from perfect central planning was in the field of labor. First, free choice of education and occupation existed to a significant degree even in the period of the most rigid labor regulations. Second, labor proved most resistant to central planning control, causing serious disproportions and inefficiencies in implementing planned targets. Thus, productivity and quality of goods significantly escaped central planning. This failure to control the quality of labor, in spite of wage policy and broad educational, political, and other measures, was one of the main reasons for abandoning the system in 1953.

---

*Except for a relatively short period when attempts were made to introduce collective farms.
**For example, obligatory delivery of crops, fixed prices for the main agricultural products, the system of taxation, etc.

Another departure was related to inefficiencies in defining pla.. targets exactly. In the first place, it was impossible to formulate production targets with full details of type and quality of goods, for technical reasons and because of lack of information. Thus, instead of individual goods, aggregates of similar types and qualities of goods were planned. The number of these aggregates amounted to not more than 10 percent of the total number of types of goods. The same was true for the planning of inputs. The impossibility of defining plan targets in complete detail left significant room for "behavioristic" variables, which could lead to deviations from expectations and result in disproportions.* In the second place, calculation of fixed prices by central planners was very arbitrary, partly because of lack of information on consumer preferences and other elements of demand, and partly because of technical inefficiency in using the information available. The arbitrary structure of relative prices blurred the problems of opportunity cost and economic allocation of savings and was one of the main reasons for the decreasing efficiency of the economy.

The fourth point of departure from a perfect central planning system involved consumer behavior. Consumers were free to decide how to use their incomes, and quite often their decisions differed from the expectations of the central planners. During the period of acute shortages of goods after World War II it was relatively easy to adjust** the structure of production to the structure of demand. As production increased, however, it became more difficult to predict consumer preferences, and the assortment and quality of goods produced increasingly deviated from what in fact consumers demanded. A shortage of some types of goods, concurrent with the overaccumulation of goods that were not desired, increasingly plagued the economy, leading to waste of resources and increased dissatisfaction on the part of consumers.

Thus, the system in effect had a dual character; one part was centrally planned while the other escaped central planning control. This duality existed in both the social-

---

*For instance, if it was easier to fulfill a planned target defined as an aggregate quantity of some type of goods that might have several sizes by producing the larger sizes, producers were inclined to do so, regardless of the demand.

**Especially with the aid of various rationing devices.

ist sector (socialist enterprises, government, other institutions, and collective farms) and the private sector (households, private producers).

This duality in the economic system resulted in a similar duality in attempted solutions of basic economic problems. Organization of production was only in part under central planning control, especially the production of private producers. Pricing also largely escaped central control on part of the goods and services produced by private producers, especially those on farmers' markets. Moreover, the quality of goods could not be controlled, so that price control on goods produced by socialist enterprises was rather deficient. Wage rates were fixed, but the application of the system of fixed wage rates led to various violations, since in practice it was impossible to control the classification of labor. Saving and investment were highly centralized and controlled, which left comparatively little room for private saving and investment. The inability to control the demand structure resulted in overaccumulation of undesired goods, which meant in effect a nonplanned correction of the saving-consumption ratio and the allocation of saving.

The dual infrainstitutional structure of the mixed central planning system resulted in a significant departure from perfect central planning. The deviation, however, was significant only in the monetary field; financial intermediation and debt management remained unimportant.* The fiscal system, summarized in the national budget, involved nearly all saving-investment flows, in addition to the standard government revenues and expenditures, as in a perfect central planning economy.

The monetary system was significantly different from that of a perfect central planning system. The main departure was the result of the dual character of the mixed system, which was reflected in the dual character of the monetary system. Money in the hands of the socialist sector had mainly the same character as in a perfect central planning system, while money in the hands of households and individual producers had the same character and functions as in a market economy. There were thus two defini-

---

*As we shall discuss later, there were two public loans in this period. However, due to their very limited role and amount, these loans cannot properly be called debt management.

tions of money:  "accounting money" and currency in circulation.*

The conversion of the socialist sector's accounting money into private-sector money was under the tight control of the "cash plans."  The cash plan was at the same time the main instrument of monetary policy in the mixed central planning system.[5]

Monetary institutions also deviated from the perfect central planning model.  In addition to the National Bank there were numerous other banks.[6]  However, since most short-term crediting was performed by the National Bank acting as both a central and a commercial bank, in practice the system was very close to the model.

The process of creation of money was different for money in the hands of the socialist sector and for that in the hands of the private sector.  Money in the socialist sector was created mainly by bank credits.  Money was obtained by the private sector through its dealings with the socialist sector.  Payments to members of the private sector were necessarily made in currency, since they did not have bank accounts, and this in effect led to an increase in the currency in circulation.  Expenditures by the private sector were also made in currency, and when they were made to the socialist sector this led to an outflow of currency to the bank accounts of the socialist sector.  The difference between the two flows resulted in a change in the amount of currency in circulation.**  The inflows (receipts by the private sector) were controlled by the cash plan, which served as the instrument of regulation of the quantity of currency in circulation.  Outflows were also part of the cash plan.  They were, however, mainly dependent upon the autonomous behavior of the private sector, particularly how much of current receipts they used for buying goods from socialist enterprises, which was far less controllable than inflow.

---

*Currency in circulation was defined as currency outside banks and post offices.  Since those in the socialist sector were not allowed to hold currency (they were obliged to deposit all currency received in a bank account), "currency in circulation" meant the currency in the hands of the private sector.

**Monetary authorities paid great attention to changes in the amount of currency in circulation, since it was considered the only type of money.  Ten-day reports were issued on both the amount and the outflow and inflow, which led to changes in the cash plan.

The demand function for money in the hands of the socialist sector was very close to that in the perfect central planning system. It was quite different, however, in the private sector, where in a very general way it resembled the demand function for money in market economies. It involved some specific variables. First, in place of the usual market-economy component of expectation of prive-level changes, expectation of changes in assortment and quality of goods was one of the main determinants of demand for money. When producers responded sluggishly to consumer preferences, the assortment of goods was usually inadequate. The expectation of its improvement was a significant reason to hold additional quantities of money in order to buy later; expectation of its deterioration led to the spending of all present holdings of money and even to borrowing.* Second, the role of the interest rate (paid on savings deposits, the only financial investment) was insignificant. Third, the relatively low incomes in the private sector left little room for saving and financial investment. Thus, the demand for money was at a relatively low level and rather unstable.

The adjustment processes also had specific characteristics. In the socialist sector they were similar to those in a perfect central planning system. In the private sector a unique feature was that supply of money adjusted to demand, instead of demand to supply. This was because the quantity of currency in circulation was created as the difference between the receipts and expenditures of the private sector in relation to the socialist sector, not as a result of bank credits. When the supply of money was greater than the demand, for example, the private sector increased its expenditures by buying goods and services

---

*If price expectation is defined in a more general way as expectation of change in purchasing power of money, under conditions of poor assortment and fixed prices purchasing power primarily means what in fact can be bought. In a market economy the assortment of goods adapts comparatively rapidly to consumer preferences, involving changes in prices in the meantime, so that the problem is not what can be bought but at what price. Thus, expectation of changes in assortment and quality of goods and services may be considered a logical counterpart to price expectation in a market economy, both of them being expectations of changes in the purchasing power of money (real money balances).

from the socialist sector, thus decreasing the amount of money to the desired level, and vice versa. The effects of the supply-to-demand adjustment processes were directly channeled to prices and/or inventories, without damaging (at least in the interim) the financial markets, e.g., financial investments, changes in interest rates, and prices of securities; and there was a relatively shorter lag than in a developed market economy. In the case of increased buying from socialist enterprises, there was only an inventory effect of deterioration of assortment. In the case of increased buying on the farmers' market, there was both an inventory and a price effect.

Since these effects were very significant, the amount of currency in circulation was followed and carefully controlled.

## Fiscal System

The fiscal system was very close to that under a perfect central planning system. Both classic budgetary and investment transactions were concentrated in the national budget, which also included the gross savings of the socialist sector and the financial saving of the private sector.

The dual character of the system resulted in significant departures from the perfect central planning system. The existence of the private sector required specific fiscal measures for "sector redistribution" purposes (in addition to fixing the prices of private-sector products at lower levels than those of socialist-sector products), to transfer savings from the private sector to the national budget. The principal taxes on which this operation depended were the turnover tax, taxes on private-sector income, and taxes on income from property.[7]

## Debt Management

There were two public loans during this period: one in 1948 (35 million dinars) to help in the implementation of the First Economic Plan, and the second in 1950 (30 million dinars) to help overcome the difficulties caused by the economic blockade imposed by the Cominform countries. In addition to the classic aim of collecting sources of public use, these loans were intended to decrease the quantity of money in the hands of the private sector, which in effect meant currency in circulation. Thus, they were used partly as an instrument of monetary policy. The amount

of these loans, however, was relatively small (free disposable saving by socialist enterprises and households was
relatively insignificant), so that neither loan really
represented a significant deviation from debt management
under a perfect central planning system.

## Economic Policy Instruments

The dual character of the mixed central planning system necessitated a combination of direct and indirect economic policy instruments instead of direct instruments only
as in a perfect central planning system. Thus, in addition to extensive direct measures such as the regulation
of organization of production, pricing, saving, investment,
and foreign transactions, there were such indirect measures
as monetary regulations in the private sector, fiscal policy, and even an element of debt management. The role of
direct measures, however, was dominant. Indirect measures
played a secondary role.

## First Stage of Decentralization

Changes in institutional infrastructure have been
widely discussed elsewhere.[8] The purpose of this section
is to underscore only the basic and the most relevant institutional modifications. To simplify the interpretation
the period under consideration (1953-64) will be discussed
as a whole, even though with some justification it may be
divided into several subperiods.

The fundamental institutional changes in this period
included both economic and sociopolitical alterations.
From the economic point of view there is a consensus that
institutional changes were aimed at improving the efficiency
of the economy. The mixed central planning system showed
increasing inefficiency in solving the country's basic economic problems. It particularly hampered the implementation of basic policy targets in the field of economic growth.

The basic idea (and it was heresy) was that the socialist economy did not necessarily imply a rigid central
planning mechanism and that the solution of economic problems should not be burdened by dogmatic and arbitrary ideas
about the socialist economic system. This nonconformist
approach led to fundamental institutional changes in the
real infrastructure first and then in the financial super-
structure.

## Infrainstitutional Changes

Preparations for fundamental institutional changes started several years before they were in fact introduced in 1953. The most important of these preparations was the passage of the Basic Law on the Management of Enterprises by Working Collectives (June 1950), which introduced the principle of workers' self-management. The actual changes were introduced in 1953, involving the basic components of the economic and sociopolitical system, such as social ownership of means of production, the planning mechanism, the organizational structure of socialist enterprises, the organization of production, the pricing mechanism, the income distribution mechanism, formation of savings, the investment mechanism, and the foreign trade and foreign exchange system.

Social ownership of the means of production remained the basic component of the economic system. However, its character was fundamentally changed by the introduction of the principle of workers' self-management, i.e., that workers are to manage enterprises independently of government and to decide how to use them. This modification had fundamental economic and sociopolitical consequences and represented the basis for all other institutional changes. It became the core of the so far unique economic system of Yugoslavia.

The planning mechanism was radically changed and with it the burden of rigid central planning. The planning mechanism was decentralized, and indicative planning was substituted for compulsory planning. The vertical structure of compulsory plans was dismantled, and individual enterprises, government bodies, and institutions made their own plans independently, without central control either in planning or in implementation. This change increased the role of the market mechanism in solving economic problems, particularly in pricing and the organization of production, so that the Yugoslav economic system became a combination of socialist planning and the market mechanism.

The organization of production was the field that underwent the most radical institutional changes. Instead of trying to reach rigid and detailed central-plan targets, enterprises were free to decide about what, how much, and how to produce, where to buy input materials, and to whom to sell their products.

The pricing-of-goods mechanism obviously had to be changed in accordance with the changes in the organization of production. Instead of a central calculation and the

19

fixing of prices of goods and services, a system with a free-market mechanism for price formation was introduced. However, because of an inherited distortion of relative prices, it was difficult to open the economy completely.

One consequence was that the prices of a significant number of goods (especially raw materials) and services remained under central control, e.g., ceiling prices, freezing of prices.

The pricing mechanism in this period left much to be desired. Pricing of goods was basically entrusted to the market mechanism, with significant limitations. The pricing of factors of production, however, remained under tight central regulation. This inconsistency remained one of the weakest points during this stage of development of the Yugoslav economic system. Its resolution is one of the basic goals of the next stage.

In the case of wages, the system of taxing the income of enterprises left relatively little room for free decisions by enterprises even in the latest years of this period. As to the interest rate, the main instrument for its regulation was the fixing of a ceiling on the rate that could be charged in granting credits.

Income distribution was largely controlled by the system of pricing goods and factors of production, as well as by a comprehensive system of taxing socialist enterprises. However, partly because of a decrease in these regulations during this period and partly because of the high rate of increase in GNP, the amount of free disposable income was increasing significantly. In addition, extensive regulation of income distribution did not mean centralization of incomes. On the contrary, an increase in the share of decentralized agencies--such as republican and local government bodies, other institutions, and socialist enterprises --in income distribution represented one of the most significant characteristics of institutional development in this period. One of the most relevant determinants of changes in the pattern of saving formation will show more clearly the significance of these changes.

Saving formation was under government control to a great extent.* There were, however, two significant

---

*The main instruments of saving regulation were tax on capital of enterprises, tax on income of enterprises, compulsory contributions of socialist enterprises to investment loan funds at all levels of government, and compulsory allocation of depreciation funds. These instruments, to-

changes in the pattern of saving formation in comparison
with the previous central planning period. First, saving
formation became highly decentralized, although largely
regulated, primarily in favor of the republican and local
governments and socialist enterprises. Second, in spite
of extensive regulations, the share of voluntary saving
in total gross saving was increased from about 10 percent
in the central planning period to about 25 percent at the
end of this period. This was partly the result of the decreasing degree of regulation (although it remained very
extensive) and partly owing to a rapid increase in GNP.

The Flow-of-Funds Accounts of the National Bank of
Yugoslavia show that the sector pattern of saving formation
was fundamentally changed in favor of decentralized savers
and that voluntary saving increased significantly although
it remained relatively small.

In the foreign trade and foreign exchange system fundamental changes occurred. In spite of this, however, it
remained the most tightly regulated area of the economy.
Institutional changes mainly referred to decentralization
of foreign trade, so that foreign trade was entrusted to
individual socialist enterprises, both specialized export-
ers-importers and other enterprises predominantly dealing
in other activities. The system was very liberal, in this
sense, so that the number of enterprises dealing in foreign
trade greatly increased. Contrary to decentralization in
the organization of foreign trade, the system of foreign
trade (particularly imports) remained highly regulated.
The same was valid for the foreign exchange system.[9] It
will be seen later that foreign trade and foreign exchange
regulations are the most conservative fields of the economic system and that they prove resistant to attempts at
radical liberalization even in the next stage of institutional development.

Investment, like saving, was under extensive government control. Roughly, the percentage of voluntary saving

---

gether with the instruments of income distribution, were
changed several times; and this pattern illustrates regulation of saving and income distribution in the later period
in this stage of institutional development of the Yugoslav
economic system. The additional, specific instrument of
saving regulation was a system of earmarking of investment
sources so that they could not be used for other purposes,
e.g., depositing of earmarked sources in separate accounts
and then control of their use.

in total gross saving (Table 1.3) illustrates how the role of free decision in the investment process was significantly increased over that of the previous central planning system. It remained, however, far less dependent on economic reasoning than in a market economy.

Financial saving, defined as the difference between gross saving and investment expenditures, reflects changes in the amount and in sector distribution. Flow-of-Funds Accounts of the National Bank of Yugoslavia show that the pattern of financial saving was also fundamentally changed in favor of decentralized savers. However, the share of households and private firms in financial saving remained insignificant, as did their share in gross saving.

Tables 1.3 and 1.4 present the effects of institutional changes in the planning mechanism, organization of production, pricing, income distribution, saving, and investment. At the same time they represent a basis for an understanding of the institutional changes in the financial field. The changed pattern of formation of saving and financial saving have created new needs for financing.

## Adjustments in the Financial System

Institutional changes in the planning mechanism, organization of production, pricing, income distribution, saving, and investment brought about fundamental changes in the financial sector and in the role of financial variables. First, changes in the planning mechanism, organization of production, and pricing resulted in a substantial increase in the role of money. Second, changes in income distribution, saving, and investment created a new need for financial intermediation and required differentiation in financial flows, financial instruments, and financial institutions. Along with these changes in the financial structure the fiscal system had to be adapted to the new institutional framework.

Financial institutions underwent a process of substantial proliferation and differentiation.* First, "investment

---

*The term "financial institutions" is interpreted in a broader sense for the purposes of this study. In addition to financial intermediaries it includes "semifinancial intermediaries," institutions that for example accept financial liabilities but do not create financial assets, and vice versa. The principal institutions of this type in Yugoslavia were "investment loan funds," which granted

TABLE 1.3

Gross Saving by Sector
(percentage of total)

| | 1950 | 1953 | 1958 | 1963 | 1964 |
|---|---|---|---|---|---|
| Socialist enterprises | | 29 | 42 | 35 | 41 |
| Local governments[a] | | 7 | 23 | 27 | 29 |
| Other organizations and un-classified | | 7 | 1 | 11 | 11 |
| Households and private pro-ducers | | 10 | 9 | 9 | 10 |
| Bank's own funds | | -- | -- | -- | -- |
| Total decentralized savings | 10[b] | 53 | 75 | 82 | 91 |
| Federal government[a] | 90 | 47 | 25 | 18 | 9 |
| Total savings, billions of dinars[c] | | 4.1 | 7.3 | 19.4 | 26.4 |
| Voluntary savings (percentage of total savings) | 10[b] | 19 | 33 | 38 | 46 |
| Percentage of GNP ratio | | 36 | 51 | 42 | 43 |

[a]Including investment loan funds (contributions to these funds by socialist enterprises, interest on loans, taxes).

[b]Rough estimate.

[c]Amounts are shown in new dinars, established after the Economic Reform of 1965, the ratio being 100 old dinars = 1 new dinar. All dinar amounts in this study are shown in new dinars..

Sources: Flow-of-Funds Accounts of the National Bank of Yugoslavia; Annual Report of the National Bank of Yugoslavia.

TABLE 1.4

Financial Surpluses and Deficits of Sectors
(billions of dinars)

| | 1953 | 1958 | 1963 | 1964 |
|---|---|---|---|---|
| Nonfinancial Sectors | | | | |
| Socialist enterprises | -2.7 | -2.9 | -7.8 | -10.7 |
| Local governments | 0.0 | -0.1 | 0.3 | -0.3 |
| Other organizations and unclassified | 0.1 | -0.3 | 0.9 | 4.2 |
| Households and private producers | 0.1 | 0.2 | 0.2 | 0.5 |
| Total decentralized | -2.5 | -3.1 | -6.4 | -6.3 |
| Federal government | 0.3 | -0.2 | -0.8 | -0.5 |
| Total nonfinancial sectors | -2.2 | -3.3 | -7.2 | -6.8 |
| Financial Sectors | | | | |
| Local investment loan funds | 0.3 | 1.3 | 3.1 | 2.7 |
| Monetary system (own funds) | -- | -- | -- | -- |
| Investment banking (own funds) | -- | -- | -- | -- |
| Total decentralized | 0.3 | 1.3 | 3.1 | 2.7 |
| Federal investment loan funds | 1.3 | 1.8 | 3.5 | 2.5 |
| Total financial sectors | 1.6 | 3.1 | 6.6 | 5.2 |
| Total domestic sectors, net (balance of payments deficits -, surpluses +) | -0.7 | -0.2 | -0.6 | -1.6 |
| Total domestic positive financial saving | 2.1 | 3.4 | 8.0 | 9.9 |
| Decentralized domestic positive financial saving, percentage of total | 9 | 50 | 66 | 80 |

Sources: Flow-of-Funds Accounts of the National Bank of Yugoslavia; Annual Report of the National Bank of Yugoslavia.

loan funds" were established at all levels of government: federal, republic, district, and commune. These funds were entrusted to investment financing according to economic plans of corresponding government bodies. As stated earlier, under central planning investment transactions were included in the national budget. The national budget now retained only classic government budget transactions, transferring investment transactions partly to investment loan funds and partly to socialist enterprises and other institutions. Thus, investment loan funds may be interpreted as a specific form of government intervention in the investment processes. The main innovation was that these funds granted investment credits instead of grants within the national budget as in the central planning period. The sources, however, remained taxes as before. In later years interest on credit and (in gross terms) repayments of credits became a very significant source for these funds.

In 1955 a new type of investment loan fund was introduced, pertaining specifically to the area of housing financing. These funds were established at the republic and commune levels. The sources were compulsory contributions by enterprises in the socialist sector. Another type of investment loan fund introduced in 1962 provided for financing of socialist enterprises that were having temporary difficulties and were not eligible for regular crediting through normal channels. These funds were also established at republic and commune levels and again relied on compulsory contributions by socialist enterprises.

At the end of this period the number of these funds had reached nearly 2,000, and a process of abolishment was started, leading to their substantial reduction.

Fundamental changes also occurred in the banking structure. First, in 1953 and 1954 all banks were merged with the National Bank of Yugoslavia, so that by the end of 1954 there was only one bank. In 1955, however, a process of decentralization was begun with the creation of a federal

---

credits for investment financing on the basis of sources mainly from taxes. The reason for using a broader definition of financial institutions is to make a broader basis for interpretation of a nondifferentiated and highly specific financial structure. The narrow definition used in developed market economies and including only financial intermediaries would exclude the majority of financial transactions and thus make interpretation of the financial structure inadequate and incomplete.

25

bank, called the Yugoslav Bank for Foreign Trade, and a great number of local banks.*  During the next years two additional federal banks were established, the Investment Bank and the Bank for Agriculture; in addition, the Postal Saving Bank and the number of local banks were increased. The process of proliferation of banks ended in 1961, when a process of merging once more began.  At the same time all local banks, except communal banks, were abolished. A new type of bank was introduced on the republic level, which was to be dominant in investment operations.  The year was very important also from the point of view of decentralization of bank operations.  Up to 1961 the major part of short-term credit operations was performed by the National Bank.[10]  In 1961 nearly all short-term credit operations were transferred to other banks.  The National Bank became in effect a central bank.

The third significant change was introduced in 1963 when all banks were authorized to perform investment crediting in addition to short-term crediting.  At the end of this period the banking structure became highly decentralized, both from the point of view of number and types of banks and from the point of view of bank operations.

By the end of 1963 the number of other banks amounted to 232, with an additional 277 branches.  Table 1.5 shows the decreasing share of the National Bank and the increasing share of investment loan funds and other banks in financial operations, based on the amount of financial assets.

Finally, a specific financial institution should be mentioned.  The Social Accounting Service, established as an independent body in 1962, had in prior years been a part of the National Bank of Yugoslavia.  Three kinds of operation are performed by this institution:

1.  Control of the legal conformity of money transactions, particularly as to the correct use of earmarked resources, and of the final accounts of socialist enterprises and other institutions.
2.  Checking on all payments.  For this purpose the institution works as an agent of banks, performing all related bookkeeping transactions on their behalf.
3.  Collection of statistics and making analyses based on them.

------

*For example, communal banks, cooperative banks (for crediting cooperatives in agriculture), and municipal savings banks.

TABLE 1.5

Assets of Financial Institutions

| | Billions of Dinars | | | | Percentage of Total | | | |
|---|---|---|---|---|---|---|---|---|
| | 1952 | 1953 | 1960 | 1963 | 1952 | 1953 | 1960 | 1963 |
| Investment loan funds | -- | 2.3 | 20.7 | 39.6 | -- | 28 | 52 | 51 |
| National Bank of Yugoslavia[a] | 5.0 | 5.8 | 9.9 | 9.5 | 100 | 72 | 25 | 12 |
| Other banks | 0.0 | 0.0 | 9.1 | 28.0 | 0.0 | 0.0 | 23 | 37 |
| Total | 5.0 | 8.1 | 39.7 | 77.1 | | | | |

[a]Excluding credits to other banks.

Sources: Statisticki bilten Sluzbe drustvenog knjigo-vodsta, No. 10 (1970); unpublished materials for 1952 and 1953.

Insurance institutions were not significant from the financial point of view. Social insurance was organized on the basis of the revenue-equals-expenditures principle, with relatively insignificant reserves. Life insurance was comparatively small, so that the premium reserves were negligible. In addition, all reserves had to be kept in bank deposits.

The first stage of decentralization ended with the following financial institutions in existence:

Financial Institutions at the
End of 1963

Banks

> National Bank of Yugoslavia (head office plus 6 offices in 6 socialist republics)

Federal banks: Yugoslav Bank for Foreign Trade,
    Yugoslav Investment Bank, Yugoslav Agricultural
    Bank (18 branches)
Republic banks (8)
Communal banks (220 banks, 259 branches)

Investment Loan Funds

General Investment Loan Fund (federal)
Republic investment loan funds (8)
District and communal investment loan funds (400
    approximately)
Republic housing funds (8)
Communal housing funds (400 approximately)
Republic Joint Reserve Funds of Enterprises (8)
Communal Joint Reserve Funds of Enterprises (400
    approximately)

All banks and investment loan funds except federal
banks, the Postal Saving Bank, the General Investment Fund,
and the National Bank of Yugoslavia were organized on a
regional principle, working only in the territory of the
governmental authority that had established the bank or
fund.

The number of financial instruments increased substantially. Their differentiation, however, did not make significant progress. The larger number of financial instruments was the result of the changed system of investment
financing, by credits instead of by grants. In addition,
this increase reflected an increase in GNP and a growth in
the need for financing.

The differentiation of financial instruments mainly
concerned deposits and credits, i.e., the field of bilateral instruments. The number of bonds in use remained insignificant. The differentiation of deposits was partly
the result of increased need for financial investments
(savings deposits, time deposits) and partly the result of
monetary fiscal regulations (restricted deposits, i.e.,
deposits that may be used only for specific purposes and
after a specified period of time). The differentiation of
bank credits reflected expansion of bank operations, particularly in the field of investment financing. Introduction of trade credits was the result of increased decision
power of enterprises and the increased role of the market
mechanism.

Financial flows increased to a large extent: first,
because of the changed mechanism of investment financing

TABLE 1.6

Financial Instruments
(billions of dinars at end of year)

|  | 1950 | 1953 | 1958 | 1963 |
|---|---|---|---|---|
| Nonfinancial Sectors |  |  |  |  |
| Money | 1.1 | 3.1 | 5.6 | 14.8 |
| Currency | 0.4 | 0.7 | 1.4 | 3.6 |
| Deposit money | 0.7 | 2.4 | 4.2 | 11.4 |
| Other sight deposits | 0.1 | 0.3 | 1.7 | 3.9 |
| Restricted deposits | 0.2 | 0.8 | 1.8 | 6.4 |
| Time deposits | -- | -- | -- | 1.1 |
| Bank bonds | -- | -- | -- | 0.1 |
| Government bonds | 0.1 | -- | -- | 0.2 |
| Trade and other direct credits | -- | 1.6 | 7.1 | 14.9 |
| Foreign assets | 0.2 | 0.4 | 0.4 | 0.3 |
| Other financial assets | 0.0 | 0.0 | 1.6 | 1.9 |
| Total | 1.5 | 5.8 | 18.2 | 43.6 |
| Financial Sectors |  |  |  |  |
| Short-term bank credits | 1.1 | 5.3 | 13.2 | 31.3 |
| Investment bank credits | -- | -- | -- | 2.7 |
| Credits by investment loan funds | -- | 1.7 | 11.5 | 37.0 |
| Other financial assets | 0.2 | 1.5 | 3.5 | 5.4 |
| Total | 1.1 | 8.1 | 28.2 | 76.4 |
| Total financial assets | 2.8 | 14.3 | 46.4 | 120.0 |
| Money supply | 1.1 | 3.3 | 5.6 | 14.8 |
| Financial assets-GNP ratio | -- | 2.9 | 2.3 | 2.6 |

Sources: Flow-of-Funds Accounts of the National Bank of Yugoslavia; Annual Report of the National Bank of Yugoslavia, 1969; unpublished sources for 1950.

and, second, because of increased GNP and saving-GNP ratio and the increased need for financing in the process of decentralization of economic decision-making power. The semifinancial intermediation flows had the highest rate of increase. Direct credits outstanding remained relatively small.

Table 1.7 distinguishes two kinds of borrowing from banks: borrowing from the monetary system and borrowing from investment banking. The former term refers to short-term bank operations and the latter to investment opera-

tions. Both types of operation were performed by each
bank. Investment operations included collection of investment resources (own funds and time deposits) and granting
credits on the basis of these resources. All other operations were classified as short-term operations. Banks were
obliged to make two separate balance sheets: one for
short-term operations and one for investment operations.
The first presented assets and liabilities of the monetary
system; the second presented those of investment banking.
These two terms thus refer to two departments of the whole
banking structure.

The establishment of investment banking in the above
sense in 1963 represented a significant change in the functions of banking. This change, introduced at the end of

TABLE 1.7

Borrowing[a]
(billions of dinars)

| | 1950[c] | 1953 | 1958 | 1963 | 1964 |
|---|---|---|---|---|---|
| Direct borrowing[b] | 0.0 | 0.3 | 1.4 | 2.4 | 2.7 |
| Indirect borrowing from: | | | | | |
| Monetary system | 0.2 | 0.7 | 1.0 | 4.6 | 3.1 |
| Investment banking | -- | -- | -- | 2.5 | 5.7 |
| Investment loan funds | -- | 1.7 | 2.5 | 4.5 | 6.1 |
| Total | 0.2 | 2.4 | 3.5 | 11.6 | 14.9 |
| Total domestic borrowing | 0.2 | 2.5 | 4.9 | 14.0 | 17.6 |
| Foreign borrowing | 0.1 | 0.2[c] | 0.6 | 0.4 | 1.9 |
| Total borrowing | 0.3 | 2.7 | 5.5 | 14.4 | 19.5 |
| Total borrowing-GNP ratio in percentage of GNP | 10 | 24 | 28 | 31 | 32 |

[a]Borrowing of nonfinancial sectors from financial sectors (indirect credits) and nonfinancial sectors (direct
credits).

[b]Net trade credits of socialist enterprises, excluding
intercrediting of these enterprises.

[c]Approximation.

Sources: Flow-of-Funds Accounts of the National Bank
of Yugoslavia; Annual Report of the National Bank of Yugoslavia, 1969; Statisticki bilten Sluzbe drustvenog knjigovodsta, No. 2 (1966), 1953 data.

the period under discussion, belongs more to the next period of institutional development. Its importance here is
that it serves as a starting point of a significant development in the field of financial intermediation.

Table 1.7 shows that even transactions that were performed by financial intermediaries were of a bilateral
character and under conditions of no open market institutions and instruments. Another specific feature of financial flows was their regional confinement owing to the
dominant influence on the banks' credit policy of local
government bodies.

Under a relatively low interest-rate policy (which
amounted to about 3 percent for investment credits and
about 7 percent for short-term credits, parallel with a
steady increase in price level at a rate even higher than
the highest interest rates for credits) and relatively
low risk elasticity, demand for credits outpaced supply.
In addition, the regional compartmentalization of financial
flows made financial disequilibrium even more pronounced.
Thus, the functioning of the financial structure during
the period was burdened by many fundamental imperfections,
which marred the economic allocation of saving. As we
shall see, improvement of the functioning of the financial
structure was one of the primary goals of the reform under-
taken during the next stage of development of the Yugoslav
economic system.

The monetary system was fundamentally changed in this
period. Changes in the quality of money, the role of
money, creation of money, demand for money, and adjustment
processes were far more significant than in the sector of
financial intermediation. It may be said that this period
was primarily a period of changes in the monetary part of
the financial structure, leaving the majority of changes
in financial intermediation for the next period of institutional development.

First, the quality of money in the hands of the socialist sector was fundamentally changed. Regular fiat
money was substituted for the previous "accounting money."
It is obvious that this change had to have very significant
monetary consequences.*

---

*This change was not without some qualifications owing
to the use of an extensive system of "earmarking." Socialist sectors were obliged to keep their money in several
accounts, for several purposes (for current transactions,
for depreciation, for investment, for "collective consump-

The role of money was fundamentally changed and became very similar to that in a market economy, although earmarking diluted the "moneyness" of the money supply and made the effects of its changes erratic and variable.

The process of money creation became far more differentiated than in the previous period of a simplified bank credit-money supply creation mechanism and cash plan regulations.* In this period the entire mechanism of monetary base creation and monetary multiplication began to operate in much the same fashion as in a market economy. This was particularly true after 1961, when crediting of customers was transferred to other banks and the National Bank of Yugoslavia became a central bank in a classic sense.**

Two specific components of this process merit particular mention. First, an extensive system of "freezing and defreezing" practices employed as a system of semifiscal, semimonetary stabilization measures had significant effects on changes in money supply. Second, a specific system of credit regulations, called "credit system" in Yugoslav terminology, made the process of credit regulation unique. The credit system in this period--defined as a system of regulations dealing with such questions as by whom and to whom credits may be granted, for what purposes, and under what conditions--was based on the selective credit regulation. This was different from the usual system of quanti-

----

tion," etc.). In this way the money supply was compartmentalized into many subgroups and it was possible for an enterprise short of money for one purpose to have an excess for other purposes. It was unable to transfer its own money from one account to the other. Although the system of earmarking was modified, even at the end of this period socialist enterprises kept their money in at least three accounts: a gyro account for current transactions and investment transactions, a depreciation account, and a "collective consumption" account.

*The cash plan survived the central planning period as a useful financial account, providing statistics related to households and individual firms. It can now be identified as the "household" sector in the Flow-of-Funds Accounts of the National Bank of Yugoslavia.

**Up to 1961 the major part of crediting of customers was performed by the National Bank, so that the monetary base-monetary multiplication mechanism was substantially dampened, relying more on monetary base creation than monetary multiplication.

tative regulation of the supply of credits in a market economy, and many components of it originated in the system of credit planning in the period of central planning.* The most characteristic regulations were those related to purposes for which credits might be granted. No general-purpose credit existed. Each credit was granted for a specific purpose, such as seasonal inventories or accounts receivable. Regulations of short-term crediting were quite different from regulations for investment crediting. The former were based on demand regulations and the latter on supply regulations.**

Under these conditions, the mechanism of credit regulation was based on purposes for which credit may be granted, how to calculate the amount of credit, and under what conditions it may be granted. By the easing of these regulations credits were increased and vice versa. This system of credit regulation involved more uncertainty than the classic system of credit supply regulation, as did the mechanism of money regulation. This may at least partly explain the volatility of bank credits and money supply during this period.

Demand for money was fundamentally changed, because of the changes in the quality and role of money. "Quasi-demand" for money decreased and even became insignificant at the end of the period.† The decreasing share of quasi-demand presumably made the problem of identification of the demand proper a very difficult task indeed.

In addition, there were significant changes in the determinants of the demand for money proper. The most significant change was the decrease in the role of expectations in the changes of the assortment and quality of

---

*Similar to credit planning in other socialist central planning economies.

**This was achieved by stating that investment credits might be granted only on the basis of investment sources and regulating the list of sources that might be considered investment sources, e.g., own funds and time deposits.

†In spite of the disappearance of "accounting money" in the hands of the socialist sector, "quasi-demand" for money did not presumably completely disappear, owing to the extensive system of earmarking. It happened very often, for example, that economic units held extra money in one account and were short of money in another and unable to transfer money from the one account to the other or to use money for other than the earmarked purposes.

TABLE 1.8

Basic Flows of Money Creation
(billions of dinars)

| | Changes | | | | | | | Position in December 1964 |
|---|---|---|---|---|---|---|---|---|
| | 1952 | 1954 | 1956 | 1958 | 1960 | 1962 | 1964 | |
| Short-term bank credits | 0.7 | 1.8 | 1.7 | 1.0 | 2.7 | 5.6 | 4.4 | 35.7 |
| Bank foreign exchange transactions | 0.0 | -0.1 | 0.2 | 0.1 | -0.1 | 0.6 | -1.3 | -0.4 |
| Transfer to nonmonetary bank deposits (increase -) | -0.7 | -0.5 | -1.0 | -0.7 | -1.1 | -2.5 | 0.4 | -13.4 |
| Money supply (increase +) | 0.0 | 1.2 | 0.9 | 0.4 | 1.5 | 3.7 | 3.5 | 21.9 |

Sources: Consolidated balance sheets of the monetary system, Statisticki bilten Sluzbe drustvenog knjigovodsta, No. 10 (1970), Table 4, No. 2 (1969), and No. 6 (1968); unpublished materials for 1952-56.

goods, though these expectations continued to play a role.*
At the same time, the importance of changes in the price
level as a determinant of demand for money increased. Interest rate and cost elasticity had started to appear as
determinants of demand for money, though they do not seem
to have been very significant.

Demand-supply adjustment processes were fundamentally
changed. In the first instance demand-to-supply-of-money
adjustments replaced the supply-to-demand adjustments of
the previous central planning period. These processes
thus became similar to those in a market economy. Second,
the monetary effects became far more significant than in
the previous period. Under conditions of decentralized
decision-making power in the field of organization of production and pricing, monetary disequilibrium resulted in
significant effects on economic equilibrium, which mani-
fested themselves in inflationary tendencies. Under the
specific conditions of this period** effects of adjustment

---

*Expectation of changes in the assortment and quality
of goods as a determinant of demand for money is less specific than it may appear. It may be argued that price expectation is a significant determinant of the demand for
money under conditions of the market formation of prices
and consumer or demand sovereignty, and expectation of
changes in assortment and quality of goods under conditions
of regulated prices and producer or supply sovereignty.
The first condition is typical for a market economy, and
so is expectation in price changes. The second condition
is typical for central planning economies, and so is expectation of change in assortment and quality of goods. In
the case of Yugoslavia, in the first stage of decentralization there occurred a process of fundamental change from
price fixing and supply sovereignty to free price formation
and demand sovereignty. The process was not completed up
to the end of this stage, so that both price expectation
and expectation of changes in assortment and quality of
goods and services presumably were significant determinants
of the demand for money. The role of price expectations
was increasing and that of expectation of changes in the
assortment of goods and services was decreasing.

**For example, the very slow responsiveness of produc-
tion to demand; tightly regulated foreign trade, which prevented prices from influencing exports and imports; and an
undifferentiated financial structure and financial markets,
which excluded dampening effects in the case of monetary
disequilibrium.

of demand-to-supply-of-money processes resulted mainly in
an increase in the price level, though apparently with a
relatively short lag and in a less roundabout way than in
a market economy. Thus, monetary disequilibrium (at least
in the case of an extra quantity of money) had more of an
orthodox quantity theory effect than might be expected in
a developed market economy with a differentiated financial
structure.

## Fiscal System

Parallel to changes in the financial structure, substantial changes occurred in the fiscal system. First,
the national budget was divided into two parts: government
budget in a traditional sense and extrabudgetary transactions related primarily to saving and investment. At the
same time, budget and other transactions were decentralized
into four independent levels: federal, republic, district,
and local. The saving-investment transactions were split
into two separate flows. Saving remained under fiscal
flows, and use of saving was entrusted to financial flows,
which involved credits instead of grants. This was the
mechanism of investment loan funds explained earlier.
Thus, these funds appeared as semifiscal, semifinancial
institutions and in a sense as semifinancial intermediaries.
In addition, a part of saving remained with socialist enterprises as a result of changes in income distribution.

Exclusion of the purposive role of saving and investment was in part compensated for by the above-mentioned
earmarking practices, which influenced directly saving and
investment and thus had a semifiscal, semifinancial (monetary) character. Decomposition of the comprehensive fiscal
system resulted in a decrease in the size and a fundamental
change in the pattern of fiscal flows, parallel with the
increase in size and appropriate differentiation of financial flows.

The targets of the fiscal system remained very comprehensive in the field of sector redistribution, aimed at
the implementing of targets in saving formation. Individual
redistribution targets, which were insignificant during
the central planning period, became increasingly important,
owing in part to increased differentiation in personal incomes. The stabilization targets of fiscal policy also
became significant, although they were mainly implemented
by such semifiscal measures as the freezing of incomes
and deposits in the socialist sector.

The sources of revenues were socialist enterprises and individuals. Socialist enterprises were required to pay a tax on their capital of up to 6 percent and averaging about 4 percent toward the end of this period. The income tax amounted to 15 percent. The contributions to investment loan funds and the turnover taxes at all levels of production provided the most important resources from the socialist sector.

Sources coming from the private sector, which included households and individual producers, comprised the tax on personal income paid to workers by enterprises, the tax on total income, the income tax paid by private producers, and the taxes on property. The income tax paid by farmers was based on cadastral income.[11] Custom duties represented a very significant part of budget revenues. Table 1.9 shows the share of individual types of taxes in total fiscal revenues.

TABLE 1.9

Fiscal Revenue in 1962
(billions of dinars)

|  | Amount | Percentage of Total |
|---|---|---|
| Income tax of socialist enterprises | 1.4 | 10.4 |
| Tax on extra profit of socialist enterprises | 0.3 | 2.2 |
| Turnover taxes | 4.1 | 30.6 |
| Customs duties | 1.2 | 9.0 |
| Taxes on incomes from private activities | 0.4 | 3.0 |
| Other taxes paid by private sectors | 2.9 | 21.6 |
| Taxes on personal income paid to workers by socialist enterprises | 2.9 | 21.6 |
| Other revenues | 0.6 | 4.5 |
| Total budget revenues | 11.1 | 82.8 |
| Contributions to investment loan funds | 1.3 | 9.7 |
| Tax on own funds of socialist enterprises | 1.0 | 7.5 |
| Total fiscal revenues | 13.4 | 100.0 |

Source: Statisticki bilten Sluzbe drustvenog knjigovodsta, No. 2 (1964), Table 22.

37

## Debt Management

Public loans were a neglected instrument of financial policy in this period. There was only one loan, and it was related to federal government borrowings for reconstruction of Skopje. The amount of bonds issued reached 0.4 billion dinars (issues of 1963-64). This loan, however, was important from the point of view of the type of bond issued: negotiable (bearer-type) medium-term bonds bearing a fairly competitive interest rate of 7 percent. If not for its amount, this loan was significant as a new approach to government borrowing.

## Economic Policy Instruments

Under conditions of fundamental decentralization of decision-making power, economic policy instruments became far more differentiated than previously. The principal change was the increase in indirect measures, especially monetary policy and fiscal policy measures. As has been noted, the degree of decentralization of power, however, was less significant in pricing, income distribution, saving, investment, and foreign trade. Thus, in these fields direct measures were very extensive.

### NOTES

1. See particularly Raymond Goldsmith, "Financial Intermediaries in the American Economy Since 1900," La Estructura Financiera y al Crecemento Economica (CEMLA [Center for Econo-Monetary Latin America], 1963).
2. The new revised series of these accounts (1958-69) is published in the Annual Report of the National Bank of Yugoslavia, 1969.
3. The Yugoslav definition of gross national product differs from definitions used in many other countries. It does not include "nonproductive services" such as government administration, education and health activities, and personal services. In view of the fact that the share of these services in GNP is increasing, the Yugoslav definition of GNP results in a downward bias both in the amount (10-15 percent less than according to Western definition) and in the rate of increase. Thus, measured in terms of the Western definition, the rate of increase in GNP would be even higher than presented in Table 1.1. For a detailed interpretation see G. Grdjić, "Comparative Computation of

Yugoslav National Income According to Material and Comprehensive Concepts of Production," Review of Income and Wealth, June 1966.

4. According to B. Horvat, the economic blockade resulted in a decrease in the economic growth rate of about 30 percent. B. Horvat, "The Characteristics of Yugoslav Economic Development," Socialist Thought and Practice, No. l, p. 4.

5. The "cash plan" represented one of the balances of a central planning system. It controlled the flow of cash receipts and expenditures of the private sector (wages, sale of goods to socialist enterprises, purchase of goods from socialist enterprises, and payment of taxes), in order to control the net difference between receipts and expenditures, i.e., changes in the amount of currency in circulation. An interesting discussion is contained in George Garvy, Money, Banking, and Credit in Eastern Europe (New York: Federal Reserve Bank of New York, 1966).

6. After the merging of all existing banks (partly by confiscation and nationalization of private banks, partly by merging of state banks) there were two banks in 1947: the National Bank and the State Investment Bank. The former was responsible for short-term credit as well as for the payment mechanism, foreign transactions, budget transactions, statistics, and savings deposits. The latter was responsible for investment financing. After 1947 three new types of bank were introduced: communal banks for short-term and long-term crediting of local enterprises, communal activities, and governments; banks for crediting cooperatives in agriculture; and local savings banks. At the end of 1951 there were 57 communal banks, 49 banks for crediting cooperatives, and 8 savings banks, in addition to 437 branches of the National Bank and 31 branches of the State Investment Bank. Miodrag Ugricic, Novcani system Jugoslavije (Beograd, 1968), pp. 166-168.

7. An interesting discussion of fiscal systems in centrally planned economies is presented in Public Finance, Proceedings of the XXIII Session in Prague, September 1967, Nos. 1-2 (The Hague: International Institute of Public Finance, 1968).

8. The most informative works are B. Horvat, Towards a Theory of Planned Economy (Belgrade: Yugoslav Institute of Economic Studies, 1964); G. Macesich, Yugoslavia, The Theory and Practice of Development Planning (Charlottesville: The University Press of Virginia, 1964); S. Pejovich, The Market-Planned Economy of Yugoslavia (Minneapolis: University of Minnesota Press, 1966); R. Stojanovic, et al.,

Yugoslav Economists on the Problem of a Socialist Economy (New York:  International Arts and Sciences Press, 1964); A. Waterston, Planning in Yugoslavia:  Organization and Implementation (Washington, D.C.:  Economic Development Institute, 1962); Economist (English issue), Zagreb, 1969; Wayne S. Vucinich, ed., Contemporary Yugoslavia:  Twenty Years of Socialist Experiment (Berkeley and Los Angeles: University of California Press, 1969).

9.  D.C., "Changes in Yugoslav Foreign Trade and For-eign Exchange System," Yugoslav Survey, No. 5 (1961); M.M., "The System and Organization of Foreign Trade," Yugoslav Survey, No. 14 (1963).

10.  At the end of 1960 credits granted by the National Bank of Yugoslavia accounted for 55 percent of total bank short-term credits and its assets, 53 percent of all bank assets.  Statisticki bilten Sluzbe drustvenog knjigovodsta (Statistical Bulletin of the Social Accounting Service), December 1969, Tables 4, 5.

11.  This pattern of taxes related to the end of the period under review.  See, for example, K. Bogoev, "The Fiscal System of Yugoslavia," Economist.

# 2

## THE ADVANCED
## STAGE OF
## DECENTRALIZATION

We shall now consider the institutional changes that occurred during 1965-67, and which in Yugoslavia are called "the reform." These changes had important consequences in the economic and social fields.[1] They represent a landmark distinguishing the previous first stage of decentralization from the present advanced stage of decentralization.

### REASONS FOR REFORM

Two sets of forces brought about the comprehensive institutional changes and other measures that have come to be called the reform. First, there was a need to correct the imperfections resulting from mistakes accumulated during the trial-and-error period of development of the country's unique economic system. Second, there was a need to adjust the economic system to the increased level of economic development brought about during a relatively long period in which the country experienced a comparatively high rate of economic growth.

It became increasingly clear during the early 1960s that many of the country's problems in the economic sphere were caused by the inadequacy of its economic system and its inability to adjust to the increasingly complex economic processes of a higher level of economic development. Growing deficiencies in solving basic economic problems stimulated discussions pointing to the conclusion that what was required to set matters straight was a new set of fundamental institutional adjustments. It also became clear that, following essential institutional adjustment in the fields of organization of production and pricing of

41

goods in the first stage of decentralization, the time had now come to introduce further decentralization measures in the fields of pricing of factors of production, income distribution, saving, and investment.

## INFRAINSTITUTIONAL ADJUSTMENTS

The main features of reform adjustments turned on a significant decrease in government intervention, an increased role of free decision-making especially on the part of socialist enterprises, an increased role of market mechanisms and autonomous adjustment processes, and an increased use of indirect economic policy measures. As noted, these changes were mainly related to the pricing of factors of production, income distribution, saving, and investment. Changes in the pricing of goods and foreign trade were also significant. The majority of these measures were implemented in 1965, although significant adjustments were introduced in 1963-64 as preparatory measures and in 1966-67 as complementary measures.*

Changes in income distribution, involving full freedom in personal income determination on the part of socialist enterprises, had fundamental consequences on sector redistribution of incomes in favor of socialist enterprises and households. At the same time, abolishment of the income tax, some other taxes, and contributions to investment loan funds increased the share of free disposable income in the total income of socialist enterprises. Both of these changes resulted in an increased share of personal income in an enterprises' income distribution and in the share of households in total income distribution.

Changes in income distribution resulted in important changes in the pattern of saving formation. It will be seen that these changes in turn required comprehensive adjustments in the financial field. Sector distribution of saving formation was substantially changed in favor of socialist enterprises and households.

Table 2.1 shows that the changed sector formation of saving was followed by further decentralization of saving formation and an increase in the share of voluntary saving in total saving. These changes are highly relevant to a

---

*Such as the abolishment of investment loan funds and contributions to these funds and the readjustment of bank operations and the banking structure.

TABLE 2.1

Gross Saving Formation by Sector
(percentage of total)

|  | 1964 | 1965 | 1966 | 1967 | 1968 | 1969 | 1970 |
|---|---|---|---|---|---|---|---|
| Socialist enter-prises | 41 | 63 | 55 | 48 | 52 | 45 | 45 |
| Local govern-ments[a] | 29 | 10 | 17 | 13 | 13 | 13 | 10 |
| Other organiza-tions and un-classified | 11 | 26 | -1 | 2 | -2 | 4 | 12 |
| Household | 10 | 11 | 25 | 26 | 26 | 31 | 28 |
| Total decen-tralized saving | 91 | 110 | 96 | 89 | 89 | 93 | 95 |
| Federal govern-ment[a] | 9 | -10 | 4 | 11 | 11 | 7 | 5 |
| Total saving (billions of dinars) | 26.4 | 30.1 | 34.4 | 37.4 | 39.5 | 45.9 | 58 |
| Voluntary saving (percentage of total saving) | 46 | 84 | 61 | 55 | 52 | 54 | 61 |
| Saving-GNP ratio | 43 | 38 | 35 | 36 | 35 | 35 | 38 |

[a]Including forced saving by investment loan funds.

Source: Flow-of-Funds Accounts of the National Bank of Yugoslavia; Annual Report of the National Bank of Yugoslavia.

further increase in the role and development of the financial system.

The evidence in the table also shows a decreased saving-GNP ratio. This may be explained in part as a correction of the previous extremely high saving ratio. It also indicates the inefficiency of existing autonomous mechanisms (including the financial mechanism) in compensating for the abolished forced saving. As we shall see, the problem of the efficiency of a financial system in encouraging voluntary flows of saving has become one of the main causes of the need for institutional readjustments in the financial field.

These changes in saving formation have resulted in significant changes in the pattern of investment financing by socialist enterprises. The increased disposable income and saving of enterprises had led to a substantial increase in self-financing of real investments, as indicated by the evidence summarized in Table 2.2.

The increased self-financing ratio did not mean a decrease in the need for financing. On the contrary, dismantling of investment loan funds, which shared a dominant part in investment financing before the reform, resulted in an increase in the role of financial intermediation in spite of an increased self-financing ratio. As suggested by the evidence in Table 2.3, the increased share of households and of decentralized and voluntary saving in total saving resulted in similar changes in the pattern of financial saving.

The increased share of voluntary saving in total saving suggests that the role of financial intermediaries in stimulating such saving has become essential for the satisfaction of financing needs. It also reveals the growing need for efficient financial markets.

The other two significant institutional changes related to the financial system were in the field of pricing and foreign trade-foreign exchange. In the field of price formation there were three groups of changes. First, the mechanism of price formation was nearly freed of government subsidies. Price formation was modified by transferring turnover taxes from all levels of production to the retail trade level. The second group of changes was related to a decrease in price distortion, resulting in an

TABLE 2.2

Self-Financing of Socialist Enterprises

|  | 1962 | 1964 | 1966 | 1968 | 1969 | 1970 |
|---|---|---|---|---|---|---|
| Percentage of self-financing in total real investment expenditures (fixed assets and stocks) | 57 | 50 | 69 | 72 | 62 | 58 |

Source: Annual Report of the National Bank of Yugoslavia, 1969, 1970.

TABLE 2.3

Financial Deficits and Surpluses
(billions of dinars)

| | 1964 | 1965 | 1966 | 1967 | 1968 | 1969 |
|---|---|---|---|---|---|---|
| Socialist enterprises | −10.7 | −3.6 | −8.5 | −11.1 | −8.1 | −12.5 |
| Federal government | −0.5 | −5.8 | −2.5 | 0.3 | 0.8 | 0.0 |
| Local governments | −0.3 | −0.4 | 0.8 | 0.0 | 0.2 | 0.5 |
| Other organizations and unclassified | 4.2 | 4.5 | −2.1 | −0.7 | −2.8 | −0.7 |
| Households | 0.5 | 1.0 | 5.6 | 3.4 | 1.8 | 4.3 |
| Total nonfinancial sectors | −6.8 | −4.3 | −6.7 | −8.1 | −8.1 | −8.4 |
| Federal investment loan funds | 2.5 | 2.6 | 3.6 | 3.5 | 3.2 | 3.0 |
| Local investment loan funds | 2.7 | 2.3 | 2.5 | 3.2 | 3.5 | 3.9 |
| Total financial sectors | 5.2 | 4.9 | 6.1 | 6.7 | 6.7 | 6.9 |
| Total domestic sectors, net (balance of payments deficits −, surpluses +) | −1.6 | 0.6 | −0.6 | −1.4 | −1.4 | −1.5 |
| Total positive financial saving | 9.9 | 10.4 | 12.5 | 10.4 | 9.5 | 11.7 |
| Voluntary financial saving in percentage of total positive financial saving | 13 | 28 | 60 | 50 | 37 | 53 |

Sources: Flow-of-Funds Accounts of the National Bank of Yugoslavia; Annual Report of the National Bank of Yugoslavia, 1969.

administrative increase in the prices of raw materials related to that for manufactured goods, with the highest (free) increase in prices of agricultural goods and services.* The severe distortion of relative prices inherited from the central planning period was one of the fundamental disturbing factors in allocation of inputs, allocation of saving, and the efficiency of foreign trade transactions.** These distortions in relative prices contributed in part to the steady increase in the price level. Thus, measures aimed at decreasing the distortion of relative prices were a significant precondition for an increase in the efficiency of the economy and for the successful pursuit of stabilization. Distortion of relative prices, which proved to be the most stubborn component of price formation, was significantly reduced.†

The third group of measures in the field of prices was to some extent in contradiction of the first two. These measures involved a broadening of price regulations to prevent reversal processes in the relative price structure, which would lead to a new increase in price distortion. Price regulations mainly in the form of price ceilings have been reduced several times since 1965. They remained nevertheless significant up to 1969.[2]

---

*The December-to-July 1965 rate of increase in producers' prices of manufactured goods was 11 percent; in raw materials, 19 percent; in agricultural goods, 14 percent; and in services, 36 percent.

**Distortion of prices was characterized by low relative prices for agricultural goods, raw materials, and services in comparison with the price relations on foreign markets. In this way opportunity cost considerations, investment financing sources, and investment decision-making were highly distorted. In foreign trade it was impossible to get rid of many regulations, leading to comprehensive restrictions and multirate practices.

†In spite of many efforts to decrease the inherited arbitrary structure of relative prices left over from the central planning period, there were many disturbing factors that prevented achievement of significant results, e.g., a closed market (rigid foreign trade and foreign trade regulations), high distortions in the efficiency of socialist enterprises, regulation of a significant part of prices parallel with free price formation, rigid regulation of income distribution, inadequate capital mobility, and a low interest rate ceiling for credits.

In the matter of pricing of factors of production, socialist enterprises were permitted to decide about income distribution, which, in effect, brought into operation a system of free wage formation. Interest rate determination in this period may be considered comparatively liberal, consisting of interest rate ceiling regulations for credits and a system of subsidized rates for specific purposes, such as export credits and credits in agriculture. However, interest rate determination has remained inflexible under a low interest rate policy, which has pegged the rate ceiling even lower than the rate of increase in prices, as suggested by the evidence in Table 2.4. It will be seen that interest rate policy has been based mainly on credit cost, neglecting financial market considerations, and that this has been one of the significant causes of inefficiency in this market.

Thus, in spite of significant liberalization steps, the system of pricing remained very controversial, including rather liberal components on the one hand (especially in personal income formation) and institutional and economic policy regidities on the other. It is little wonder that problems of pricing stand in the forefront of current discussion in Yugoslavia. These discussions no doubt will serve to prepare the way for significant changes in this field.

In the field of foreign transactions significant changes have occurred, although these are not fundamental and are important primarily as a new step in the direction of liberalization in these transactions. The principal purpose of change in this field was to open the economy to foreign influence and for such influence to have an impact on the economy's efficiency. Three groups of changes were introduced during 1965-67: first, in the field of foreign trade; second, in the foreign exchange systems; and third, in foreign borrowing regulations.

In the field of foreign trade, exports were almost fully liberalized. Import restrictions also were liberalized significantly, so that liberalized imports from convertible currency countries reached more than 50 percent of total convertible currency imports in 1968.[3]

In the field of foreign exchange regulations one of the significant changes was substitution of "everything is permitted that is not forbidden" for "everything is forbidden that is not permitted." As a result, exporters are authorized to keep their export proceeds and use them according to their needs. They cannot use them for selling to other importers, except to the amount of their "reten-

47

## TABLE 2.4

### Interest Rates and Increase in Price Level

| | 1961 | 1962 | 1963 | 1964 | 1965 | 1966 | 1967 | 1968 | 1969 | 1970 |
|---|---|---|---|---|---|---|---|---|---|---|
| Retail prices, percent increase in the average level | 8 | 6 | 5 | 9 | 16[a] | 6 | 7 | 5 | 8 | 10 |
| Interest rate ceiling (on bank credits) | 10 | 7.5 | 7.5 | 7.5 | 8 | 8 | 10 | 8 | 8 | 8 |
| Interest rate on savings deposits (sight) | 5 | 5 | 5 | 5 | 5 | 5 | 6 | 6 | 6 | 6 |
| Interest rate on time savings deposits | 6 | 6 | 6 | 6 | 6 | 6 | 7 | 7 | 7.5 | 7.5 |

[a]Excluding increase due to reform measures.

Sources: "Kamata u nasem privrednom sistemu" (Interest in Our Economic System) (Belgrade: Udruzenje banaka Jugoslavij [Yugoslav Banking Association], 1969), p. 35; unpublished materials.

tion quota," but they can sell to banks.  In using their
balances in these accounts they must follow foreign trade
regulations.

Significant changes also were introduced in the exchange rate.  The previous "settlement exchange rate"
(parallel to the official exchange rate) and the system of
coefficients for specific groups of goods and services
were replaced by a unit exchange rate amounting to 12.5
dinars to a U.S. dollar.[4]  Introduction of the unit exchange
rate and abolishment of coefficients and premiums led to
a new role for tariffs.  They were adjusted to the new foreign exchange and foreign trade systems.  In addition to
readjustment of individual customs duties, the average
tariff rate was reduced from 23 to 11 percent of the value
of imports.[5]

The third field in which significant changes occurred
was foreign borrowing.  The new regulations permitted substantial room for foreign borrowing by banks and socialist
enterprises within limits regulated by the National Bank of
Yugoslavia.  As a result, foreign borrowing was significantly liberalized and decentralized.[6]  A specific innovation in this field was the introduction of "joint venture"
legislation, which permits joint domestic-foreign enterprises on a partnership basis.[7]

These three groups of measures may be considered as
important adjustments to the institutional framework,
brought about largely by the growing complexity of economic
processes in the country's rapidly developing economy.
There is general agreement, however, that these measures
represent a minor part of the adjustments that are necessary at the present level of development of Yugoslavia's
economy and economic system.  Further significant changes
may be expected.[8]

Two general observations may be made regarding these
infrainstitutional changes.  First, in spite of the important institutional adjustments to the economy's needs, the
economic system continues to retain significant inconsis-
tencies and deficiencies.  Second, this fact suggests that
further significant infrainstitutional adjustments are to
come even though the 1965 reform has significantly improved
the efficiency of the economy.


## ROLE OF FINANCIAL VARIABLES

The infrainstitutional adjustments in the 1965 reform
have had fundamental consequences in the financial field.

Further decentralization of economic decision-making power, an increase in the role of autonomous economic processes, and particularly the substantial increase in the share of voluntary saving and financial saving formation have resulted in a significant increase in the role of financial variables.

In the monetary field, the institutional changes made monetary processes more complex and effective. Demand and supply functions of money involved new and important behavior variables. As a result, the adjustment processes of demand to the supply of money have become more complicated. Moreover, stabilization goals have become at least as important as production and development goals. This requires an efficient monetary equilibrium policy and involves the entire complicated body of problems related to monetary policy formation and monetary policy implementation. Thus, the institutional changes of the reform have brought about a substantial increase in monetary effects. Monetary policy has now become one of the strategic economic policy instruments.

The consequences of these changes in the field of financial intermediation were even more important. The changes in saving formation and investment decision-making required comprehensive adjustments of financial institutions, financial instruments, and financial operations, including organization of efficient financial markets. Under the new conditions brought about by the reform the financial structure has become responsible for a significant part of saving and financial saving formation on the one hand and economic allocation of the essential part of saving on the other. The efficiency of the financial mechanism has become the essential precondition for smooth functioning of economic processes and promotion of a high rate of economic growth. Failure of the financial mechanism would hamper the efficient functioning of the economic system and in effect require a backward readjustment of infrainstitutional structure. The following chapters are devoted to an examination of how adequately these requirements have been met for the adaptation of the financial structure and what remains to be done.


## FINANCIAL INSTITUTIONS

Before the reform the structure of financial institutions involved a central bank, deposit banks, and investment loan funds. It was recognized very early that this structure of financial institutions and their operations had many deficiencies and that plans for the reform would have to include significant institutional adjustments in this area.

The principal deficiencies in the financial institutions came from their administrative character and the strong government influence. Investment loan funds were, in fact, government institutions. Their resources came mainly from taxes, and the allocation of these resources was under tight government control, although effected through granting credits and usually involving competitive bidding.*

Banks also were under comprehensive government control. They were established by government bodies. These bodies appointed the management and had strong influence on bank policy formation. Banks were authorized to operate only within the territory of the government that had established them. There was little room for economic reasoning and free decision-making. Such a structure for financial institutions was obviously inappropriate for a system where autonomous economic processes play a strategic role, especially in saving and investment. These shortcomings are reinforced in the new system, where monetary processes and financial intermediation now are based on a large body of behavior variables and where financial institutions have to perform a significant degree of economic calculation. This structure was inappropriate even before the reform period, so that plans for its readjustment became urgent relatively early. It is for this reason that institutional changes in the financial field were begun even before the reform, partly to make urgent corrections and partly as preparation for the reform. As a result, two groups of institutional adjustments were implemented before the reform of 1965.

---

*These funds were administered by banks, which were obliged to follow the economic plans of the relevant government bodies. In addition to specified projects that had to be financed, the economic plans stipulated for one part of the resources only the purpose for which it should be used, e.g., a sugar factory, so that the bank administering the fund had relatively more room for decision-making, mainly in deciding which project among many in competitive bidding was the best.

First, nearly all investment loan funds were abolished,
beginning with the Federal Investment Loan Fund in 1964.*
Second, new banking legislation was passed in March 1965,**
introducing fundamental changes in organization, management, and functions of banks. Both of these groups of
changes have significantly adjusted the financial structure
to the new needs of financing. It will be seen, however,
that institutional adjustment does not necessarily mean
functional adjustment, and that the above measures have
only created a suitable institutional basis for a long-run
process of adjustment of functioning of financial institutions to the new financing needs.

## BANKING STRUCTURE

The present banking structure was introduced in 1965-
66, after a relatively long period of discussion and investigation.[9] Banks were given far more responsibility
for saving formation, stimulation of supply of financial
resources, and economic allocation of saving. In effect,
changes introduced by the new legislature included both
organizational and conceptual modifications.

First, the basic conceptual change was to decrease
the influence of government and increase the influence of
socialist enterprises on bank policy formation, in order
to make policy formation more sensitive to economic calculation and to the changing needs for financing. Second,
in order to improve the degree of fluidity of financial
flows, all banks were made interregional and authorized to
operate throughout the country. They also were vested
with the right to perform foreign transactions with both
domestic and foreign residents provided specific conditions

---

*Abolishment of investment loan funds does not mean
abolishment of a government role in investment financing.
Sources of these funds remained under government control,
and it continued to play a significant role in investment
financing, e.g., using repayments and interest on credits
as a source of financing.

**The new banking legislation could not be implemented
at once, and a one-year period was granted to banks to adjust to the new legal provisions. These adjustments were
not performed until the first quarter of 1966, so that for
all practical purposes the banking structure remained unchanged until the reform in July 1965.

were fulfilled. Third, the new legislation stimulated bigger banks in order to improve the efficiency of bank operations.

The reorganization of banking involved the National Bank of Yugoslavia as a central bank, commercial banks, investment banks, and savings banks.

## The National Bank of Yugoslavia

The role, organization, and operations of the National Bank of Yugoslavia* have not been changed significantly.** It remains the central bank of Yugoslavia, performing regular central banking operations, including monetary regulations, issue of banknotes and coins, holding of foreign exchange reserves, etc.

The National Bank of Yugoslavia is an independent federal institution, established by federal law. The bank is managed by the governor, who is appointed by the Federal Assembly on the recommendation of the Federal Executive Council. He is responsible to both of these institutions for the implementation of bank operations and targets. There is another managing body in the bank: the Council of the Working Community. Its organization and election are similar to those of the Workers' Councils in socialist enterprises. Its responsibility, however, is rather limited, and involves labor relations, working conditions, decision-making in the field of personal income and investment, fixing fees for bank services, and establishment of

---

*The bank was established in 1883 as the Privileged National Bank of the Kingdom of Serbia (Privilegovana Narodna banka) by virtue of the Law of the National Bank. Thereafter the name was changed several times. It was the National Bank of the Kingdom of Serbs, Croats, and Slovenes in 1920, the National Bank of the Kingdom of Yugoslavia in 1929, and the National Bank of the Federal People's Republic of Yugoslavia in 1946. The present name was introduced in the Constitution of the Socialist Federal Republic of Yugoslavia, 1963, Art. 29.

**The operations of the National Bank of Yugoslavia were significantly adjusted to the new needs in 1961, when crediting of customers was transferred to other banks and the National Bank of Yugoslavia became a regular central bank. Consequently it was not necessary to introduce significant changes in 1965.

bank bylaws. The council is not responsible for monetary regulations or performance of other bank operations.

The bank's head office is in Belgrade. In addition, there are six central offices in the capitals of the six republics.

One of the significant questions in interpreting a central bank's position is its relation to the government. As has been stated, the National Bank is an independent institution. It is not, however, independent in monetary policy formation. The Federal Assembly and the Federal Executive Council decide monetary policy targets, and the National Bank is responsible only for their implementation. In policy formation the National Bank plays a significant role by preparing proposals and furnishing policymakers with the appropriate analysis for relevant economic developments and forecasts. The National Bank's monetary planning is particularly significant in this connection.[10] Proposals by the National Bank are usually accepted by policymakers without significant corrections. As a consequence the National Bank's influence is considerable in monetary policy formation.

The role of the federal secretary of finance is reduced to supervision of the legal conformity of bank operations and regulations.

The balance sheet of the National Bank gives a useful indication of its operation. The assets side of this balance sheet is characterized by three peculiarities. First, there are no securities (because of the negligible amount of bonds issued). Second, the main part of the bank's assets consists of discount credits, showing that these credits are the strategic instrument of monetary policy. Third, there is no item relating to a gold (or foreign exchange) cover of bank liabilities. On the liability side there are no specific elements, except the existence of the item related to monetary float.*

## Other Banks

The banking structure involves three other types of bank, called "business banks" in Yugoslav terminology.

------------------------

*Monetary float is on the liability side in the "gyro" payment system (European practice). In the checking payment system monetary float is on the asset side (net), as is the case with the Combined Balance Sheet of the Federal Reserve System of the United States.

TABLE 2.5

Combined Balance Sheet of the National Bank of Yugoslavia,
End of 1971
(billions of dinars)

| Assets | | Liabilities | |
|---|---|---|---|
| Gold and foreign exchange | 3.6 | Foreign liabilities | 2.7 |
| Other foreign assets | 1.7 | Foreign exchange deposits (domestic residents) | 0.1 |
| Foreign exchange credits to other banks (domestic) | 0.9 | Deposits | 8.8 |
| Short-term credits[a] | 13.9 | Currency in circulation | 11.9 |
| | | Money float[b] | 2.3 |
| Discount credits and other credits to other banks | 17.6 | Bank deposits | 12.5 |
| | | Gyro accounts | 1.1 |
| | | Reserve requirements | 7.3 |
| Other assets | 1.7 | Other deposits | 4.1 |
| | | Other liabilities | 1.1 |
| Total | 39.4 | | 39.4 |

Source: Statisticki bilten Sluzbe drustvenog knjigovodsta, No. 2 (1972), Table 5.

[a]Mainly to the federal government.

[b]The combined balance sheet of the National Bank of
Yugoslavia includes only assets and liabilities related to
it as a monetary institution. Thus, buildings, inventories,
equipment, its own funds as a "working organization" (the
same as in other working organizations), etc., are not included.

These are commercial banks, investment banks, and savings
banks. Commercial banks may grant short-term credits,
consumer credits, and investment credits* for working assets

_____

*In Yugoslav official terminology short-term credits
are defined as credits granted on the basis of short-term
resources (sight deposits, discount credits, etc.), regardless of maturity. Consumer credits are credits granted to
individuals on the basis of savings deposits. Investment

of enterprises, for communal investments, and for housing. Investment banks may grant all credits granted by commercial banks and, in addition, investment credits for fixed asset financing.* Savings banks accept savings deposits and grant credits to individuals. They also may perform other services for individuals. Both commercial and investment banks may accept savings deposits and grant consumer credits to individuals. In effect, there is no fundamental difference between commercial and investment banks, and both are "mixed." The mixed character of the banking structure is even more evident in the case of commercial banks with an additional amount of "credit fund." They are authorized to grant all credits granted by investment banks including credits for fixed asset financing. This does not mean, of course, that all banks are commercial and investment in the same degree. Usually, individual banks are predominantly investment or commercial according to their traditional orientation and position on the market.

As shown in Table 2.6, at the end of 1969 there were 67 "business banks" in Yugoslavia. Thus far there are no savings banks in the proper sense.**

A cross-section analysis of short-term bank credits by banks shows that in mid-1968 there was a significant concentration of bank crediting. Indeed, the evidence presented in Table 2.7 suggests that 12 percent of all business banks shared 57 percent in total short-term credits. Concentration of credit operations is even stronger if investment credits are involved. Nearly all of these questions are concentrated in 10 banks.

The method of establishing business banks has been fundamentally changed. Instead of a government decision, the procedure is based on the decision of a number of socialist enterprises, other working organizations, and government bodies. If legal requirements are fulfilled the bank is chartered, provided it meets certain conditions. The conditions include a minimum amount of "credit fund,"

---

credits are defined as credits granted on the basis of "investment resources" (own funds, time deposits, etc.), regardless of maturity.

*Investment banks in the Yugoslav banking structure are quite different from those that in Western terminology perform "investment banking," e.g., banques d'affaires.

**The Postal Savings Bank accepts savings deposits but does not grant credits. It is required to hold all resources in an account with the National Bank of Yugoslavia.

56

TABLE 2.6

Number of Business Banks
(end of year)

|                                         | 1965 | 1966 | 1967 | 1968 | 1969 | 1970 |
|-----------------------------------------|------|------|------|------|------|------|
| Commercial banks                        |      | 62   | 54   | 28   | 22   | --   |
| Combined commercial-investment banks    |      | 40   | 40   | 36   | 36   | 55   |
| Investment banks                        |      | 9    | 9    | 9    | 9    | 9    |
| Total                                   | 233  | 112  | 103  | 73   | 67   | 64   |

Source: Annual Report of the National Bank of Yugoslavia, 1969.

TABLE 2.7

Share of Individual Banks in Total Short-Term Credits
(end of May 1968)

|                                                             |    |    |    |    |    |    |    |     |
|-------------------------------------------------------------|----|----|----|----|----|----|----|-----|
| Number of banks in descending order of short-term credits (accruals) | 5  | 10 | 15 | 20 | 30 | 40 | 50 | 82  |
| Percentage share in total number of banks                   | 6  | 12 | 18 | 24 | 37 | 49 | 61 | 100 |
| Percentage share in total amount of short-term credits      | 41 | 57 | 65 | 72 | 82 | 88 | 92 | 100 |

Source: Balance sheets of individual business banks, May 1968.

number of founders (25), and a minimum amount of deposits.*
For the establishment of an investment bank the agreement
of the republic assembly is also required.

The decision on the establishment of a bank is made
in a "foundation meeting," which verifies the list of
founders and their shares in the credit fund, the amount of
the credit fund, and the type and name of the bank. During
a foundation meeting temporary management is elected and
temporary bylaws are drafted. Afterward the management of
the bank applies for a charter. The charter is issued when
the Economic Court verifies that the minimum requirements
are fulfilled.

The credit fund represents the bank's own capital.
The shares in this fund are transferable, and the bank is
required to issue appropriate certificates to the owners of
the shares.** These certificates are regarded as securities, and legal regulations for securities are applied to
them. In this way banks are organized as specific "corpor-
ations" whose shareholders are limited to socialist working
organizations and government bodies, with individuals excluded.

The management of a business bank is composed of several bodies and the manager. The highest managing authority
of the bank is its assembly, the members of which are the
founders of the bank and representatives of the working community of the bank. Each member has voting power corresponding to the share in the credit fund but not more than
10 percent of the total voting power. The assembly decides
on strategic questions of bank activity, such as guidelines
for credit policy, basic conditions for granting credits
and accepting deposits, income distribution, organization

---

*The minimum amount of credit fund (own capital) to be
subscribed by the founders for commercial banks is 10 million dinars; for investment banks, 150 million dinars; and
for savings banks, 1 million dinars. Republic governments
are authorized to introduce a higher minimum amount for the
credit fund. Commercial banks that also intend to grant
investment credits for fixed asset financing must have an
additional amount of 15 million dinars subscribed in the
credit fund. The requirement for a minimum amount of sight
deposits applies to establishment of a commercial bank and
amounts to 20 million dinars.

**These certifications were introduced at the end of
1969 in order to promote differentiation of the financial
market and its fluidity.

of the bank including establishment of branches, changes in bank bylaws, charges for bank operations, approval of final account, election of other managing bodies and the manager of the bank. The assembly is required to meet once a year.

The next managing body is the executive board, which is elected by the assembly. It is charged with the implementation of the guidelines and decisions of the assembly and prepares proposals for the assembly.

The third managing body is the credit committee. The committee decides on granting individual credits according to guidelines established by the assembly with additional interpretations of these guidelines by the executive board. Members of this committee are appointed by the assembly from among members of the working community of the bank, with the manager of the bank as chairman.

Finally, the manager of the bank is responsible for the efficient working of the bank and implementation of decisions made by the managing bodies. He is appointed by the assembly and is a member of the executive board.

The management structure governs the bank as a financial institution. Another group of managing bodies deals only with labor relations, distribution of the part of the income allocated to the working community, improvement of working conditions, promotion of productivity, professional education, and similar activities. The highest body in this group is the council of the working community, elected by all members of the organization. Larger banks have an executive board of the council, which is responsible for the implementation of the decisions made by the council.

Income distribution is decided by the assembly. Net income is defined as the difference between receipts--interest on credits granted, commissions, and charges for bank services--and expenditures for interest on borrowings, deposits, bonds, tax on own capital, and write-offs of uncollectable credits. The net income may be allocated to the credit fund ("anonymous" part or individual shares), the reserve funds, to long-term depositors as extra interest, and to founders of the bank according to their share in the credit fund. One part is given over to the free disposal of the working community to be used for personal income, investment, and "collective consumption," according to the decision of the council of the working community.

In the event a bank suffers a loss, it is to be covered first by using reserve funds. If these are insufficient, the remaining part of the loss is to be covered by using the credit fund. If the credit fund is decreased below the minimum, the founders of the bank are to subscribe additional amounts to meet legal requirements. If the founders refuse to do so, or if there is no reason to expect improvement in the future, the founders have the option to liquidate.

Sources of business banks are legally classified as "short-term" and "investment" sources. The list of investment sources is regulated by legal provisions and National Bank decisions. The rest of the bank sources are considered short-term.* This classification of sources is one of the significant instruments of both monetary and investment policy.

A specific characteristic of short-term sources of banks is a relatively high share of borrowing from the central bank. This is partly due to relatively high reserve requirements and partly to lack of a developed financial market where banks could turn to borrow.**

In addition to borrowings from the central bank, a considerable part of the sources of business banks comes

---

*It should be mentioned that this classification does not necessarily involve short-term/long-term maturity of bank liabilities, although a dominant part of this classification corresponds to a short-term/long-term maturity. The classification has primarily legal consequences, in that short-term sources may be used only for short-term credits, which are regulated in many respects. Investment credits, which may be granted on the basis of investment sources only, are far less regulated, so that banks are nearly free in their use.

**At the end of 1969 the reserve requirements ratio amounted to 30 percent of deposits. However, some deposits were exempted from this obligation, so that the average reserve requirements ratio was lower (13 percent of total deposits). Obligatory reserves are held in separate accounts and cannot be used by banks even in the case of a heavy drain of reserve money and difficulties in payments. Thus, banks hold reserve money for current payments on gyro account with the National Bank of Yugoslavia in the full amount necessary for liquidity purposes. In addition, business banks are obliged to allocate a special reserve fund account for the occasion of an unexpected drain of reserve money. In this way, business banks, as we shall see, have to hold relatively large amounts of reserve money in accounts with the National Bank of Yugoslavia, which increases their need for borrowing from the central bank.

TABLE 2.8

Short-Term Sources of Business Banks
(end of 1971)

| | Billions of Dinars | Percent-age of Total |
|---|---|---|
| Foreign liabilities | 2.9 | 4.4 |
| Foreign exchange deposits of working | | |
| organizations and individuals | 6.6 | 10.1 |
| Foreign exchange borrowings from | | |
| domestic banks | 0.4 | 0.6 |
| Deposits | 37.3 | 56.8 |
| Gyro and similar accounts | 17.2 | 26.2 |
| Other sight deposits | 10.2 | 15.5 |
| Restricted deposits | 9.9 | 15.1 |
| Borrowings from the National Bank of | | |
| Yugoslavia | 14.8 | 22.5 |
| Borrowings from other banks | 2.2 | 3.4 |
| Other liabilities | 1.4 | 2.2 |
| Total | 65.7 | 100.0 |

Source: Statisticki bilten Sluzbe drustvenog knjigovodsta, No. 2 (1972), Table 6.


TABLE 2.9

Short-Term Sources of Business Banks According to Origin
(end of year)

| | Billions of Dinars | | Percentage of Total | |
|---|---|---|---|---|
| | 1965 | 1969 | 1965 | 1969 |
| Borrowings from the National | | | | |
| of Yugoslavia | 14.7 | 14.8 | 35.3 | 22.5 |
| Socialist enterprises | 13.2 | 15.7 | 31.7 | 23.9 |
| Individuals | 1.9 | 6.9 | 4.6 | 10.5 |
| Other domestic sectors | 9.7 | 16.1 | 23.3 | 24.5 |
| Rest of the world | 2.2 | 12.2 | 5.3 | 18.6 |
| Total | 41.7 | 65.7 | 100.0 | 100.0 |

Source: Flow-of-Funds Accounts of the National Bank
of Yugoslavia; Annual Report of the National Bank of Yugoslavia, 1969; unpublished materials.

from socialist enterprises and, particularly in the last few years, from individuals and foreign sources. This is a significant indication of changes in the pattern of ultimate lending, reflecting changes in the pattern of income distribution and formation of saving and also the future orientation of bank activity pursuing a policy of attracting new sources.

Investment sources consist of investment sources proper and housing sources. The second may be used only for housing. The first may be used for all kinds of credits and for all purposes. As a result, this group of sources has always been considered preferential, and banks are ready to pay a higher interest rate--or provide additional services to attract depositors or press borrowers to deposit some balances amounting in effect to compensatory deposits. The sources for these funds are mainly the bank's own funds (credit funds), time deposits, and domestic borrowings, as indicated in Table 2.10.

The sector distribution of investment sources shows that, in addition to their own funds, the most important sectors are governments and then socialist enterprises. The share of foreign lenders and individuals in investment sources of banks is the least significant.

Parallel to the two groups of sources are the two groups of bank investments dealing with short-term credits and investment credits. It already has been mentioned that the essential attribute of short-term credits is that they are granted on the basis of short-term sources, regardless of their maturity, although they are predominantly short-term. The same is valid for investment credits, which are granted on the basis of investment sources.

The difference between these two types of credit is in the system of regulations and the purpose for which they are used. Short-term credits are significantly regulated as to maturity, to whom they may be granted, and for what purpose. Investment credits are restricted in that they cannot exceed the amount of investment sources. The exception is housing credits (granted on the basis of housing sources), which may be granted only for housing and communal investments.

Short-term investments of business banks are nearly all in the form of credits to customers. There are no investments in securities. Investments in foreign assets are not very significant.

The specific feature of uses of business bank sources is a relatively high amount of deposits with the central bank. Business banks hold large amounts of compulsory re-

TABLE 2.10

Investment Sources of Business Banks
(end of 1971)

| | Total | |
| --- | --- | --- |
| | Billions of Dinars | Percentage of Total |
| Own funds | 13.8 | 13.6 |
| Time deposits | 21.7 | 21.3 |
| Bonds | 0.4 | 0.4 |
| Restricted deposits | 3.3 | 3.2 |
| Borrowings from other financial institutions[a] | 37.9 | 37.3 |
| Foreign borrowings | 2.6 | 2.6 |
| Housing sources | 18.2 | 17.9 |
| Other liabilities | 3.8 | 3.7 |
| Total | 101.7 | 100.0 |

[a]Up to October 1969 this item accounted for the major part of investment sources originating in bank borrowings by government bodies. Government bodies thus used sources coming from the abolished investment loan funds (after using one part of them for investment in credit funds of business banks). In October 1969 it was decided to change the legal status of these sources. The existing borrowing contracts were concealed and sources entrusted to banks as government agents (commissioners), so that these borrowings were sharply reduced. They are classified as sources of investment loan funds in the flow-of-funds accounts and balance sheets of financial institutions.

Source: Statisticki bilten Sluzbe drustvenog knjigovodsta, No. 2 (1972), Table 7; unpublished sources.

## TABLE 2.11

Investment Sources of Business Banks According to Sectors
(end of 1971)

|  | Billions of Dinars | Percent- age of Total |
|---|---|---|
| Own funds (including housing funds) | 24.7 | 24.3 |
| Socialist enterprises | 15.6 | 15.3 |
| Government | 38.9 | 38.3 |
| Individuals | 4.3 | 4.2 |
| Other domestic sectors | 15.5 | 15.3 |
| Rest of the world | 2.6 | 2.6 |
| Total | 101.6 | 100.0 |

Source:  Unpublished sources.


## TABLE 2.12

Uses of Short-Term Sources of Business Banks
(end of 1971)

|  | Billions of Dinars | Percent- age of Total |
|---|---|---|
| Foreign assets | 1.6 | 2.4 |
| Foreign exchange credits to domestic sectors | 0.8 | 1.2 |
| Short-term credits | 40.5 | 61.6 |
| Consumer credits | 4.5 | 6.9 |
| Use of short-term sources for invest- ment crediting | 2.7 | 4.1 |
| Credits to other banks | 2.2 | 3.4 |
| Deposits with the National Bank | 12.6 | 19.2 |
| Gyro accounts | 1.1 | 1.7 |
| Compulsory reserves | 7.3 | 11.1 |
| Special reserve fund accounts | 1.0 | 1.5 |
| Other deposits | 3.2 | 4.9 |
| Other assets | 0.8 | 1.2 |
| Total | 65.7 | 100.0 |

Source:  Statisticki bilten Sluzbe drustvenog knjigovodsta, No. 2 (1972), Table 6.

serves on separate accounts, in addition to regular gyro
accounts, liquidity reserve accounts, and other accounts.
The relatively large amounts of these deposits require
large bank borrowings from the central bank.  The main
users of short-term credits are socialist enterprises (33
percent of dinar credits, total of foreign exchange credits
at the end of 1969).

Uses of investment sources also are confined to bilateral investments in the form of credits to investors.
The amount of securities is negligible.  There are no data
on the term structure of these investments.  Scattered
evidence suggests that investment credits are granted in
a wide variety, beginning with terms shorter than one year
to terms longer than 22 years.  Housing credits are predominantly granted on terms longer than 20 years.

The main users of investment credits are socialist
enterprises (nearly all of these credits), except for housing credits, part of which are granted to other organizations and individuals, and credits for communal investments,
which are granted to local governments.

The combined balance sheet of all banks (including
the National Bank of Yugoslavia) and all bank operations

TABLE 2.13

Uses of Investment Sources of Business Banks
(end of 1971)

|  | Billions of Dinars | Percent- age of Total |
| --- | --- | --- |
| Investment credits | 66.5 | 65.5 |
| Housing credits and credits for communal investment | 17.3 | 17.0 |
| Credits to other financial institu- tions | 11.1 | 10.9 |
| Investment credits in foreign ex- change to domestic sectors | 2.1 | 2.1 |
| Unused sources | 4.1 | 4.0 |
| Other assets | 0.5 | 0.5 |
| Total | 101.6 | 100.0 |

Source:  Statisticki bilten Sluzbe drustvenog knjigovodsta, No. 2 (1972), Table 7.

65

presented in Table 2.14 shows a relatively simplified pattern of bank operations, their investments and sources.

## Experience and Prospects

The new banking structure has been in operation since 1966, a period not long enough for full adjustment to have taken place to the new institutional background and more sophisticated needs for financing. During this period banks have indicated a significant progress under conditions of substantial increase in free competition and economic determination of bank policy.

The process of adjustment of bank operations to new requirements was hampered by many obstacles. First, the existing structure of investments, which were made during a period when economic calculations played a minor role, proved resistant to attempts to readjust them to the new banking principles. Important external barriers existed that hampered improvement in the efficiency of banking, for example, the still-important influence of governments; an inadequate interest rate policy, which insisted on relatively low interest rates; a demand for financial resources that outpaced the supply because of relatively low risk elasticity, a low interest rate, and requirements for a high rate of economic growth; and a relatively undifferentiated financial structure that overloaded banks. Their net effect was to hamper stronger economic determination of bank behavior, to induce regional confinement of financial flows (under the influence of government bodies), and to weaken bank stimulation of saving and supply of financial resources and economic allocation of these resources. These facts suggest that the main causes of deficiencies in the banking structure come from external sources. This is a significant observation regarding future developments of banking structure, indicating that further improvement of its efficiency depends in the first place on improvement of the external conditions of its functioning, rather than on new institutional adjustments. This is also consistent with the old rule that the banking system shares the advancement of efficiency of the whole economy.

## FINANCIAL SEMI-INTERMEDIARIES

The second group of financial institutions consists of financial semi-intermediaries, i.e., financial institu-

TABLE 2.14

Combined Bank Balance Sheet
(end of 1969)

| | Short-Term Operations | | Investment Operations | | Total | |
|---|---|---|---|---|---|---|
| | Billions of Dinars | Percentage Share | Billions of Dinars | Percentage Share | Billions of Dinars | Percentage Share |
| Assets | | | | | | |
| Foreign assets | 8.0 | 10.6 | 0.2 | 0.2 | 8.2 | 4.6 |
| Foreign exchange credits | 4.2 | 5.6 | 2.4 | 2.3 | 6.6 | 3.7 |
| Credits to customers | 62.2 | 82.6 | 84.4 | 82.6 | 146.6 | 82.6 |
| Short-term credits | 57.4 | 76.2 | -- | -- | 57.4 | 32.2 |
| Consumer credits | 4.8 | 6.4 | -- | -- | 7.8 | 2.7 |
| Investment credits | -- | -- | 67.1 | 65.7 | 67.1 | 37.8 |
| Housing credits | -- | -- | 17.3 | 16.9 | 17.3 | 9.8 |
| Other assets | 0.9 | 1.2 | 15.2 | 14.9 | 16.1 | 9.1 |
| Total | 75.3 | 100.0 | 102.2 | 100.0 | 177.5 | 100.0 |
| Own funds | -- | -- | 24.7 | 24.2 | 24.7 | 13.9 |
| Deposits | 60.3 | 80.0 | 26.4 | 25.8 | 86.7 | 48.9 |
| Gyro accounts and similar | 32.6 | 43.3 | -- | -- | 32.6 | 18.4 |
| Other sight-term deposits | 13.3 | 17.6 | -- | -- | 13.3 | 7.5 |
| Restricted deposits | 14.1 | 18.7 | 3.3 | 0.3 | 17.4 | 9.8 |
| Time deposits | 0.3 | 0.4 | 23.1 | 22.5 | 23.4 | 13.2 |
| Bonds | -- | -- | 0.4 | 0.4 | 0.4 | 0.2 |
| Foreign borrowings | 12.4 | 16.5 | 3.4 | 3.3 | 15.8 | 8.9 |
| Other liabilities | 2.6 | 3.5 | 47.3 | 46.3 | 49.9 | 28.1 |
| Total | 75.3 | 100.0 | 102.2 | 100.0 | 177.5 | 100.0 |

Source: Annual Report of the National Bank of Yugoslavia, 1969, pp. 44 and 48.

tions that create only financial assets or only liabilities, but not both as in the case of regular financial intermediation. It was shown that these institutions are "investment loan funds" and that they accounted for the major part of financing before 1964.

In 1963-65 the major part of these institutions disappeared (first the federal investment loan fund, and then republican, district, and communal investment loan funds, and housing funds as well), so that in 1966 only one type of these funds existed: republican and communal "joint reserve funds of enterprises." However, very soon afterward federal funds were established: the Federal Fund for Financing of Less-Developed Regions, the Fund for Reconstruction of Skopje, and the Fund for Financing of Export Credits.

Sources of all these funds predominantly come from taxes or government grants. However, there is a tendency to finance these funds on the market (by issues of bonds, etc.), and first steps in this direction may be expected in the near future.

The joint reserve funds represent a specific type of fund that comes from compulsory contributions by socialist enterprises. It already was explained that they grant credits to enterprises that are not eligible for regular financing for temporary financial difficulties. Their role becomes increasingly important in view of the growing complexity of economic processes and the increasing responsibility of socialist enterprises in their own affairs.

The resources of the abolished investment loan funds (1963-65) were used partly for investment in bank credit funds and partly for the establishment of government investment accounts at all levels of government. As indicated in Table 2.15, these sources account for the major part of investment loan funds. They are not allocated by new contributions but by the amount of interest on credits, and repayments amount to a substantial portion of disposable resources.


OTHER FINANCIAL INSTITUTIONS

In addition to the deposit banks and public-sector financial institutions, a full list of financial institutions would include such organizations as insurance and provident institutions, specialized credit institutions financed on the market (banques d'affaires), unit and investment trusts and investment companies, and open market

TABLE 2.15

Investment Loan Funds, End of 1971
(billions of dinars)

| Uses | | Sources | |
|---|---|---|---|
| Credits to socialist | | Federal sources | 41.8 |
| enterprises | 26.6 | Investment accounts | 34.2 |
| For fixed assets | 21.9 | Investment loan | |
| For working assets | 4.7 | funds | 7.6 |
| Credits to other or- | | Other government | |
| ganizations | 1.9 | sources | 18.8 |
| Credits to banks | 30.9 | Investment accounts | 10.3 |
| Monetary balances | 0.5 | Investment loan | |
| Other uses | 0.7 | funds | 8.5 |
| Total | 60.6 | Total | 60.6 |

Source:  Statisticki bilten Sluzbe drustvenog knjigovodsta, No. 2 (1972), Table 7.

institutions (share and bond market institutions).[11] The
answer to the question of which of these types of financial
institutions exist in Yugoslavia will serve both as a summary and as a comparison with a developed financial market
economy.

Insurance and provident institutions exist in Yugoslavia.  They cannot, however, be classified as financial
institutions.  Social security institutes are organized on
the current-expenditures-equal-current-receipts basis and
do not have premium reserves (as in the first stage of decentralization).  Insurance institutes provide life insurance and accumulate premium reserves.  The amount of these
reserves is negligible and, in addition, has to be held on
deposit with banks.

The problem of making insurance and provident institutions active in the financial field deserves increased attention in the post-reform period.  In the pre-reform period the operations of these institutions were adjusted to
a relatively low level of personal income.  The increased
share of personal income in total income since reform has
changed these conditions fundamentally, making room for
significant increases in different types of financial investment.  There may be a good chance for extending social

security by introducing an appropriate second, voluntary line for this insurance in addition to the existing compulsory line, which would be based on premium reserves. The voluntary line of social security may involve additional services, such as better hospitalization, additional remuneration coverage, additional pension, and similar benefits. This may be an important stimulation for saving and financial investment by households. There are significant obstacles for an efficient implementation of such an extension. Among these obstacles may be mentioned the low interest rate policy, continued increase in prices, and an adverse attitude toward insurance based on several bad experiences in the past. A plan for the extension of services of provident and insurance institutions to the financial field would require comprehensive preparations.

Specialized credit institutions financed on the market do not exist in Yugoslavia thus far. The same is true of trusts and investment companies and of open market institutions as well. Institutions that may be classified as (at least) quasi-open market institutions are arrangements organized by the Yugoslav Banking Association and other regional banking associations for interbank borrowing of call money to cover an unexpected drain of reserve money, something similar to the "federal funds market" in U.S. banking terminology. However, a demand that has thus far outpaced supply has hampered satisfactory development of these arrangements.

Finally, the Social Accounting Service should be mentioned. It performs the same three functions as in the first stage of decentralization. It does not perform financial operations (accepting deposits, granting credits, etc.) and cannot be considered a financial institution.


SUMMARY AND OUTLOOK

The structure of financial institutions in Yugoslavia is relatively simple. More of its deficiencies can be traced to its functioning than to its institutional pattern. The fact that there are only two of six possible types of financial institution does not mean very much. There are very few developed market economies whose financial structure includes the full list of financial institutions. There are many economies more developed than Yugoslavia's whose financial structure does not include all types of financial institutions.

The above analysis of the structure of financial institutions in Yugoslavia shows that its deficiencies stem
from both internal and external causes, though the external tend to dominate. Further development of the structure
of financial institutions may be expected to take place in
the field of operation rather than in institutional modification. In this connection, the main improvements may
come from a more realistic interest rate policy, reduction
in government influence on bank policy, more energetic
participation of socialist enterprises in bank policy formation, and a surmounting of the historical barrier of the
administrative approach to the banking business and the
structure of bank investments related to this approach,
which have been inherited from the previous periods of
rigid central planning.


## NOTES

1. See, for example, G. Macesich, "Major Trends in
the Postwar Economy of Yugoslavia," in Wayne S. Vucinich,
ed., Contemporary Yugoslavia: Twenty Years of Socialist
Experiment (Berkeley and Los Angeles: University of California Press, 1969), pp. 203-235.
2. In 1969 about 40 percent of industrial products
were under price regulation and 30 percent of retail trade
goods. Prices of agricultural goods were not restricted.
D. Vukovic, "Prices after the Economic Reform," Yugoslav
Survey, No. 25 (1966), and "Price Formation and Social
Price Control," Yugoslav Survey, No. 1 (1968).
3. In addition to liberalized imports in the proper
sense, there have been imports of "general goods" (about
40 percent of total imports from convertible currency
countries); the remaining 10 percent involves "commodity
quotas" and "import permits." L. Janičić, "The New External Trade and Foreign Exchange System," Yugoslav Survey,
No. 4 (1967). If one keeps in mind that "general quota"
need not be used in the year of issue, and that there always have been substantial amounts of unused quotas, it
appears that a significant part of this type of import may
be considered "free." In addition, it appears that socialist enterprises have been authorized for free imports
covered by "retention quota" and to 10 percent of their
allocations to depreciation funds. Taking all these liberal imports together, they account for far more than one-
third of total imports in convertible currencies (according to some estimates more than half).

4. The official exchange rate was 300 old dinars for a U.S. dollar. The settlement rate was 750 old dinars for a U.S. dollar (7.5 new dinars). D.C., "Changes in Yugoslav Foreign Trade and Foreign Exchange System," Yugoslav Survey, No. 5 (1961); M.M., "The System and Organization of Foreign Trade," Yugoslav Survey, No. 14 (1963).

5. A. Domandžić, "Custom Tariffs," Yugoslav Survey, No. 24 (1965).

6. L. Janičić, "New External Trade."

7. M. Radovanović, "Joint Investment by Domestic Enterprises and Business and Financial Cooperation Between Yugoslav and Foreign Firms," Yugoslav Survey, No. 1 (1968).

8. Lj. Adamović, "Foreign Trade Policy in Yugoslavia," Economist (English issue), Zagreb, 1969.

9. Two banking laws were passed in 1965: the National Bank of Yugoslavia Law (Zakon o Narodnoj banci Jugoslavije), February 1965, and the Banking and Credit Law, March 1965. Both are published in the Official Gazette, No. 12 (1965). An English translation is available in H. Aufricht, "Central Banking Legislation," International Monetary Fund, Vol. II (Washington, D.C., 1967).

10. D. Dimitrijević, "Use of Flow-of-Funds Accounts for Monetary Planning in Yugoslavia," Review of Studies in Income and Wealth, No. 1 (1969).

11. See, for example, Capital Markets Study, General Report (Paris: Committee for Invisible Transactions, OECD, 1967), p. 152.

# 3

Let us consider now the implications of the reform in the field of financial instruments, primarily as to their size and pattern, whether they have adapted to the new requirements, and what may be expected in the future.

The increased role of financial variables presumably requires an increase in the size and differentiation of financial instruments. It would oversimplify the problem if only the amount of financial assets and the number of types of financial instrument were considered. The experience of many developed countries indicates that a less differentiated structure of financial instruments may be efficient.[1] This is because the efficiency of a set of financial instruments involves many qualitative determinants, so that nominal lists and amounts of these instruments may be misleading.

## SIZE OF FINANCIAL ASSETS

The amount of financial assets has increased significantly since 1965. This increase has not exceeded the rate of growth of GNP, so that the financial assets-GNP ratio substantially outran ratios reached before the reform. The rate of increase in financial assets was also higher than that of gross saving, so that financial assets-gross saving ratio has been significantly increased.

The financial interrelations ratio may be estimated to be about 0.6, which is far less than in developed market economies, where it is about 1.0 or more.[2] Although comparisons between the Yugoslav and market economy ratios are difficult to make, there is no doubt that the difference

TABLE 3.1

Financial Assets
(end of year)

| | 1963 | 1964 | 1965 | 1966 | 1967 | 1968 | 1969 | 1970 |
|---|---|---|---|---|---|---|---|---|
| Total (billions of dinars | 120.0 | 151.0 | 186.5 | 267.7 | 307.7 | 370.4 | 429.0 | 514.4 |
| Ratio to GNP | 2.62 | 2.48 | 2.35 | 2.70 | 2.97 | 3.31 | 3.25 | 3.26 |
| Ratio to gross saving | 6.20 | 5.73 | 6.19 | 7.79 | 8.24 | 9.37 | 9.35 | 8.87 |

Sources: Flow-of-Funds Accounts of the National Bank of Yugoslavia; Annual Report of the National Bank of Yugoslavia, 1969.

74

is an indication of the relatively low state of development of the Yugoslav financial structure.

## STRUCTURE OF FINANCIAL INSTRUMENTS

To judge from the evidence presented in Table 3.2, the structure of financial instruments has remained undifferentiated. A large share of deposits in the total financial assets of nonfinancial sectors and an insignificant amount of securities (and in a very simplified pattern) characterize financial instruments in nearly the same way as before the reform.

This does not mean that differentiation in financial instruments has failed to advance. In the first place, the share of time and savings deposits in total financial assets of nonfinancial sectors has increased. In addition to the existing seven types of deposits (savings deposits, time deposits, housing deposits, other sight deposits, restricted deposits, foreign exchange deposits—of working organizations and individuals—and monetary deposits), banks are preparing additional types of deposit to meet the new needs and preferences of individuals. One type would be individual checking accounts adapted to the need of an increasing number of persons to receive personal income through a bank account and to pay through this account. Second, in spite of the insignificant amount of securities outstanding, important progress has been made in this field. In 1969 a particularly significant development occurred involving the issue of bonds by socialist enterprises and new regulations for bond issues and a bond market. Two socialist enterprises issued bonds: the Automobile Factory in Kragujevac (subscribed 114 million dinars) and the Yugoslav Railways (subscribed 167 million dinars). The new regulations cover such points as who may issue bonds (governments, banks, socialist enterprises), under what conditions, how bonds can be bought and sold, regulation of the bond interest rate, which states that this interest rate is not under ceiling rate regulations. The Federal Executive Council was at the same time authorized to issue detailed regulations in the field of bond financing following the guidelines involved in this legislation.[3] A specific stipulation in these regulations obliged banks to issue negotiable certificates of shares in their credit funds. These certificates would have the status of securities. Third, a significant increase in the share of foreign exchange assets also indicates a differentiation of financial

# TABLE 3.2

Financial Instruments According to Type, Domestic Sectors
(end of year)

| | Billions of Dinars | | Percentage of Total | |
|---|---|---|---|---|
| | 1963 | 1969 | 1963 | 1969 |
| **Nonfinancial Sectors** | | | | |
| Money | 14.8 | 30.3 | 12.3 | 7.1 |
|   Currency | 3.6 | 11.9 | 3.0 | 2.8 |
|   Deposit money | 11.2 | 18.4 | 9.3 | 4.3 |
| Other sight deposits | 3.9 | 13.3 | 3.3 | 3.1 |
| Restricted deposits | 6.3 | 14.0 | 5.3 | 3.2 |
| Time deposits | 1.2 | 23.2 | 1.0 | 5.4 |
| Bank bonds | 0.1 | 0.8 | -- | 0.2 |
| Government bonds | 0.1 | 2.0 | -- | 0.5 |
| Direct credits (including | | | | |
|     trade credits) | 14.9 | 80.1 | 12.4 | 18.7 |
| Foreign assets | 0.3 | 8.9 | 0.3 | 2.1 |
| Other financial assets | 2.0 | 16.4 | 1.8 | 3.8 |
|     Total | 43.6 | 189.0 | 36.4 | 44.1 |
| **Financial Sectors** | | | | |
| Short-term credits | 31.3 | 62.2 | 26.1 | 14.5 |
| Investment credits | 2.7 | 109.8 | 33.0 | 25.6 |
|   Bank credits | 39.7 | 81.3 | 2.2 | 19.0 |
|   Credits by investment loan | | | | |
|     funds | 37.0 | 28.5 | 30.8 | 6.6 |
| Foreign assets | 1.9 | 15.7 | 1.6 | 3.7 |
| Other financial assets | 3.5 | 52.3 | 2.9 | 12.1 |
|     Total | 76.4 | 240.0 | 63.6 | 55.9 |
| Total financial assets | 120.0 | 429.0 | 100.0 | 100.0 |
| Total money supply | 18.4 | 32.6 | -- | -- |

Sources: Flow-of-Funds Accounts of the National Bank of Yugoslavia; Annual Report of the National Bank of Yugoslavia, 1969.

TABLE 3.3

Financial Assets of Nonfinancial Sectors
(end of year)

| | Billions of Dinars | | Percentage of Total | |
|---|---|---|---|---|
| | 1963 | 1969 | 1963 | 1969 |
| Socialist enterprises | 28.1 | 135.1 | 64.3 | 71.5 |
| Individuals | 6.2 | 31.1 | 14.2 | 16.4 |
| Other domestic sectors | 9.4 | 22.8 | 21.5 | 12.1 |
| Total | 43.7 | 189.0 | 100.0 | 100.0 |

Sources: Flow-of-Funds Accounts of the National Bank of Yugoslavia; Annual Report of the National Bank of Yugoslavia, 1969.

instruments. Thus, in addition to traditional types of foreign exchange accounts (foreign exchange accounts of banks with foreign banks, foreign exchange accounts of domestic residents with domestic banks, e.g., socialist enterprises and individuals), foreign assets of individuals became relatively significant. Fourth, the share of money supply in total financial assets of nonfinancial sectors decreased significantly.

Sector distribution of financial assets of the nonfinancial sectors shows significant change in favor of individuals and socialist enterprises, who had an increased share of total income and saving.

FUTURE DEVELOPMENT

The main features of the changes in financial instruments since the reform have been a significant increase and differentiation in bank deposits and the first preparatory steps in the field of securities. The problem of future development of financial instruments and their amount is related primarily to the questions of how long the development will manifest itself in an increase in deposits and when a higher increase and differentiation in securities may be expected.

The question of size of financial assets is less difficult to answer. The increasing share of individuals and
socialist enterprises in total income and saving and the
increased role of financial intermediation will presumably
require a relatively significant increase in financial
assets.

The deposits-securities dilemma will very likely be
resolved by a higher increase in deposits than in securities, at least in the near future. The reason for this expectation is that an increase in securities requires, as
its foundation, more financial sophistication on the part
of individuals and enterprises. It requires well-organized
open-market institutions and information in the field of
securities. Investments in deposits, on the other hand,
do not require these preconditions, and in addition individuals are very familiar with them. A good bank policy
may manage to overcome some of the difficulties and make
securities more attractive. However, it was shown that
there are many external reasons for a successful bank policy:
it depends in part on a more realistic interest rate policy
and a relatively stable price level.

Nevertheless, these problems should not be exaggerated.
An undeveloped pattern of securities and a relatively small
quantity of them does not necessarily mean that financial
structure is inefficient. It is reasonable to expect further improvement in the pattern of financial instruments
by further differentiation of deposits and improvement of
facilities related to deposits, with a parallel increase in
the rate of growth of securities. It is difficult to predict the time required for this process; it will depend
both on the ability of banks to create appropriate instruments attractive to savers and on changes in the behavior
of buyers of financial instruments.

A specific problem that should be mentioned concerns
provident institutions. It was shown that there may be
good reason to expect a significant increase in the types
of financial instrument created by these institutions. An
increase in these instruments may be expected to improve
the pattern of financial instruments significantly.


NOTES

1. Capital Markets Study, General Report (Paris:
Committee for Invisible Transactions, OECD, 1967), pp. 111-
114.

2. According to R. Goldsmith, this is the ratio of total financial assets to total tangible assets. See R. Goldsmith, "Financial Intermediaries in the American Economy Since 1900," La Estructura Financiera y al Crecemento Economica (CEMLA [Center for Econo-Monetary Latin America], 1963).

3. "The Law of Changes of Banking and Credit Law," Official Gazette, No. 55, 1969.

# CHAPTER
# 4

## FINANCIAL
## FLOWS

Three aspects of financial flows are interpreted in this chapter: ultimate lending, ultimate borrowing, and financial intermediation.

## ULTIMATE LENDING

The term "ultimate lending" refers to financial investments by nonfinancial domestic sectors. Where there is a more rapid increase of demand relative to the supply of credits, the term means the same as credit availability, or supply of credits. Thus defined, ultimate lending includes investments in both nonmonetary and monetary assets. This may seem too broad, at least as it includes an increase in holdings of currency. However, holdings of currency may be considered as lending to the monetary authority (bank of issue), having the same consequences as holdings of deposits with the bank of issue.

The reform's institutional adjustments have had very significant consequences on the determinants, size, and pattern of ultimate lending. In the field of determinants of ultimate lending, the main outcome of these institutional adjustments has been an increase in the role of economic calculations. In this connection the main changes have been an increase in the role of interest rate and the risk factor, including expectations of price-level changes. These changes have made interest rate policy and stabilization policies essential preconditions for an efficient stimulation of saving and indeed for the functioning of the whole financial mechanism.

The size of ultimate borrowing has increased more than proportionally in comparison with the increase in GNP, as shown in Table 4.1. The rate of increase in ultimate borrowing was also higher than the rate of increase in saving.

A higher rate of increase in ultimate borrowing than in GNP and saving reflects the increased role of the financial mechanisms and variables, particularly if the parallel increase in the self-financing ratio is taken into account (see Table 2.2). A higher rate of increase than GNP reflects the decrease in the saving ratio. Comparison with other countries shows that the above ratios are very high, exceeding those in many developed market economies.[1]

When there is an increased share of households and socialist enterprises in total income and saving, their share in ultimate lending has also increased, as shown in Table 4.2. The same reasons have resulted in a further increase in decentralizing ultimate lending and particularly in a substantial increase in voluntary ultimate lending.

The "term structure" evidence presented in Table 4.3 shows a substantial change to short-term lending, mainly in the form of deposits and trade credits. The development of long-term lending has involved a decreasing share of own funds and an increasing share of time deposits and bonds.

Another significant classification of the ultimate lending of domestic sectors relates to direct-indirect lending channels. As noted elsewhere, there were several bond issues by socialist enterprises and governments. These types of direct crediting (outside financial institutions) have remained insignificant in amount, although very significant as a starting point in a process of increase in size and differentiation of direct crediting. Direct crediting has remained mainly related to trade credits, and a significant increase in the size and differentiation of these credits may be considered an important change in the role of direct crediting. Thus, in addition to the old types of short-term trade crediting--which include prolonged account receivables--there has been a tendency to increase the share of medium-term trade credits to domestic and foreign buyers of equipment, transportation equipment (especially ships), and consumer credits.

Another form of direct financial flow that has become increasingly significant is the "joint fund" resulting from "joint-venture" arrangements among domestic and between domestic and foreign firms, such as joint financing of some investment projects, financing within "cooperation" arrangements, and partnerships.

TABLE 4.1

Ultimate Borrowing, GNP, And Gross Saving

| | 1963 | 1964 | 1965 | 1966 | 1967 | 1968 | 1969 | 1970 |
|---|---|---|---|---|---|---|---|---|
| Ultimate borrow-ing (billions of dinars) | 14.4 | 18.8 | 24.7 | 24.2 | 27.3 | 39.2 | 45.8 | 63.2 |
| Ratio to GNP | 0.32 | 0.31 | 0.31 | 0.24 | 0.26 | 0.35 | 0.35 | 0.40 |
| Ratio to gross saving | 0.73 | 0.70 | 0.84 | 0.69 | 0.70 | 0.96 | 0.99 | 1.00 |

Sources: Flow-of-Funds Accounts of the National Bank of Yugoslavia; Annual Report of the National Bank of Yugoslavia, 1969, 1970.

TABLE 4.2

Ultimate Lending According to Sectors
(percentage of total)

| | 1963 | 1964 | 1965 | 1966 | 1967 | 1968 | 1969 | 1970 |
|---|---|---|---|---|---|---|---|---|
| Socialist enterprises | 24.5 | 28.4 | 55.8 | 46.6 | 55.4 | 65.5 | 58.3 | 58.5 |
| Republican and local gov- ernments[a] | 24.6 | 29.2 | 3.0 | 11.5 | 12.1 | 9.7 | 11.0 | 8.1 |
| Other organizations and unclassified | 8.5 | 13.9 | 28.1 | 8.4 | 5.1 | 3.9 | 6.6 | 5.3 |
| Household | 11.9 | 9.6 | 4.4 | 20.4 | 13.4 | 13.1 | 16.3 | 17.0 |
| Total decentralized | 69.5 | 81.1 | 91.3 | 86.9 | 86.0 | 92.2 | 92.2 | 88.9 |
| Federal government[a] | 30.5 | 18.9 | 8.7 | 13.7 | 14.0 | 7.7 | 7.8 | 11.1 |
| Voluntary ultimate lend- ing | 38.3 | 56.4 | 78.7 | 71.0 | 73.2 | 76.5 | 73.7 | 77.7 |

[a]Including investment loan funds.

Sources: Flow-of-Funds Accounts of the National Bank of Yugoslavia; Annual Report of the National Bank of Yugoslavia, 1969, 1970.

TABLE 4.3

Term Structure of Ultimate Lending by Domestic Sectors
(percentage of total)

| | 1963 | 1964 | 1965 | 1966 | 1967 | 1968 | 1969 | 1970 |
|---|---|---|---|---|---|---|---|---|
| Short-term | | | | | | | | |
| Deposits | 18.6 | 24.8 | 23.8 | 18.8 | 9.1 | 27.1 | 24.9 | 25.0 |
| Other types | 26.0 | 17.5 | 51.6 | 35.8 | 50.4 | 45.9 | 45.6 | 45.9 |
| Total | 44.6 | 42.3 | 75.4 | 54.6 | 59.5 | 73.0 | 70.5 | 70.9 |
| Long- and medium-term | | | | | | | | |
| Deposits | 7.3 | 7.1 | 2.7 | 21.0 | 17.3 | 10.6 | 14.4 | 13.5 |
| Bonds | 1.9 | 1.9 | -0.1 | 1.2 | -0.5 | -0.4 | 0.1 | 1.7 |
| Own funds[a] | 46.2 | 48.7 | 22.0 | 23.2 | 23.7 | 16.8 | 15.0 | 13.9 |
| Total | 55.4 | 57.7 | 24.6 | 45.4 | 40.5 | 27.0 | 29.5 | 29.1 |

[a]Mainly receipts by investment loan funds.

Sources: Flow-of-Funds Accounts of the National Bank of Yugoslavia; Annual Report of the National Bank of Yugoslavia, 1969, 1970.

Finally, total ultimate lending (ultimate lending by domestic sectors plus foreign borrowing) should be considered. The evidence is summarized in Table 4.4. As noted, the reform's institutional changes introduced new types of foreign borrowing, making it possible for banks and socialist enterprises to borrow freely within the borrowing ceilings determined by monetary authorities. These institutional changes resulted, however, in a diversification of borrowers, but the share of this borrowing (foreign lending to domestic sectors) in total ultimate lending has not been increased.

## ULTIMATE BORROWING

The term refers to borrowing by the nonfinancial sectors. The size of ultimate borrowings has followed the path of ultimate lending under demand conditions that have outpaced the supply of financial resources. The reform's institutional adjustments have not introduced significant modifications in this area. The main determinants of ultimate borrowing have remained low risk elasticity, expectation of price increase, and a relatively low interest rate policy (nearly a zero or even a negative real interest

TABLE 4.4

Total Ultimate Lending

|  | 1963 | 1964 | 1965 | 1966 | 1967 | 1968 | 1969 | 1970 |
|---|---|---|---|---|---|---|---|---|
| Billions of dinars | 16.0 | 19.6 | 27.4 | 29.6 | 30.9 | 45.1 | 50.3 | 62.2 |
| Percentage of total Domestic sectors | 88.6 | 90.9 | 88.1 | 89.7 | 90.3 | 88.5 | 90.1 | 92.1 |
| Rest of the world | 11.4 | 9.1 | 11.9 | 10.3 | 9.7 | 11.5 | 9.9 | 7.9 |

Sources: Flow-of-Funds Accounts of the National Bank of Yugoslavia; Annual Report of the National Bank of Yugoslavia, 1969, 1970.

rate). These determinants necessarily have brought about a very high demand for financial resources. This does not mean that reform adjustments have had no influence, but thus far the influence has been comparatively small.

The sector pattern of ultimate borrowing has also remained unchanged, as indicated by the evidence presented in Table 4.5. Socialist enterprises have been the major borrowing sector, as before the reform.

The term structure of ultimate borrowing has been changed in favor of short-term credits, mainly due to expansion of trade credits and accounts payable (which increasingly overpass the normal maturities and are really used as a source of short-term financing). If this type of borrowing is excluded, short-term borrowing has decreased its share in total borrowing. A decreasing share of long-term financing reflects the increased share of self-financing of investment by socialist enterprises.

A comparison of Table 4.6 with Table 4.3 shows an increasing discrepancy between term structures of ultimate lending and ultimate borrowing. This is leading to a higher share of medium- and long-term borrowing and lending respectively, which measures the increased role of the transformation function of financial intermediaries.

## FINANCIAL INTERMEDIATION

The basic features of financial intermediation were explained in the discussion of the financial institutions structure. It remains to explain credit system and to summarize recent changes in the field of determinants, effects, and the efficiency of intermediation flows.

According to the definition used here, the credit system consists of a system of regulations covering by whom, to whom, for what purposes, and under what conditions credits may be granted. These regulations encompass short-term crediting by banks, investment crediting by banks and other financial institutions, and direct crediting by non-financial institutions.

The majority of these regulations relate to bank short-term credits.* Regulations in the other two fields of crediting are relatively simple. For investment credits

---

*Credits granted on the basis of short-term resources (borrowings from the National Bank of Yugoslavia, sight deposits, etc.).

TABLE 4.5

Ultimate Borrowing According to Sectors

| | 1963 | 1964 | 1965 | 1966 | 1967 | 1968 | 1969 | 1970 |
|---|---|---|---|---|---|---|---|---|
| Total (billions of dinars) | 14.6 | 18.8 | 24.7 | 24.2 | 27.3 | 39.2 | 45.8 | 63.2 |
| Percentage of total | | | | | | | | |
| Socialist enterprises | 77.4 | 84.0 | 69.2 | 86.5 | 97.5 | 87.4 | 84.9 | 83.3 |
| Federal government | 7.0 | 6.0 | 21.7 | 9.3 | 0.7 | -2.2 | 1.3 | 4.2 |
| Other governments | 0.5 | 0.8 | 1.4 | -0.8 | 0.7 | 0.5 | 1.3 | 1.8 |
| Other organizations | 1.8 | 0.4 | 2.8 | 5.3 | -0.9 | 0.5 | 2.2 | 2.0 |
| Households | 10.4 | 6.7 | 0.3 | -0.8 | 1.1 | 8.8 | 6.8 | 8.0 |
| Total domestic sectors | 97.1 | 97.9 | 95.4 | 99.5 | 99.1 | 95.0 | 96.5 | 99.3 |
| Rest of the world | 2.9 | 2.1 | 4.6 | 0.5 | 0.9 | 5.0 | 3.5 | 0.7 |

Sources: Flow-of-Funds Accounts of the National Bank of Yugoslavia; Annual Report of the National Bank of Yugoslavia, 1969, 1970.

TABLE 4.6

Ultimate Borrowing According to Term Structure
(percentage of total)

|  | 1963 | 1964 | 1965 | 1966 | 1967 | 1968 | 1969 | 1970 |
|---|---|---|---|---|---|---|---|---|
| Short-term borrowing | 47.5 | 32.6 | 55.7 | 53.8 | 60.3 | 61.5 | 58.9 | 57.9 |
| Bank credit | 31.0 | 18.4 | 25.0 | 16.1 | 14.3 | 24.3 | 19.2 | 17.9 |
| Trade credit, accounts payable and unclassified | 16.5 | 14.2 | 30.7 | 37.7 | 46.0 | 37.2 | 39.7 | 40.0 |
| Long- and medium-term credit | 52.5 | 67.4 | 44.3 | 46.2 | 39.7 | 38.5 | 41.1 | 42.1 |

Sources: Flow-of-Funds Accounts of the National Bank of Yugoslavia; Annual Report of the National Bank of Yugoslavia, 1969, 1970.

88

there is only one rule: they cannot be granted except on the basis of "investment sources," such as own funds, time deposits, borrowing of investment sources, etc. This rule was introduced in 1963 and has remained unchanged. In the field of direct crediting there is a rule that socialist enterprises are allowed to grant credits within their basic business operations, such as trade credits, joint investment projects financing, and subscription of shares in bank credit funds. Other credit operations by nonfinancial sectors are not allowed. Regulations in this field of crediting, however, are considered rather vague and obsolete, so that there have been several attempts to introduce financial operations that are in fact inconsistent with the rule.* Future developments can be expected to lead to further extension of credit operations in this field and significant modification in the restrictive approach to this type of crediting.

In the field of short-term crediting there have been fundamental changes since the reform. In place of the previous system of demand regulation, a system of credit supply regulation was introduced in 1967. This change meant replacement of an extensive system of regulations covering to whom credits may be granted, for what purposes, etc., by a system based on the regulation of credit availability. This change, however, was less than a substitute for the credit availability regulation. The new system of credit regulation has carried over significant regulations from the previous one.** These regulations have been modified several times, so that the system of short-term crediting has become very close to a system of general-purpose short-term credits, bank responsibility for credit worthiness, and its freedom to decide about conditions and amount of crediting, similar to systems in market economies.

---

*For example, the previously mentioned borrowing by socialist enterprises from households by issuing bonds.

**For example, regulations covering to whom credits cannot be granted (governments, other organizations), for which purposes short-term credits may be granted (for working assets financing), and basic conditions for credit worthiness. These regulations were changed later, reducing credit regulations. In addition to listing purposes for which short-term credits may be granted, for instance, it has been said that they can be granted "for other purposes," which in effect has meant introduction of general-purpose credit.

Transition to a system of increasing bank decision-making power in granting credits and bank responsibility for the credit worthiness of borrowers and economic allocation of sources was consistent with the institutional changes in the reform. These changes, in addition to those mentioned above, were aimed at enabling banks to include broader economic determination in their credit operations parallel with the broader economic determination of socialist enterprise.

The increased role of economic calculation of financial flows has presumably improved their efficiency. As stated, they are still deficient in stimulating saving and ultimate lending, discouraging inefficient borrowing, and allocating financial sources economically. The basic causes of these deficiencies appear to have been the poor differentiation of the financial structure, inadequate interest rate policy, unadjusted fiscal policy, the relatively high influence of government administrative reasoning in bank policy formation, and a relatively high disequilibrium on financial markets, a heritage from the pre-reform period of heavy credit regulations and regional compartmentalization of bank crediting.

Developments since the reform have led to an abatement of these deficiencies and an improvement of efficiency in both ultimate lending and ultimate borrowing, and in financial intermediation as well. This is, however, a long-term process. Thus far, the reform's effects have prepared a favorable institutional basis for a successful development of this process. The functioning of the new institutional basis has not yet been satisfactorily adjusted to meet the new needs for financing. Although comparisons with the pre-reform period show significant improvement in the efficiency of financial flows, the process of their adjustment to the new needs for financing has advanced relatively slowly; and the major part of this adjustment is yet to come.

## NOTE

1. According to the Capital Markets Study, acquisition of financial assets-GNP ratio in 1965 amounted to 0.9 in France, 0.13 in Germany, 0.32 in Japan, 0.12 in the United Kingdom, and 0.13 in the United States. The average 1960–65 ratio between acquisition of financial assets and gross saving amounted to 0.56 in France, 0.47 in Germany, 1.05 in Japan, 0.63 in the United Kingdom, and 0.50 in the

United States. <u>Capital Markets Study, General Report</u> (Paris:  Committee for Invisible Transactions, OECD, 1967), pp. 97, 144.

# 5

## SOCIALIST ENTERPRISES

There is nothing specific in the general pattern of
uses of socialist enterprises. As shown in Table 5.1, they
consist of investments in fixed assets, inventories, and
financial assets. The pattern of sources is also very common, except allocations to the "business fund." This fund
represents the value of social capital in the hands of
socialist enterprises, and it comes partly from government
grants and partly from allocations from enterprises' income. The specific character of this fund means that it
is socially owned, but socialist enterprises are free to
use it in the way they find suitable. The only limitation
is that they are not allowed to use it for personal income
and other consumption purposes or for purposes that would
entail disinvestment. The other types of sources are the
same as in market economies: short-term credit, long-term
credit, and lately even bonds. Comparisons with sources of
firms in some developed market economies show that their
pattern lies within limits observed in these economies.[1]

The most significant changes in the pattern of uses
of socialist enterprises in comparison with the pre-reform
period relate to the sharp decrease in the share of investments in fixed assets and the increase in trade credit and
accounts receivable in total uses. On the sources side
there have been a substantial reduction in the share of
long-term borrowing (reflecting an increased self-financing
ratio) and a sharp increase in the share of trade credits
received and accounts payable. Considerable growth in
foreign borrowing is reflected in the relatively high increase in its share in the total sources of socialist enter-

TABLE 5.1

Sources and Uses of Socialist Enterprises
(percentage of total)

|  | 1961-64 | 1966-67 |
|---|---|---|
| Uses |  |  |
| Gross investment in fixed assets | 56.7 | 39.4 |
| Increase in inventories | 19.9 | 20.1 |
| Trade credit and accounts receivable | 8.8 | 27.5 |
| Money and other financial investments | 10.2 | 8.6 |
| Foreign assets | 0.0 | 1.2 |
| Other | 4.4 | 3.2 |
| Sources |  |  |
| Allocations to own funds | 40.1 | 39.3 |
| Long-term debt | 39.1 | 21.2 |
| Short-term debt | 10.6 | 9.8 |
| Trade credit and accounts payable | 7.5 | 22.7 |
| Foreign liabilities | 2.7 | 7.0 |
| Total uses-sources, annual average (billions of dinars) | 19.1 | 49.9 |

Sources:  Flow-of-Funds Accounts of the National Bank of Yugoslavia; Annual Report of the National Bank of Yugoslavia, 1969.

prises.  The sharp increase in the share of trade credit and accounts receivable-payable in total uses and sources partly reflects increased interfinancing of socialist enterprises and partly is caused by the shortage of liquidity (under a tighter monetary policy) which contributed to significant postponement of payments for goods and services.

## GOVERNMENT

After the reform there was a clear determination to stop financing the various levels of government by short-term bank credits.  This rule has been strictly implemented in the case of the republic and local governments.  In the case of the federal government the rule has been transformed in the attempt to reduce short-term crediting as much as possible.  Table 5.2 summarizes the situation as regards the various levels of government.  As to the other credits,

TABLE 5.2

Sources and Uses of Government Financing

(billions of dinars)

|  | 1960-64 | | | 1965-69 | | |
|---|---|---|---|---|---|---|
|  | Federal Government | Other Government | All Government | Federal Government | Other Government | All Government |
| Sources |  |  |  |  |  |  |
| Receipts | 29.6 | 34.3 | 64.0 | 47.2 | 73.0 | 120.2 |
| Financial sources |  |  |  |  |  |  |
| Short-term bank credits | 4.8 | 0.2 | 5.0 | 2.7 | -0.2 | 2.5 |
| Investment credits | 0.3 | 0.4 | 0.7 | 1.3 | 0.6 | 1.9 |
| Other credits | 4.0 | 0.7 | 4.6 | 3.5 | 0.8 | 4.3 |
| Bonds | 0.4 | -- | 0.4 | -0.1 | -- | -0.1 |
| Total | 9.5 | 1.3 | 10.7 | 7.5 | 1.1 | 8.6 |
| Total sources = total uses | 39.1 | 35.6 | 74.7 | 54.7 | 74.1 | 128.8 |
| Uses |  |  |  |  |  |  |
| Expenditures | 36.4 | 34.8 | 71.2 | 54.5 | 71.9 | 126.3 |
| Acquisition of financial assets | 2.7 | 0.8 | 3.5 | 0.2 | 2.3 | 2.5 |

Sources: Flow-of-Funds Accounts of the National Bank of Yugoslavia; Annual Report of the National Bank of Yugoslavia, 1969.

banks are allowed to grant investment credits (including housing credits) and socialist enterprises may grant trade credits.

The issue of bonds is recognized more and more as a significant source of government financing. The amount of bonds outstanding is relatively small so far.

## INDIVIDUALS

This sector consists of households and private firms, including individual farmers. The major part of the financial sources of individuals is comprised of consumer credits. For a long time before the reform these credits had been the only credits granted to individual households. Now the list of credits granted to individual households includes several types, such as consumer credits, which still account for the major part of all credits granted to individuals; housing credits, which stay very close to consumer credits in their importance and amount; investment credits to individual producers and to households for expanding of tourist capacities; and other specific credits to households. Consumer credits and housing credits account for about 95 percent of total outstanding credits to individual households, so that the other types of credit are relatively insignificant.

Intercrediting among individuals is considered illegal. This rule, however, is far from being strictly applied.* It is very likely that the amount of intercrediting is growing, but there is no reason to assume that it has reached a significant level as yet.

A specific type of crediting of individuals is crediting of private farmers by socialist enterprises in agriculture. The enterprises perform for private farmers who are under contract (e.g., plowing, sowing, reaping, transporting and selling of goods), including use of their own materials (seeds, fertilizers, etc.). The individual farmer pays for these costs of production when the products are sold. The main reason for this cooperation is to help individual producers, who possess more than 80 percent of the country's total cultivable land, to become familiar with modern technology and better types of product and

---

*Advertisements in daily newspapers are full of individual requirements for credits, offering in one way or another an attractive interest rate, share in profit, etc.

TABLE 5.3

Sources and Uses of Individuals
(billions of dinars)

| | Transactions | | Position at end of | |
|---|---|---|---|---|
| | 1960-64 | 1965-69 | 1964 | 1969 |
| Sources | | | | |
| Receipts (excluding inter-payments) | 106.1 | 325.7 | | |
| Financial sources | | | | |
| Consumer credits | 3.3 | 0.5 | 4.2 | 4.7 |
| Housing credits | 0.7 | 3.3 | 1.2 | 4.5 |
| Other bank credits | -- | 2.9 | -- | 2.5 |
| Total | 4.0 | 6.8 | 5.4 | 11.7 |
| Total sources-uses | 110.1 | 332.5 | | |
| Uses | | | | |
| Expenditures | 104.6 | 309.6 | | |
| Acquisition of financial assets | | | | |
| Currency | 2.7 | 7.0 | 4.4 | 11.4 |
| Deposit money | 0.1 | 0.1 | 0.2 | 0.3 |
| Savings deposits | 1.9 | 6.8 | 2.5 | 9.3 |
| Time deposits | 0.4 | 4.5 | 0.4 | 4.3 |
| Foreign exchange accounts | -- | 2.0 | -- | 3.0 |
| Foreign currency holdings | 0.1 | 2.2 | 0.1 | 2.3 |
| Other | 0.3 | 0.3 | 0.3 | 0.6 |
| Total | 5.5 | 22.9 | 7.9 | 31.2 |

Sources: Flow-of-Funds Accounts of the National Bank of Yugoslavia; Annual Report of the National Bank of Yugoslavia, 1969.

cattle. When combined with a system of guaranteed prices, this system of cooperation has proved very successful.

On the uses side, the most significant development has been the increase of investments in financial assets. The situation is summarized in Table 5.3.

NOTE

1. Thus, Capital Markets Study shows the share of equity in total liabilities from 24 percent (Japan) to 61 percent (the United States); the share of long-term debt

from 13 percent (the United Kingdom) to 27 percent (Japan); the share of short-term liabilities from 23 percent (the United States) to 49 percent (Japan). All data are for 1964-65 and cover France, Germany, Italy, Japan, the United Kingdom, and the United States. Capital Markets Study, General Report (Paris: Committee for Invisible Transactions, OECD, 1967), pp. 97, 144.

# 6

# THE FISCAL
# SYSTEM

There is a close interrelationship between the development of the financial structure and the fiscal system. Moving from a central planning system there has occurred a decrease in fiscal flows and an increase in financial flows. Both have had a tendency toward a differentiation of goals, flows, and instruments. The reform's institutional changes have had significant consequences on the fiscal system, requiring significant adjustments in the pattern of fiscal flows and fiscal actions.

The most relevant of the reform's changes in this connection have been related to the sectoral pattern of income distribution and saving formation. It was shown that reform measures resulted in a substantial increase in the share of socialist differentiation of personal income, further diffusion of saving, and an increase in voluntary saving. On the one hand, this resulted in an increase in the role of the financial structure. On the other hand, it led to a new role for the fiscal system.

Changes in the role of the fiscal system involved several fields of fiscal action. First, the "sector-redistribution" role, which was dominant in the pre-reform period, has been substantially reduced; and the role of "individual redistribution" has become increasingly significant. Second, the increased role of financial (including monetary) variables has required adequate adjustment of fiscal policy measures, especially to implement stabilization goals and to promote the development and efficient functioning of financial markets. In addition to the usual questions of fiscal policy and the proper combination of monetary policy, fiscal policy in this connection has become increasingly responsible for the stimulation of specific financial investments on the part of nonfinancial sectors, encouraging or discouraging some types of uses of saving. Third, the role of the fiscal system and fiscal action has generally increased with the increased role of autonomous economic processes and the growing need for indirect economic policy intervention. At the same time, its role in the field of direct intervention was substantially reduced, particularly in saving formation.

A general result of these changes was a decrease in taxes paid by socialist enterprises and an increase in taxes paid by individuals. The other general development was a decrease in taxes for investment purposes (forced saving) and an increase in taxes for classic government expenditures.

Individuals now pay the following taxes:

1. Taxes on personal income amounting to 12.7 percent (in 1968), of which 4.7 percent is federal and 8 percent republic and local. This tax accounts for the highest percentage of total tax revenues.[1]

2. Taxes on income from private activities, including a tax on income from agricultural activity--which accounts for the major part of all these taxes--a tax on the incomes of artisans and professional persons, and a tax on royalties.[2]

3. Taxes on incomes from property, including buildings, agricultural implements, and hybrid grapevines.

4. Tax on income from labor paid by individual firms that hire labor.

5. Tax on inheritances and gifts, including real property located in Yugoslavia.

6. Tax on total income paid in addition to the above taxes if total income exceeds 20,000 dinars plus 3,000 per member of the family if none has any income. This tax is progressive, starting at 3 percent and going to 70 percent of taxable income. In the case of a four-member family, for example, with only one member having earnings, a 70 percent tax rate is reached if total income exceeds nine times the average personal income (in 1969).[3]

7. Turnover tax, now paid by consumers when buying goods or services. Before the reform it was paid at all levels of production.[4] It includes two types of tax: retail sales tax and service sales tax. There are three levels of turnover taxes: federal, republic, and local. The federal general turnover tax rate is 12 percent. In the case of so-called "luxury goods" it may reach 20 percent. Republic turnover tax cannot exceed 2 percent and local turnover tax, 6 percent. Basic agricultural products,

books, newspapers, drugs, tobacco, and all exports are exempted from republic and local turnover taxes.

Taxes levied on socialist enterprises and other working organizations were significantly reduced following the reform. Four types of tax have disappeared (some of them on the eve of reform): 15 percent income tax; basic contributions to investment loan funds; tax on mining rent; tax on "extra" profit. And, as we have noted, the turnover tax has been shifted from producers to consumers.

In effect, socialist enterprises were obliged to pay two types of tax, one of them temporary, through 1970. The main tax was a specific tax on own funds (in Yugoslav terminology, interest on business funds), aimed at providing resources for the financing of investments in less-developed regions (the "Federal Fund for Financing of Less-Developed Regions"). This tax was introduced in 1957 and before the reform amounted to 6 percent maximum. After the reform the maximum rate was reduced to 4 percent, but many exemptions and differential rates were abolished, so that the average rate remained the same as before the reform, or about 4 percent. This tax was scheduled to disappear at the end of 1971. The other tax paid by enterprises also relates to financing purposes; it concerns the contribution to joint reserve funds of enterprises, local and republic. The rates amount to from 2 to 5 percent of income (according to republic government decision).*

Finally, there are customs duties paid by both enterprises and individuals. After the reform the system of customs duties was adjusted to most GATT standards.** The average customs rate was reduced after the reform to 12 percent, compared to 24 percent before the reform.[5] The tax situation is presented in Table 6.1.

Thus, the fiscal system has been significantly adjusted to its more differentiated role following the reform. More important than its institutional structure is how the existing fiscal system is used. Fiscal activity has been too little involved in stabilization policy programs to relate to the problems of development and functioning of financial markets. Moreover, there has been poor coordination between

---

*In addition, there are other contributions of a temporary character, e.g., contributions for reconstruction of Skopje, or of minor importance—such as for children's protection, for roads, for water protection, etc.
**Yugoslavia is a member of GATT.

TABLE 6.1

Fiscal Revenues, 1969

|  | Billions of Dinars | Percent- age of Total |
|---|---|---|
| Taxes on personal income (employees) | 7.9 | 24.8 |
| Taxes on income from agricultural activity of private farmers | 1.3 | 4.2 |
| Taxes on incomes from other activities of individuals | 1.4 | 4.4 |
| Turnover taxes | 12.1 | 37.9 |
| Duties | 0.7 | 2.3 |
| Other taxes paid by individuals | 0.4 | 1.1 |
| Custom duties | 4.3 | 13.6 |
| Other revenues | 0.2 | 0.7 |
| Total budget revenues | 28.3 | 89.0 |
| Contributions to investment loan funds | 1.1 | 3.6 |
| Tax on own funds (interest on business fund) | 2.4 | 7.4 |
| Total fiscal revenues | 31.8 | 100.0 |

Source: Statisticki bilten Sluzbe drustvenog knjigo-vodsta, No. 2 (1970), Tables 29, 31.

monetary and fiscal policy actions. These deficiencies of fiscal policy are now recognized, and it may be expected that future development in this field will be related to a more sophisticated use of fiscal instruments.

NOTES

1. See B. Jovanović, "Taxation of Workers' Personal Income," Yugoslav Survey, No. 3 (1968).
2. See M. Djurbabić, "Citizens' Contributions and Taxes," Yugoslav Survey, No. 26 (1966), and "Taxation of Private Farmers," Yugoslav Survey, No. 4 (1968).
3. Djurbabić, "Citizens' Contributions and Taxes."
4. Before the reform there were several forms of turn-over tax: general turnover tax, producers' turnover tax,

purchase tax on specified products, service sales tax, communal sales tax, and tax on transfer of real estate.  However, producers' turnover tax was the most important, accounting for about 60 percent of total turnover taxes.  This was paid by producers at all levels of production.  B. Lazarevic, "Turnover Tax," <u>Yugoslav Survey</u>, No. 23 (1965).

5.  For details see A. Domandžić, "Custom Tariffs," <u>Yugoslav Survey</u>, No. 24 (1965).

# 7

## CREATION
## OF MONEY

Our purpose in this section is to investigate the basic questions of monetary theory in the Yugoslav institutional framework. To this end we shall consider the role of money, the definition of money supply, creation of money, demand for money, and adjustment processes of demand to the supply of money.

This chapter is devoted to an examination of the definition of money supply used by monetary authorities and to an empirical investigation of the determinants of changes in money supply.

### DEFINITION AND DEVELOPMENT
### OF MONEY SUPPLY

A recent definition of money supply includes currency in circulation (notes and coins outside banks and post offices), balances on bank gyro accounts,* bank checks and other similar bank instruments, balances on budgetary and similar transitional accounts,** and money float.† Thus,

---

*Accounts of socialist enterprises and governments with banks used for payment by issuing gyro orders (similar to checking accounts in the United States).

**Accounts used for the collection of budgetary receipts and their distribution among federal, republican, and local budgets.

†Under the Yugoslav gyro order system of payments, money float is an additive item rather than a subtractive item as in a checking system of payment. This is because in the

the definition of money supply in recent use among monetary authorities belongs to a group of narrow definitions covering only transaction balances.

This definition of money supply differs both from that used in the central planning stage and that used in the first stage of decentralization. Compared to the definition used in the central planning stage it is far broader, including deposit money in addition to currency in circulation. In comparison with the definition used in the first stage of decentralization it is narrower, excluding sight deposits, which are not used for payments.*

In addition to the above definition the concept of "quasi-money" is used, including sight deposits that are not included in the definition of money supply. The sum of the money supply and quasi-money corresponds to the definition of money supply used in the first stage of decentralization. The broader monetary aggregate relates to the concept of "total liquidity," including "restricted deposits" and time deposits up to one year of maturity in addition to money supply and quasi-money. The basic monetary aggregate used in both monetary analysis and monetary policy, however, is money supply in the above narrow sense. To simplify the problem we shall restrict our investigation of the money creation processes in this chapter to the narrow definition of the money supply.

Table 7.1 presents the amounts and relative shares of these three concepts of monetary aggregates in total liquidity.

The pattern of money supply according to types of money and sector has changed significantly during this period. The proportion of currency in money supply, about 20 percent before 1965, has substantially increased, reaching

---

gyro system the first payment transaction is a debiting of the payer's, and the final transaction a crediting of the payee's, account, contrary to the procedure used in the checking system. The amount of the payment is in the meantime floating outside the accounts, resulting in a subtraction of monetary balances on gyro accounts (in the checking system it results in an addition to balances on checking accounts). Therefore, to correct these effects, the money float should be added in the gyro system and subtracted in the checking system of payments.

*The main deposits of this type, which are excluded from the concept of the money supply now, are sight savings deposits.

TABLE 7.1

Money Aggregates
(billions of dinars)

| | Posi-tion 1969 | Increase | | | Percentage of Total (position end of 1969) |
|---|---|---|---|---|---|
| | | 1968 | 1969 | 1970 | |
| Money supply | 32.6 | 5.6 | 3.5 | 5.8 | 57 |
| Quasi-money | 13.3 | 1.5 | 2.6 | 2.5 | 23 |
| Other liquid balances | 11.8 | 0.8 | 2.2 | 1.1 | 20 |
| Total liquid-ity | 57.7 | 7.9 | 8.3 | 9.4 | 100 |

Source: Annual Report of the National Bank of Yugo-slavia, 1969, p. 28, and 1970, p. 29.

TABLE 7.2

Currency in Circulation and Deposit Money

| | Bil-lions of Dinars End of 1969 | Percentage of Total End of Year | | | | | | |
|---|---|---|---|---|---|---|---|---|
| | | 1964 | 1965 | 1966 | 1967 | 1968 | 1969 | 1970 |
| Currency in cir-culation | 11.9 | 21.0 | 22.5 | 29.1 | 33.9 | 33.0 | 36.6 | 38.7 |
| Deposit money | 20.7 | 79.0 | 77.5 | 70.9 | 66.1 | 67.0 | 63.4 | 61.3 |

Source: Statisticki bilten Sluzbe drustvenog knjigo-vodsta, No. 2 (1970), Table 4.

37 percent in 1969.  This change reflects primarily the change in demand for money by households and individual firms owing to the increased share of personal income in total income; expansion of private activities (especially tourism, transport, and other services); increases in agricultural production (mainly in the hands of individual producers) and in prices of agricultural products; and increase in interindividual transactions (buying and selling of land, houses, small equipment, and cars).  Under these conditions both transaction demand and demand for money as an asset were significantly increased.  These conditions also led to a higher rate of increase on currency in circulation.*  Recent increased holding of dinars aborad also has contributed to a greater increase in currency in circulation.

## DETERMINANTS OF MONEY SUPPLY

We have based our consideration of the determinants of changes in the money supply on two methodological approaches.  The first is based on a bank balance sheet identity.  This method presents changes in the money supply as a result of changes in assets and nonmonetary liabilities on the consolidated balance sheet of the monetary system. It shows direct flows determining changes in the money supply without explaining underlying determinants of these flows.  This method is suitable for the practical purposes of monetary management, giving a quick glance at basic groups of determinants of changes in the money supply.

The second and more advanced method is based on the Friedman-Schwartz monetary multiplier identity.[1]  This method provides greater insight into the complex processes of money creation but omits explanation of "ultimate determinants" of changes in money supply.  The method, however, is a suitable tool for monetary analysis.[2]

The balance sheet identity approach shows that bank credit has been the dominant determinant of changes in money supply, both short- and long-term.  Changes in nonmonetary liabilities of banks rank second in determining changes in money supply.  Their influence, however, has been more significant from the short- than from the long-

---

*It was explained earlier that currency in circulation is mainly in the hands of individuals, since socialist enterprises and other organizations are forbidden to hold and use currency for payments (except "small payments").

TABLE 7.3

Basic Flows of Money Creation
(billions of dinars)

| Changes in | Bank Credit | Nonmonetary Deposits | Foreign Assets (net) | Money Supply |
|---|---|---|---|---|
| 1966 | 2.4 | -2.9 | 1.5 | 1.0 |
| 1967 | 1.7 | -1.9 | -0.3 | -0.4 |
| 1968 | 7.2 | -2.1 | 0.5 | 5.6 |
| 1969 | 8.4 | -4.4 | -0.5 | 3.5 |
| 1966-69 | 19.9 | -11.2 | 1.1 | 9.7 |
| 1969: I | -0.2 | 0.5 | -0.2 | 0.1 |
| II | 0.9 | 0.3 | -0.6 | 0.6 |
| III | 1.0 | -0.5 | -0.4 | 0.1 |
| IV | 1.5 | -0.6 | -0.2 | 0.8 |
| V | 0.3 | -0.4 | -0.2 | -0.3 |
| VI | 1.7 | -1.6 | -0.4 | -0.2 |
| VII | -0.5 | 0.9 | 0.3 | 0.8 |
| VIII | 0.7 | -0.6 | 0.3 | 0.4 |
| IX | 0.2 | -0.9 | 0.3 | -0.4 |
| X | -0.5 | 0.8 | 0.2 | 0.4 |
| XI | 1.1 | -0.6 | 0.1 | 0.6 |
| XII | 2.1 | -1.6 | 0.2 | 0.6 |
| Position end of 1969 | 62.2 | -30.3 | 0.7 | 32.6 |

Source: Statisticki bilten Sluzbe drustvenog knjigovodsta, No. 10 (1970), Table 4.

term point of view, involving rather volatile short-run fluctuations. The third and least significant determinant has been changes in the foreign assets-liabilities of the monetary system. However, they also from time to time may produce very significant short-term changes in money supply.

Although bank credit may be considered the dominant, and a very stable, determinant of the long-term development of the money supply, it is a far less significant determinant of short-term changes, owing in part to erratic fluctuations of nonmonetary deposits and changes in the foreign assets-liabilities of the monetary system. This conclusion is very significant from the point of view of practical monetary management. It shows that bank credit (which is the main instrument of monetary management) is a rather poor substitute for the money supply as a monetary indicator, so that monetary policy cannot rely on it as the sole target.

The dominant role of bank credit in money creation reflects the country's undifferentiated structure of financial assets and bank investments. The relatively greater effects of changes in nonmonetary deposits come partly from the readjustments in individuals' portfolios (especially the increase in savings deposits) and partly from the extensive use of freezing-thawing of deposits as an instrument of anticyclical policy. Finally, the rather weak effects of foreign exchange transactions reflect the relatively small amount of foreign capital transactions and the policy of holding a minimum amount of foreign exchange reserves (only for transactional purposes) under the prevailing balance-of-payments deficit.

The Friedman-Schwartz approach to the determinants of the money supply is used in a modified form and adjusted to the specific institutional framework of the Yugoslav economic system. The monetary multiplier identity used in this book involves eight variables instead of the three used in the Friedman-Schwartz formula. The identities used in this investigation are as follows:

(1)  $M = B \cdot m$

(2)  $m = \dfrac{d_m \cdot z + c + p}{r_o + r_1 + c + p}$

where

$M$ = money supply; $m$ = monetary multiplier;

$B$ = high-powered money (monetary base);

$$d_m = \frac{D_m}{D} \qquad z = \frac{D}{D_b} \qquad c = \frac{C}{D_b} \qquad p = \frac{P}{D_b}$$

$$r_o = \frac{R_o}{D_b} \qquad r_1 = \frac{R_1}{D_b}$$

$D_m$ = deposit money, involving balances on gyro and other accounts comprised by the definition of money supply (float is not included); deposit money is held mainly by socialist enterprises and

other organizations; the share of individual
holdings in this type of money is negligible;

$D$ = total deposits of nonbanking sectors with the
monetary system, including deposits with the central bank; time deposits of more than one year's
duration are not included, since they form part
of the "investment banking" sector and not of the
monetary system;

$D_b$ = total deposits ($D$) excluding deposits with the
central bank;

$C$ = currency in circulation;

$P$ = money float;

$R_o$ = obligatory reserves, involving three kinds of
reserve held on separate accounts: reserve requirements in the proper sense (maximum 35 percent of deposits, excluding savings deposits and
time deposits), balances on "special reserve
funds" accounts (aimed at meeting extraordinary
needs for reserve money), and special deposits
of banks with the central bank (as an instrument
of anticyclical policy, especially in the area
of balance-of-payments management*;

$R_1$ = other bank reserves on gyro accounts with the
central bank, including notes and coins in vaults.

High-powered money ($B$) is defined ("sources" method)
as the amount of total assets of the central bank minus
foreign liabilities and minus central bank deposits by nonbank sectors (mainly the federal government). According
to the "uses" method it includes reserves of other banks,
plus currency in circulation plus money float. Thus, the

---

*This aggregate is obviously rather heterogeneous from
the point of view of factors determining changes of these
three types of reserves. It is, however, homogeneous from
the point of view of their effects on the credit capacity
of banks, which justifies their aggregation for reasons of
simplicity. For the same reason, autonomous changes in
obligatory reserves proper are not investigated separately
from changes due to changes in reserve requirement rates.

amount of high-powered money depends partly on central bank action (mainly credits to other banks, as may be seen from Table 2.3), and partly on exogenous determinants (foreign exchange transactions, deposits by nonbank sectors) involving a significant degree of uncertainty.

The seven ratios used in the above identity reflect the five groups of determinants of the monetary multiplier. The liquidity reserve ratio ($r_1$) reflects behavior of the other banks; behavior of the "public" (individuals, socialist enterprises, and other organizations) is presented in currency to deposits ratio (c) and deposit money to total deposit ratio ($d_m$); fiscal policy action is presented in the ratio of total deposits to other bank deposits (z); effects of the payments mechanism are expressed by the float to deposit ratio (p); finally, obligatory reserves to deposits ratio ($r_o$) represents the influence of monetary authorities on the monetary multiplier (in addition to their influence on high-powered money). Investigation of these ratios suggests that fluctuations in the monetary multiplier are strongly influenced by exogenous variables outside the control of monetary management. In view of the fact that uncontrollable variables also may effect changes in high-powered money, it appears that monetary management in Yugoslavia involves a rather significant degree of uncertainty.

The evidence suggests that in the short run both high-powered money and the monetary multiplier significantly determine changes in the money supply. Long-run development of the money supply (increase in money supply) is exclusively produced by the increase in high-powered money. The monetary multiplier has been decreased in the period under consideration and contributed to a decrease in the money supply.

Table 7.4 shows a 42.6 percent increase in the money supply in 1966-69. This increase in money supply was accompanied by a 51.1 percent increase in high-powered money and a 5.6 percent decrease in the monetary multiplier. From equation (1) in logarithmic form, it is evident that high-powered money contributed to the 116 percent increase in the money supply, while the contribution of the monetary multiplier was 16 percent in the opposite direction. The contributions of both high-powered money and the monetary multiplier to changes in the money supply were rather erratic. Thus, the contributions of high-powered money to annual changes in the money supply accounted for from +161 to -107 percent. At the same time, contributions of monetary multipliers ranged from +207 to -61 percent. Variations in the contributions of high-powered money and the

TABLE 7.4

High-Powered Money and Monetary Multiplier as
Determinants of Money Supply
(end of period)

| | | Percent Increase in the Period | | | Percentage of Contribution to Changes in Money Supply | |
|---|---|---|---|---|---|---|
| | | M | B | m | B | m |
| 1966 | | 4.5 | 4.1 | 0.4 | 91 | 7 |
| 1967 | | -1.7 | 1.9 | -3.6 | -107 | 207 |
| 1968 | | 23.9 | 18.5 | 4.6 | 79 | 21 |
| 1969 | | 12.1 | 20.2 | -6.7 | 161 | -61 |
| 1966-69 | | 42.6 | 51.1 | -5.6 | 116 | -16 |
| 1969: | I | 0.3 | -4.1 | 4.6 | -1661 | 1761 |
| | II | 2.2 | -0.6 | 2.8 | -30 | 130 |
| | III | 0.5 | 1.3 | -0.8 | 239 | -139 |
| | IV | 2.6 | 4.1 | -1.4 | 158 | -58 |
| | V | -1.0 | -2.7 | 1.7 | 265 | -165 |
| | VI | -0.8 | 1.3 | -2.1 | 154 | -54 |
| | VII | 2.5 | 2.5 | 0.0 | 97 | 3 |
| | VIII | 1.2 | -0.2 | 1.5 | 21 | 79 |
| | IX | -1.4 | 1.2 | -2.5 | 94 | 6 |
| | X | 1.3 | 1.7 | -0.5 | 121 | -21 |
| | XI | 2.0 | 6.7 | -4.4 | 340 | -240 |
| | XII | 2.0 | 8.0 | -5.6 | 376 | -276 |

monetary multiplier to monthly changes in the money supply
were necessarily far more volatile, involving seasonal in
addition to presumably more powerful stochastic variables.

Table 7.4 reveals, in addition to erratic fluctuation
in high-powered money and monetary multiplier, a negative
association between changes in high-powered money and the
monetary multiplier. This may be explained in part as a
result of distributed lag in adjusting the monetary multiplier to changes in high-powered money, so that in the
meantime the monetary multiplier appears lower in the case
of an increase and higher in the case of a decrease in
high-powered money.

Table 7.5 suggests that the central bank's credit to
other banks and especially to the federal government is the
main source of high-powered money, both in long- and short-

TABLE 7.5

Sources and Uses of High-Powered Money
(billions of dinars)

| | Position End of 1969 | Changes | | | |
|---|---|---|---|---|---|
| | | 1966 | 1967 | 1968 | 1969 |
| Sources | | | | | |
| Central bank's credit to other banks | 18.4 | 1.1 | 0.9 | 0.4 | 1.7 |
| Federal government and other nonbank sectors | 15.8 | -1.6 | -0.6 | 2.9 | 1.6 |
| Total | 34.2 | -0.5 | 0.3 | 3.3 | 3.3 |
| Foreign assets (net) | 2.5 | 1.0 | 1.1 | 0.0 | 0.0 |
| Total creation of high-powered money | 36.7 | 0.4 | 1.3 | 3.4 | 3.4 |
| Minus: deposits of nonbank sectors with the central bank | -9.9 | 0.3 | -0.9 | 0.1 | 1.1 |
| High-powered money, total | 26.8 | 0.7 | 0.4 | 3.5 | 4.5 |
| Uses | | | | | |
| Obligatory reserves of other banks | 11.4 | -1.1 | 0.7 | 0.7 | 2.5 |
| Liquid reserves of other banks | 1.1 | 0.2 | -0.7 | 0.2 | -0.4 |
| Currency in circulation | 11.9 | 1.8 | 1.0 | 1.6 | 2.4 |
| Money float | 2.3 | -0.2 | -0.6 | 0.9 | 0.0 |
| Total | 26.8 | 0.7 | 0.4 | 3.5 | 4.5 |

Source: Statisticki bilten Sluzbe drustvenog knjigo-vodsta, No. 10 (1970), Table 5.

114

run considerations. On the uses side, high-powered money is absorbed mainly by bank obligatory reserves with the central bank and by currency in circulation.

The volatile fluctuations of individual sources and uses of high-powered money reveal the complexity of the problem of monetary management. Thus, even this determinant (presumably the most controllable) of the money supply involves a rather significant degree of uncertainty. This imposes the need for an appropriate method of planning of high-powered money management and an efficient means for the implementation of planned targets.

Erratic short-run behavior of the monetary multiplier reflects volatile fluctuations in nearly all its determinants. The long-run decreasing trend of monetary multiplier has been caused by the increase in currency-deposits ratio (c), deposit money-total deposits ratio ($d_m$), and total deposits-other bank deposits ratio (z). The other three ratios have contributed in the opposite direction: decrease in obligatory reserves ratio ($r_o$), liquidity reserves ratio ($r_1$), and money float-deposits ratio (p).

The evidence suggests that the process of money creation is under rather loose control and that monetary management in Yugoslavia involves a significant degree of uncertainty. The pessimistic conclusions suggested by the evidence in Tables 7.2 and 7.3 should be tempered, however, by the fact that the period under consideration involves fundamental institutional changes that presumably have significantly reduced comparability within the period under

TABLE 7.6

Determinants of Change in Monetary Multiplier

| Deter-minant | End of | | Marginal Multipliers | | | | |
|---|---|---|---|---|---|---|---|
| | 1965 | 1969 | 1966 | 1967 | 1968 | 1969 | 1966-69 |
| m | 1.287 | 1.217 | 1.495 | -1.254 | 1.600 | 0.780 | 1.079 |
| $d_m$ | 0.435 | 0.332 | -0.196 | 0.286 | 0.413 | 0.184 | 0.145 |
| z | 1.426 | 1.223 | 0.700 | 1.524 | 1.094 | 0.882 | 0.973 |
| c | 0.205 | 0.263 | 0.424 | 0.543 | 0.241 | 0.316 | 0.335 |
| $r_o$ | 0.341 | 0.252 | -0.256 | 0.452 | 0.179 | 0.347 | 0.137 |
| $r_1$ | 0.075 | 0.025 | 0.038 | -0.392 | 0.028 | -0.050 | -0.037 |
| p | 0.087 | 0.050 | -0.043 | -0.329 | 0.139 | -0.006 | 0.005 |

consideration (and also with the period before 1965). The rather unstable behavior of determinants of money supply in this period should not be taken as a rule necessarily valid for the future. The expectation that determinants of changes in money supply may very likely become significantly more stable in future periods is supported by the fact that their variations in the second half of the period under investigation were less than in the first half. This expectation, however, is justified only if significant new institutional changes are not introduced. If that happens, monetary management should expect disturbing new effects on the determinants of changes in money supply and consequently a new increase in the degree of uncertainty of money control.

## NOTES

1. M. Friedman and A. Schwartz, <u>A Monetary History of the United States, 1867-1960</u> (Princeton: Princeton University Press, 1963), pp. 776-98.

2. Another and perhaps more sophisticated method used is based on a money creation function, involving "ultimate determinants of the behavior of banks and public in the process of money creation, e.g., interest rates, risk elasticities, amount of wealth and its structure, cost of reserve deficiency elasticity, etc. This is the approach used by K. Brunner and A. Meltzer in "Some Further Investigations of Demand and Supply for Money," <u>Journal of Finance</u>, May 1964, and "Liquidity Traps for Money, Bank Credit and Interest Rates," <u>The Journal of Political Economy</u>, January-February 1968. This approach, however, does not appear particularly useful in the Yugoslav case of frequent institutional changes and presumably rather unstable functional relationships in the field of money creation.

# 8

**DEMAND
FOR MONEY**

It has been shown that the demand function for money changed fundamentally during the first stage of decentralization, approaching closer and closer to a demand function for money typical of market economies. This process has been continued since 1964, so that the specific properties of the demand for money in Yugoslavia are not greatly at variance with the usual range of country-to-country differences. It is nevertheless useful to underscore some basic determinants of the demand for money in Yugoslavia.

## DETERMINANTS OF DEMAND
FOR MONEY

Demand for money in Yugoslavia can be classified into two broad groups according to at least two specific types of demand for money: demand by socialist enterprises and demand by individuals* (employees, individual producers, etc.).

Demand for money by socialist enterprises is determined by a set of variables that are partly the same as in a market economy and partly reflect the specific nature of the Yugoslav economic system. These determinants are the following:

1. Amount of money transactions, time pattern of receipts and expenditures or income representing transactions.

---

*For purposes of simplification other sectors (government, other institutions) are considered similar to individuals, at least in their consumer-minded nature.

2.  Cost of holding money, represented by interest rates and price changes.

3.  Rather low sensitivity to consequences of illiquidity (expecting that social considerations will prevent full legal sanctions from being applied, especially in the case of large enterprises), inducing a lower demand for money.

4.  Relatively inefficient money market, inducing a high degree of uncertainty for borrowing money and requiring a larger margin of security for precautionary purposes.

5.  Obligation to hold money in separate accounts for separate purposes.  Reduction of this obligation, which ended during this period with the abolishment of the system of compartmentalization of money held by enterprises, worked in the direction of removing the last vestiges of "quasi-demand" for money, which in effect resulted in a decrease in the demand for money by socialist enterprises.

To simplify, it may be said that the first two variables influence the demand for money by socialist enterprises (similar to the demand for money by enterprises in market economies) and the last three determine the effects of the first two.  In this way the demand function for money by socialist enterprises may be investigated in much the same way as in market economies.

The more important determinants of the demand for money by individuals appear to be the following:

1.  Income.

2.  Amount of transactions, time pattern of receipts and expenditures.

3.  Cost of holding money, represented by interest rates and price changes.

4.  Simplified pattern of financial instruments and poor financial market mechanism, which makes choice for financial investments narrow and discourages nonmonetary financial investments, particularly those in long-term instruments.

5.  Further significant monetization of economic activity by the agricultural population, partly by decreasing the share of the agricultural population in total population and partly by increasing the monetized part of income, consumption, and investment of individual farmers.

6.  Increasing investments in foreign currency, partly by workers abroad, partly by domestic residents (although illegal) particularly in tourist regions, and partly in foreign exchange accounts with domestic banks.

118

The income variable deserves additional explanation. The reform measures have resulted in a substantially higher rate of increase in income of individuals in comparison with the rate of increase in total GNP. This has been the result of a higher rate of increase in personal incomes of employees rather than in the incomes of socialist enterprises, as well as increases in production and prices of agricultural goods produced by individuals; extension of private activities, especially in transport and tourism; and increased transactions in selling-buying of land and houses and substantial increase in their prices. The higher rate of increase in the income of individuals than in total GNP has induced a decrease in the demand for money by individuals (parallel with the increased saving ratio) and in total demand for money (because of the above effect and because of the increased share of individuals' income in total income.)*

## DISTRIBUTED LAG EQUATIONS AND MONETARY DEMAND ANALYSIS

Monetary demand analysis has shown a strong relation between permanent income and the amount of money demanded.[1] Since permanent income is a calculated value determined by approximately nine quarters of past income as it is weighted through consumption, it seems logical to wonder whether money demand might be as effectively estimated by using the lagged values of income directly. In this model money demand would be a direct function of current income and past incomes, where the appropriate weights for each lagged value would represent a part of the time pattern of incomes on money demand. Hence we expect current and more recent incomes to play a larger role in money demand than less recent incomes, so that the coefficients of the income variable should increase to a peak and then decrease as the variable is lagged by a greater number of periods.

$$M_{t,\ j} = f(Y_t,\ _jY_{t,\ j-1},\ \cdots,\ Y_{t-1},\ _jY_{t-1,\ j-1},\ \cdots,\ r)$$

---

*The best illustration of the effect of this change is the increase of the share of currency (mainly held by individuals) in total money supply from less than 20 percent before 1965 to 37 percent in 1969.

$$M_{t, j} = a + \beta_1 Y_{t, j} + \beta_2 Y_{t, j-1} + \cdots + \beta_k Y_{t-1, j} + \cdots + r$$

where $0 < \beta$

and $\dfrac{N}{\Sigma \beta_i}$ is finite

$i = 1$

The several techniques that may be used to estimate the distributed lag equation of this model are most efficient when a priori knowledge of the properties of the coefficients and the equation is used. For example, the coefficients of the income variable in this model can be assumed to be positive and to increase for several quarters and then to decrease to zero after a sufficiently long lag. This assumption allows the model to be estimated by techniques applicable to autoregressive equations and/or ordinary multiple regressions on transformed variables. Solow suggested using a Pascal distribution for the coefficients in order to allow them to increase for the first few terms of the sequence and then to decrease geometrically (Solow, 1960). I. Fisher proposed that the coefficients be allowed to decrease arithmetically from a certain point in time backward (Fisher, 1937). Almon made Fisher's proposal more general by suggesting that the coefficients be parameters of a polynomial function of a time in a specified interval where the degree of the polynomial is chosen prior to estimation and is less than the number of lagged periods used in the regression (Almon, 1965). Any of these, or other assumptions about the coefficients, reduce the number of parameters to be estimated.

In the absence of lagged dependent variables, these estimates are unbiased using ordinary regression techniques or asymptotically unbiased under autoregressive techniques whenever the error terms are strictly random. In this model there is no a priori reason to assume that the error terms are autocorrelated; but, if such correlation exists, knowledge of the exact correlation could be used to transform the exogenous variables in a manner that eliminates the asymptotic bias. In principle other techniques including instrumental variables might be used to remove the bias. These techniques appear to give only mediocre precision for the estimates compared to a direct fitting because of compounding variables (Malinvaud, 1966, p. 492).

If the legnth of the interval over which income variables are considered is not known, it might be chosen by estimating the equation for several interval lengths and choosing the one with the smallest sum of squares of the residuals (largest multiple correlation coefficient adjusted for sample size when the sample is small). Other techniques, such as a sequence of analysis of variance tests on successive regressions, or a test for coefficients of specified precision or stability, are also available. All of these latter methods favor models with short lags and are sensitive to the number of observations available for estimation, since the number of degrees of freedom is critical (Malinvaud, 1966, p. 483).

This study's model did not appear to have significant correlation among the error terms when the time shape of the income variable's influence was assumed to be a polynomial. The technique of linear interpolation among the polynomial functions of time used as weights for the lagged income variables in this model is described by Almon (1965). This study of money demand has assumed that a fourth degree polynomial should yield a sufficiently detailed time shape considering the approximately 50 quarterly observations that are usually available. The polynomial's coefficients weighted the monetary variable for various period lengths and the best time period was chosen on the basis of the coefficient of determination. This results in an estimate that may be biased toward shorter lags than the true ones, but such bias does not lead to severely misleading results (Malinvaud, 1966, p. 483). The income elasticities are calculated using the mean values for each variable in the equations presented for each country.

## TEST PROCEDURES AND RESULTS

The basic equations presented in this chapter have been estimated using ordinary least squares for the permanent income model and an interest rate.

Recent empirical studies indicate that the permanent income weights of Cagan and Friedman may not be the appropriate weights to use (Wright, 1969). Hence we have used other weights as well and present the results for the following sections.

The distributed lag equation, using income over time as one of the independent variables, has been estimated using Almon's technique of linear interpolation of a polynomial. Because the length of the lag was not known a priori several lengths were estimated and the best equations were chosen on the basis of high coefficients of determination, smooth time patterns for the coefficients, and the significance of the added terms in the equations. The equations showed no significant multicolinearity between the independent variables (Farrar, et al., 1967).

For Yugoslavia the testing procedures were the following. First, the demand for money is treated explicitly as a function of the lagged values of income and of interest rates. Eight different equations were estimated using the Almon technique, where the first equation contained no lagged values of income; the second equation contained three lagged values of income; the third equation, four lagged income values; and so on up to the eighth equation, with nine lagged values of income. The results do not show significant increases in the equation's explanatory value or stability for more than nine periods. From these eight equations the best is chosen on the basis of explanatory power $(R^2)$, stability of coefficients, and significant addition to explanatory power over previous equations.

Second, the demand for money is treated explicitly as a function of permanent income and interest rates in an effort to compare this specification's performance with the direct estimate using distributed lag techniques. The estimation required a set of three equations depending on the weights used to estimate permanent income. We have estimated the coefficients for equations using permanent income calculated with weights of 0.4, 0.7, and 0.8 in an effort to judge what might determine the weight choice. The calculation of appropriate weights uses the first eight observations of income, and thus the number of observations remaining for each country is reduced by eight in these equations.

Third, the income elasticities for each equation were estimated directly around the mean values of the variable. None of these equations were specified as logarithmic functions since Almon's technique lends itself more easily to a linear specification.

The estimate for income used in the analysis for Yugoslavia for the period 1956-68 is the nominal income of individuals and individual private enterprises. Money supply was defined as the amount of currency plus total gyro accounts and savings of individuals and individual private enterprises. The interest rate estimates were constructed using only the interest rate on sight savings deposits.

Table 8.1 first presents the results of fitting the demand for money in Yugoslav economy to the lagged income variables. The best fit was obtained using a three-period income lag. Equations with longer lag lengths did not sub-

TABLE 8.1

Yugoslavia--Permanent Income Variables

| Intercept (standard error) | Interest Rate [t value] | Permanent Income [t value] | Income [t value] | $R^2$ [F value] | Income Elasticity |
|---|---|---|---|---|---|
| 1. 100.533 (68.532) | -34.8996 [.6667] | | $.59341\ Y_t$ + $.83748\ Y_{t-1}$ + $1.40908\ Y_{t-2}$ [2.3400] [1.9850] [3.4500] | .9802 [556.418] | 1.27 |
| 2. 352.771 (48.779) | -96.1647 [-2.4674] | 3.39170 [30.5901] | | .9906 [2106.25] | 1.23 |
| 3. 192.217 (74.295) | -63.9596 [-1.0868] | 3.19307 [20.2239] | | .9805 [1005.55] | 1.26 |
| 4. 95.306 (81.132) | -43.2055 [-.6778] | 3.10079 [18.3446] | | .9767 [839.998] | 1.25 |

N = 51 for equation 1 and 43 for equations 2, 3, 4.

stantially increase the explanatory value of the model.
Second in the table is the demand for money as a function
of permanent income and interest rates, where permanent
income is again calculated with three different weights.
The income elasticities for the country are all slightly
higher than unity and do not vary significantly with the
choice of income variable.

In Yugoslavia the permanent income variables performed
as well as the direct lagged values of income. There is
no statistically significant difference between the first
and second equation even though the second equation has
slightly higher $R^2$. Apparently the model is indifferent
between permanent and directly estimated lagged income.
However, the unsteady nature of the intercept leaves the
appropriateness of this model for Yugoslavia in doubt.

One reason is certainly the important institutional
changes that have occurred in the country during the period
under review. For this reason the periods should be broken
into three subperiods (1947-52, 1953-64, and 1965-69) and
the equations recalculated.

We can test this hypothesis by dividing the time period into three periods--1947-52, 1953-64, and 1965-69,
which mark periods of significant institutional change--
and estimating the money demand equation for each period.
It would be best statistically if we could obtain a set of
income data and money data that is consistently measured
across all three time periods and with as many observations
as possible (back to 1947, monthly). However, the definition of money has changed over these three periods. In
addition, the income series, correlated with the money
definition and available in monthly estimates, does not
extend back past 1953 (personal income for individuals and
individual private enterprises). Although nine observations were lost when we used permanent income (using a
weight of 0.4), it is a much better variable to represent
income in Yugoslavia. Hence we are able to run only periods
1955 to 1962 using money supply, old definition (MSO), and
deposit money, old definition (DMO), for the money variable for equation 1 in Table 8.2, and 1965 to 1969 using
either money supply plus quasi-money, recent definition
(MSQ) equation 2, or total liquid resources, recent definition (TLR) equation 3, or total liquid resources in hands
of individuals, recent definition (LIR) equation 4, or
money plus quasi-money in the hands of individuals, recent
definition (QIR) equation 5.

These equations in Table 8.2 were compared with the
original data. The middle period (1955-62) shows money

TABLE 8.2

Yugoslavia--Permanent Income Variables

|   | Intercept (std. error) | Permanent Income [t value] | $R^2$ [F value] | Income Elasticity |
|---|---|---|---|---|
| 1. | 2.2145 (10.424) | .03317 [51.1815] | .9650 [2619.55] | .10 |
| 2. | -548.626 (161.913) | .09158 [20.1888] | .8828 [407.588] | 1.18 |
| 3. | -1081.456 (223.325) | .07982 [16.9823] | .8418 [288.399] | 3.17 |
| 4. | 1053.522 (67.7583) | .28144 [25.6562] | .9228 [658.242] | .61 |
| 5. | 1034.325 (66.5020) | .28432 [26.4189] | .9269 [697.958] | .61 |

N = 96 in equation 1; 55 in equations 2, 3; and 56 in equations 4, 5.

demand a function of personal income of individuals with a small, insignificant constant term and an income coefficient and correlation coefficient that are comparable to our original estimates in Table 8.1.

The latter period (1965-69) shows significant, large, constant terms and a significant income coefficient that is statistically different from those in our original estimates, as well as a lower correlation coefficient from other estimates. LIR and QIR perform similarly with a significant constant of approximately +1053.00 and an income regression coefficient of 0.2814. On the other hand, TLR had a significant constant of -1081 and a coefficient for income of 0.0798, and MSQ had a significant constant of -548.63 and an income coefficient of 0.0916. Both of these equations had lower correlation coefficients. This poor fit for the latter period and extreme variation in the constant term suggests the significant institutional changes occurring in the country during this particular period.

NOTES

1. This section draws on the following sources: S. Almon, "The Distributed Lag Between Capital Appropriations and Expenditures," Econometrica, Vol. XXXIII (January 1965); G. C. Chow, "On the Long-Run and Short-Run Demand for Money," The Journal of Political Economy, Vol. LXXIV (April 1966); D. E. Farrar and R. P. Glauber, "Multicolinearity in Regression Analysis: The Problem Revisited," The Review of Economics and Statistics, Vol. IL (February 1967); I. Fisher, "A Note on a Short-Cut Method for Calculating Distributed Lags," Bulletin de Institut International de Statistique, Vol. 29 (1937); M. Friedman, "The Quantity Theory of Money: A Restatement," in M. Friedman, ed., Studies in the Quantity Theory of Money (Chicago: University of Chicago Press, 1956), "The Demand for Money--Some Theoretical and Empirical Results," Journal of Political Economy, LXVII (June 1959), 327-51, "Interest Rates and the Demand for Money," Journal of Law and Economics, IX (October 1966), 71-85; D. Laidler, "Some Evidence on the Demand for Money," Journal of Political Economy, LXXVI (February 1966), 55-58, "Rate of Interest and the Demand for Money-- Some Empirical Evidence," Journal of Political Economy, LXXIV (December 1966), 543-55; G. S. Laumas, "The Permanent Income Hypothesis, Interest Rates and the Demand for Money," Weltwirtschaftliches Archiv, Bank 103, 1969, Hefti, 131-52; G. Macesich and J. G. Haworth, "Interest Rates, Money Demand and Distributed Lag Function in Five Countries" (forthcoming); E. Malinvaud, Statistical Methods of Econometrics (New York: Rand McNally, 1966); A. H. Meltzer, "The Demand for Money: The Evidence from the Time Series," Journal of Political Economy, LXII (June 1963), 219-46; R. Mundell, "Inflation and Real Interest," Journal of Political Economy, XXI (June 1963), 280-83, "Growth, Stability and Inflationary Finance," Journal of Political Economy, LXXIII (April 1965), 97-109; P. Samuelson, "The Role of Money in National Economic Policy," Controlling Monetary Aggregates (Boston: Federal Reserve Bank of Boston, 1969); R. Selden, "Monetary Velocity in the United States," in M. Friedman, ed., Studies in the Quantity Theory of Money; R. Solow, "On a Family of Lagged Distribution," Econometrica, Vol. XXVIII (April 1960); C. Wright, "Estimating Permanent Income: A Note," Journal of Political Economy, LXXV (September-October 1969), 845.

# 9

## ROLE OF
## MONEY

The functions of money in Yugoslavia are much the same as in a market economy. Therefore, we shall consider here the adjustment processes of demand to supply of money.

### SPECIFIC DETERMINANTS

In Yugoslavia specific institutional and other determinants have a rather controversial influence on adjustment processes of demand to supply of money and the strength, pattern, variability, and time lags of their effects. Some of them presumably contribute to the strength, stability, and shorter-lagged effects. Others work in the opposite direction. The time pattern of individual determinants, moreover, is changeable, so that prevailing determinants of strength, stability, and shorter-lag effects in one period are frequently replaced by a stronger influence of determinants working in the opposite direction in the next period and vice versa. Although the time pattern of this interchange of effects appears erratic, it seems logical to assume a tendency of increasing roles of determinants contributing to an increasing variability and uncertainty of effects and extending time lags of these effects. This would appear to be particularly valid for future developments.

The basic determinants contributing to the strength of monetary effects, their stability and shorter lags come from the rather undifferentiated financial structure and the inefficient financial markets. Relatively simple structure of financial institutions and instruments, rigid formation of interest rates, and relatively low interest-rate elasticities under the existing low interest-rate ceiling result in reduced roundabout processes related to developed financial markets, small pyramiding effects (both in a positive and negative sense) of initial monetary impacts; simple substitution effects in the case of higher or lower money holdings than desired, the choice between goods and money holdings accounting for the major part of this effect, rather simple portfolio adjustments under conditions of a simplified pattern of financial instruments, and lack of a developed open market for financial instruments.

Second, these determinants lie in the field of balance-of-payments transactions. The basic contribution in this direction comes from the relatively low capital transactions and the fact that the dinar is not a convertible currency. In addition, the rather poor differentiation of financial markets in comparison with the markets of foreign partners reduces foreign capital transactions to a few easily controllable bilateral channels of foreign borrowing and lending.

Both of these determinants have been significantly weakened recently by increasing financial investments (savings deposits, beginning steps in the issuing of bonds, foreign exchange deposits, even holdings of foreign currency) and significant extension and differentiation of foreign borrowing-lending. Presumably this tendency will be continued in the future, inducing an additional source of variability in the effects of monetary processes and in the time lags of these effects.

Determinants inducing variability of effects of adjustment processes, extension and variability of time lags, and weakening of these effects have come primarily from frequent institutional changes and from direct regulations.

Frequent institutional changes may bring about significant changes in variables relevant to the adjustment processes of demand to supply of money. In addition to behavior variables, these changes may influence modifications of market mechanisms, income distribution, and saving and investment processes. One of the most significant recent changes in this field has been the change in the sector pattern of income distribution, which has influenced fundamental changes in the demand for money by households and ultimately in total demand for money.

Direct regulations represent a particularly powerful source of variations in the effects of monetary processes. The best example of these effects is regulation of prices of goods and services, interest rates, and personal incomes (or wage rates in Western terminology). We have already noted that personal income formation has been fully liberalized but the prices of goods and interest rates are still under rather tight control. Thus, processes based on the assumption of flexible price formation are strongly distorted. In addition to price control, significant rigidities in price formation originated in relatively higher distortion in relative prices and distortion in efficiency of individual enterprises. Another specific feature of price formation is relatively weaker influence of foreign prices owing to extensive foreign trade controls.

# 10

**THE APPROACH
TO MONETARY
POLICY**

We shall now consider standard problems of monetary policy, which includes formation of monetary policy goals and targets, instruments for their implementation, and efficiency of monetary policy in Yugoslavia. This chapter will examine the dominant views on the role of monetary policy, the transmitting mechanism of monetary policy, the problem of monetary vs. fiscal policy, and the problem of rule vs. discretion in deciding on monetary policy.

## THE DOMINANT VIEWS

The changes brought about by the reform have contributed to a significant extension of the role, scope, and responsibility of monetary policy. The reform has generated an increase in consumer sovereignty in the role of individual free decision-making. This process has spilled over into both financial and nonfinancial fields and induced stronger disturbing effects of monetary disequilibrium. These changes have also required a more efficient and effective monetary regulation. The effect in general is to make the role of monetary policy similar to that in developed market economies.

Although there are close similarities with market economies, monetary policy in Yugoslavia also involves significant differences. These include relatively strong price controls whose effects are to distort relative prices; rigid control of interest-rate formation and low interest elasticity; a very liberal system of "personal income" formation, escaping any control*; an inadequate and inefficient financial market; a relatively small amount of foreign capital transactions because of tight control measures; and nonconvertibility of the dinar. Thus, the peculiar mixture of rigidities and strong exogenous impacts on the one hand and very liberal mechanisms and autonomous adjustment processes on the other make the problems of goals, targets, and their implementation noteworthy in the case of Yugoslavia.

Under specific Yugoslav conditions there has always been a prevailing "monetarist" approach. There are several reasons for it. First, the prewar quantity theory has never been interrupted by Keynesian views. Keynesian monetary theory did not reach Yugoslav economists before the World War II, and after the war the central planning framework was unsuited to Keynesian views. By the end of the 1950s when Yugoslavia was more receptive, the rigid Keynesian views already had been substantially revised, and at the same time a revised and sophisticated quantity theory was rapidly gaining worldwide acceptance.

Second, Keynesian monetary theory appeared oversophisticated for the simple, rather undifferentiated financial structure of the Yugoslav economy, particularly in light of the rigid mechanism of interest-rate formation. Thus, even if somebody insisted on the application of a simple Keynesian model, it would be reduced to a quantity theory model by excluding interest rate as a significant variable. Using the Hicksian IS-LM version of the Keynesian model, this would mean that the LM equation is transformed into the Cambridge version of the quantity theory model or some other form of demand function for money and that there is no crossing point between LM and IS lines defining monetary and general equilibrium.

Third, the prewar quantity theory was not inconsistent with the dominant Marxian theory after the war. Both the

---

*In addition to the natural bias of a liberal system of personal income formation to a higher rate of increase in income than in production and productivity, there has been a new cause for increase in personal incomes: higher-paid Yugoslav workers employed abroad (nearly one million recently). Thus, personal incomes have to increase at a higher rate than production and productivity to become competitive (or at least to decrease the discrepancy) with foreign wage rates.

theoretical and practical approaches* to monetary problems
were very close to the quantity theory views under conditions of noncommodity, fiduciary money.

Finally, one of the most decisive arguments for the
prevailing monetarist approach has been the experience of
strong inflationary impacts produced by sharp monetary expansion.

As a result, there always has been a general consensus
that "money matters" and that there is a need for an efficient monetary policy. However, this does not mean that
there has been complete agreement about the goals and targets of monetary policy or about its efficiency. It is
possible to distinguish two groups of views. On the one
hand there are "neutral money policy" views and on the
other there are "easy money policy" views. The first
group of views is related to recent post-reform developments,
when stabilization goals became as significant as production
and development goals. The basic idea is that under complex contemporary economic interrelationships, where there
is economic determination of decision-making and an increase
in the role of autonomous economic processes, stabilization
goals represent an essential precondition for efficient
production, economic allocation of resources, and reasonable rate of economic growth. Thus, monetary policy has
to avoid creation of extra money, and if this happens any-
way it has to respond quickly and resolutely with the appropriate tight monetary policy measures.

The "easy money views" dominated the monetary policy
before the reform. They continue to exist and exert some
influence. The rationale for these views is that production and economic growth are the basic economic policy
goals and that an easy money policy is more helpful toward
these goals than a neutral, not to mention tight, money
policy. The risk of inflation ranks lower than the risk
of deceleration of production and economic growth. And,
if monetary policy creates inflationary pressures, it
should, as a rule, decrease moderately the rate of its
"easiness." Application of a tight money policy usually
results in sharp recessionary effects, so that the costs
of restoration of equilibrium are far higher than the
damage caused by a mild inflation. Therefore, a tight money
policy may be used only exceptionally, in cases of sharp

_____

*As already indicated, even in the central planning
system the quantity of money (currency in circulation) was
strongly regulated by cash planning.

inflationary developments, and for as short a period as possible.

The most recent development is an integration of these views in the argument that monetary policy alone cannot be an efficient instrument of economic policy. It should be combined with fiscal policy (or what is called "incomes policy"), personal income policy, and the like, so that the problem of monetary policy formation should be included as a subproblem of the more general problem of creation of an optimal blend of all relevant policies. This approach takes from the "neutral policy" views the idea of strong countercyclical and stabilization components and at the same time justifies the "easy money" views that disturbing consequences of a tight money policy may be more costly than the consequences of the alternative inflationary disturbances if monetary measures are not combined with other appropriate policies. This, in effect, has been the dominant approach to monetary policies in the post-reform period.

## THE TRANSMITTING MECHANISM

The effects of monetary policy measures are transmitted to goals of economic policy by processes that necessarily involve specific components that reflect institutional and other peculiarities of the Yugoslav economy.

First, monetary policy in Yugoslavia may control supply of funds more efficiently than in developed market economies, since banks are the main suppliers of funds, so that control of bank credit for all practical purposes means control of the major part of supply of funds. The reason for this is the simplified structure of financial institutions, including control of banks by monetary authorities. In addition, the mixed character of these banks (including both short- and long-term operations) means that monetary measures may influence both short-term money and capital market.

Second, processes initiated by monetary measures lead to relatively stronger and shorter-lagged effects on demand for goods and services than in developed market economies, as was discussed earlier. Monetary policy measures influence, first, investment expenditures through decreasing investment credits, and then consumption expenditures. However, relatively sharp deceleration-acceleration effects on these expenditures and subsequent strong impacts on the rate of increase in production may be considered peculiarities that make this process different from those in developed market economies.

Third, the effects of changes in demand for goods and services on prices, production, and imports and exports are strongly distorted by a number of specific exogenous causes. It is for this reason that these effects, at least in the short run, may strongly deviate from logical expectations.

Finally, the entire process of transmitting the effects of monetary measures is relatively simpler than in developed market economies, for it excludes the processes related to interest-rate effects and the existence of a differentiated pattern of financial instruments and institutions. It is for this reason that the transmitting mechanism includes less uncertainty, in addition to stronger and shorter-lagged effects.

## MONETARY VS. FISCAL POLICY

Recent developments have led to an increasing need for cooperation between monetary and fiscal policy. Deficiencies in implementing monetary policy as the only instrument of economic policy (in addition to direct measures) have raised the problem of a proper combination of monetary and fiscal policy measures. Instead of a "monetary vs. fiscal policy" problem, there is the problem of the "mix" of "monetary and fiscal policy."* In other words, instead of investigating the problem of the comparative advantages of monetary over fiscal policy, investigations are devoted to the problem of creating an optimal combination of monetary and fiscal measures.

The basic idea is to combine the efficiency and effectiveness of monetary policy in influencing demand for goods

*The "monetary vs. fiscal policy" problem in some developed market economies historically came after the dominating Keynesian approach that "money does not matter" and that fiscal policy is the main instrument of economic policy. In Yugoslavia the problem of monetary-fiscal policy comes historically after the approach that monetary policy is the main indirect instrument of economic policy and after a period of neglected use of fiscal policy as an instrument of economic policy. Thus, the problem is approached from different points of view and necessarily has a different content in Yugoslavia in comparison with other economies.

and services with that of fiscal policy in influencing re-
source allocation, investment decision-making, and other
related phenomena beyond the control of monetary policy.
Though the idea is clear enough, its implementation is hampered by several specific difficulties.

The main difficulties arise from the existence of an
inadequate financial market. The federal government cannot
borrow on the market. Its only source of borrowing is the
central bank. This has at least two consequences that hamper the use of fiscal policy. First, fiscal surplus-deficit
necessarily leads to changes of high-powered money in the
same amount, so that expenditure effects of fiscal deficit-
surplus are necessarily accompanied by monetary effects.
Second, lack of an efficient financial market makes it very
difficult for individual enterprises to borrow on the market.
In particular, a demand for funds, which tends in the normal course to outpace supply when coupled with strong ter-
ritorial barriers, makes the borrowing possibilities very
narrow and uncertain. It is for this reason that discount
policy includes a broad system of selective channels for
discounting, which work as a substitute for inadequate borrowing facilities in the market. This means, however, that
high-powered money cannot be created in large amounts by
granting credit to the federal government. The major part
of creation of high-powered money has to be left to selective discounts. As a consequence, there is relatively little room left for the government financing required by the
fiscal policy action.

Thus, the essential precondition for using fiscal
policy in combination with monetary policy is the development of an active financial market. At present the use of
forced lending to government as a substitute for market borrowing is being considered. Such an approach, however,
may have serious disadvantages in frustrating positive development of financial markets, absorbing a substantial
part of scarce funds, and creating additional disturbances
in the market.

The use of fiscal policy, moreover, is significantly
hampered by the complicated and time-consuming processes of
decision-making. This is in marked contrast to the rather
simplified procedure for monetary policy action. On this
score Yugoslav experience is very similar to that of developed market economies.

Finally, discussion of the monetary-fiscal policy mix
problem should include a system of quasi-monetary/quasi-fis-
cal policy measures. These measures are related to the
above-mentioned earmarking and freezing-defreezing of re-

stricted deposits.  These measures have an expenditure effect influencing expenditures of socialist enterprises,
other institutions, and government bodies.  At the same
time, they have monetary effects by inducing withdrawals
from or additions to the money supply, and even cause
changes in high-powered money if deposits are held with
the central bank.  Since these measures may have strong
monetary effects, a careful examination of these effects
is necessary.

## RULE VS. DISCRETION

Discretionary monetary policy dominates the scene in
Yugoslavia.  This is reasonable in view of frequent and
significant institutional changes in the country, which in
turn have produced considerable changes in the conditions
underlying the demand function for money and adjustment
processes of demand to the supply of money.

The same reasons that make "discretion" preferred over
"rule" are contributing to a preference for short-run small
changes in monetary measures and targets instead of longer-
run policy formation.  It will be seen later that this attitude is reflected in quarterly monetary planning as well
as in annual plans.

## BRONFENBRENNER TESTS FOR
## RIVAL MONETARY RULES

Let us consider now how well the monetary authority in
the country has managed the money supply and compare its
performance with what might have happened had the money supply been managed according to some well-defined "automatic
rules."  Such a comparison provides some gauge as to the
difficulty of the task of properly managing the money supply in a country undergoing vast and important institutional
changes.  It also sheds light on the continuing controversy
over "rules vs. discretion" in monetary management.

The empirical tests that follow are those designed by
Martin Bronfenbrenner[1] to test the performance of the monetary authority in the United States for various concepts of
the money supply under given assumptions as to the nature
and timing of the effects of monetary changes, the actual
price-level history of the United States with its hypothetical history under alternative monetary rules.  For the purposes of his tests, Bronfenbrenner defines as "ideal" mone-

TABLE 10.1

Pairwise Tests: Average Values of $d_{ij}$ Statistic,
Yugoslavia, Quarterly 1961-68

| Narrow M | | Broader M | |
| --- | --- | --- | --- |
| Wholesale | Consumers | Wholesale | Consumers |
| P | P | P | P |
| (judgment vs. 3 percent) | | | |
| .031 | .015 | .036 | .007 |
| (judgment vs. 4 percent) | | | |
| .031 | .015 | .034 | .009 |
| (judgment vs. lag) | | | |
| .058 | .066 | .098 | .084 |
| (3 percent vs. 4 percent) | | | |
| .000 | .000 | -.001 | .002 |
| (3 percent vs. lag) | | | |
| .027 | .051 | .062 | .077 |
| (4 percent vs. lag) | | | |
| .027 | .051 | .063 | .075 |

tary behavior the constancy of the price level and thus
leaves to other branches of economic policy such other objectives of policy as stabilizing interest rates, protect-
ing the gold stock, promoting full employment, balance-of-
payments equilibrium, and so on. The alternative rules
tested by comparison with Bronfenbrenner's "ideal" rule
are as follows:

1. The "judgment rule," which holds that monetary
authorities deal with each situation as it arises according
to their best judgment of circumstances present and future.
This particular rule is assumed to have been the one actually
in practice during the period under review.
2. The "inflexible rule," under which the money stock
grows at a steady annual rate of 3 percent and which he
calls the "3 percent variant of the inflexible rule."
3. The "4 percent variant of the inflexible."
4. A "lag rule," which provides for money stock expansion according to a percentage equal to the sum of the

prior year's percentage <u>increase</u> in the labor force, the prior year's percentage <u>increase</u> in man-hour labor productivity, and the prior year's percentage <u>decrease</u> in the velocity of circulation of money. In effect, if M is the money supply, N the labor force, O an index of output per employed workers, and V the income velocity of circulation of money, the rule may be written as

$$(1) \quad \frac{dM}{M_t} = \frac{dN}{N} + \frac{dO}{O} - \frac{dV}{V_{t-1}}$$

The equation for Bronfenbrenner's "ideal" rate of monetary growth is derived from Irving Fisher's equation of exchange in its income form. MV = PY and differentiating so that

$$(2) \quad \frac{dM}{M} + \frac{dV}{V} = \frac{dP}{P} + \frac{dY}{Y}$$

The "ideal" pattern preserves price level stability or in effect

$$(3) \quad \frac{dM}{M_O} = \frac{dY}{Y} - \frac{dV}{V}$$

When, however, the price level has not remained constant the actual rate of growth of the money supply is determined by

$$(4) \quad \frac{dM}{M} = \frac{dY}{Y} - \frac{dV}{V} + \frac{dP}{P}$$

so that

$$(5) \quad \frac{dM}{M_O} = \frac{dM}{M} - \frac{dP}{P}$$

Thus, the "ideal" pattern can be defined as the growth rate of real income minus the growth rate in velocity or the observed growth in the money supply minus the growth rate in the price level. We have

$$\frac{dM}{M_O}$$

as the "ideal" pattern or growth rate and

$$\frac{dM}{M_i}$$

as any annual growth rate other than the "ideal." The actual growth rate observed is indicated by

$$\frac{dM}{M_1}$$

the 3 percent rule is presented by

$$\frac{dM}{M_2}$$

the 4 percent rule is

$$\frac{dM}{M_3}$$

the "lag" rule is

$$\frac{dM}{M_4}$$

If we let $d_i$ stand for the annual growth rate of the price
level, then

$$(6) \quad d_i = \frac{dM}{M_i} - \frac{dM}{M_O} = \frac{dM}{M_i} - \frac{dY}{Y} - \frac{dV}{V}$$

when

$$i = 2, \ 3, \ 4$$

The changes in real income and velocity are observed
changes in (6). The $d_i$ indicates the deviation of the
growth of the money supply from the "ideal" under the various rules. The lower on the average is $d_i$, the better is
the performance of the rule being tested.

Two principal assumptions underlie Bronfenbrenner's
tests both of which may be debilitating. One is that the
effect of the money supply changes in the price level is
worked out usually within one year or one quarter depending

upon whether annual or quarterly data are used in the analysis. The evidence cited elsewhere in this study clearly
indicates the lags in the effect of money supply changes on
economic activity including prices that are variable. The
other assumption is that changes in velocity are independent
of monetary policy and changes in the money supply.* The
tests and their results do provide, as a first approximation,
useful insights into problems of monetary management, especially in a country such as Yugoslavia.

For the purposes of this study two definitions of
the money supply are employed. One is the narrow definition and includes demand deposits and currency outside the
commercial banking system. The second includes time deposits held in commercial banks. The consumer price index
and the wholesale price index are used as a measure of the
price level.

We may compare the performance of the several rules
by means of a pairwise test, which we may represent sym-
bolically as

$$(7) \quad d_{ij} = \left| d_j \right| - \left| d_i \right|$$

The statistic $d_{ij}$ measures the extent to which rule i comes
closer than does rule j to the "ideal" behavior in any
given year. If $d_{ij}$ should be negative, then the performance
of rule j is judged superior to rule i.

Yugoslavia's experience during the period 1961-68 sup-
ports the judgment rule, followed closely by the 3 percent
and 4 percent variants of the inflexible rule and last by
the lag rule. The test results for Yugoslavia are obtained
by using quarterly data for the period 1961-68. The tests
deal primarily with the private sector of the economy and
the cash balances of individuals. They exclude cash balances held by the socialist enterprises. Thus, the tests
and their results could be viewed as only suggestive and
not as definitive.

The absolute deviations test scores in favor of the
judgment rule with the results most pronounced when a narrow

---

*This is not in effect a simple version of the quantity
theory of money. Professor Bronfenbrenner has indicated
to one of us in correspondence that he does not interpret
V as a constant but only assumes it to be unresponsive to
changes in M. Moreover, his later work scraps the "lag
rule" in favor of having the monetary authority adapt dM
to its own autonomous or induced changes in V, N, O, etc.

definition of the money supply is used together with consumer prices.  The 3 percent and 4 percent rules yield
roughly similar results.  Again, the lag rule is the poorest
performer.  Algebraic deviations test results indicate
that the judgment and 4 percent rules have a slight inflationary bias.

The pairwise test results presented in Table 10.1 indicate that the judgment rule outperforms the other rules,
though the 3 percent and 4 percent rules are still contend-
ers, particularly when broader definitions of money are
used together with consumer prices.  In any case they out-
distance the lag rule, which again is the poorest performer.


## NOTE

1.  M. Bronfenbrenner, "Statistical Tests of Rival
Monetary Rules," Journal of Political Economy, February
1961, pp. 7-14, and "Statistical Tests of Rival Monetary
Rules:  Quarterly Data Supplement," Journal of Political
Economy, December 1961, pp. 621-25.  See also F. Modigliano,
"Some Empirical Tests of Monetary Management and of Rules
Versus Discretion," Journal of Political Economy, June
1964, pp. 211-45; and D. P. Tucker, "Bronfenbrenner on
Monetary Rules:  A Comment," Journal of Political Economy,
April 1963, pp. 173-79.

# 11

## GOALS AND
## TARGETS OF
## MONETARY
## POLICY

The term "goals" is used for "ultimate ends" of monetary policy, which are at the same time basic goals of
economic policy. The term "targets" relates to "interme-
diate" goals of monetary policy, involving changes in monetary indicators aimed at achieving goals of monetary policy.
Major parts of this chapter will be devoted to interpretation of specific components of definitions of goals and
targets of monetary policy and to the problem of trade-offs
in Yugoslavia.

### DEFINITIONS OF GOALS

Institutional and other changes after the reform have
required significant adjustments in the pattern of monetary
policy goals and produced fundamental changes in interrelationships of individual goals, their conflicting effects
and complementarities. The basic change in the pattern of
monetary policy goals has been the increased importance
of stabilization and balance-of-payments goals, so that
they have become as significant as the previously dominating
economic growth and employment goals. Thus, the list of
basic goals of monetary policy was extended fundamentally
after the reform. It is obvious that this change has made
the problem of trade-offs far more complex than before and
similar in difficulty to that in developed market economies.
The contents of these goals are similar to those in
market economies, at least along broad lines. However,
under specific Yugoslav conditions they also contain peculiarities that require explanation.

## Economic Growth

Definition of economic growth in Yugoslavia includes the effects of monetary policy on the rate of saving and on the economic allocation of saving. This goal has always had high priority in Yugoslavia, particularly before the reform.

## Employment

The employment goal in Yugoslavia is defined in very broad terms. It involves not only decrease in unemployment in the narrow sense (registered unemployment) but also in hidden unemployment, which is rather large.* It also includes employment of other factors of production as well as utilization of productive capacity. The usual narrow concept of employment as a monetary policy goal, including only decrease in the percentage of unemployment, is quite inappropriate to the Yugoslav situation of large hidden unemployment and very scarce capital goods. In fact, goals related to decrease in hidden unemployment and increase in the rate of use of capacities are more important than the goal of decrease in registered unemployment. Thus, the employment goal is related to the highest possible rate of employment of all factors of production. For practical purposes, both economic growth and employment goals are defined by the rate of increase in GNP.

Monetary policy may influence the employment goals by affecting demand for goods and services on the one hand and creating favorable conditions for financing of increased employment on the other. Economic growth and employment goals are closely and positively correlated so that monetary policy works in favor of one by promoting the other.

---

*The large share of agricultural population in total population (nearly 50 percent) illustrates how serious is the problem of hidden unemployment. Large hidden unemployment makes it extremely difficult to decrease the rate of registered unemployment. Thus, during the years 1968-69 average employment increased by 4 percent (from 3.561 million in 1967 to 3.706 million in 1969) and at the same time about 500,000 workers were employed abroad so that new employed workers outnumbered natural additions to the labor force several times. However, the number of registered unemployed has not decreased. On the contrary, it increased from 291,000 in 1967 to 316,000 in 1969 (average).

## Stable Price Level

In view of strong built-in nonmonetary causes of price increase, it is obvious that the goal of price stability cannot be defined as the goal of "no increase in the price level." Instead, the goal is defined so as to minimize the rate of increase in the price level. The evidence suggests that this minimal increase is about 5 percent yearly.*

The question of which prices becomes complicated. In practice retail prices are taken as a measure of changes in price level. Though the problem has not been discussed at length in Yugoslavia, there is increasing suspicion that the index numbers of retail prices involve significant upward bias owing to failure to take improvements in growth into adequate account. Other problems are indicated by the significantly higher increase in the retail prices of industrial goods compared to the rate of increase in producers' prices of these goods.** For the moment, however, this is the most representative index of prices,† and under the circumstances its use as a measure of changes in price level is justified.

The effects of monetary policy on the price level are similar to those of market economies, that is, through its influence on demand for goods and services. As already indicated, the effects are relatively stronger and shorter-lagged than in developed market economies in the case of

---

*This is the rate of increase in price level in years of "tight money policy" and decreasing demand for goods. The best example is 1967, when money supply decreased by 2 percent, demand for goods and services decreased by 1 percent in real terms, GNP in real terms increased by 1 percent, while the level of retail prices increased by 5 percent. The 4-5 percent increase in prices represents the lowest rate of increase in the entire period since 1952.

**Thus, in the period 1966-69 retail prices of industrial goods were increasing at a rate of 5 percent annually, whereas producers' prices of these goods were increasing at a rate of 2 percent annually.

†In addition to retail price index numbers, there are index numbers for producers' prices of industrial goods, cost of living index numbers, and some other partial index numbers. Indexes are published in Index, a monthly publication of the Federal Statistical Institute, Belgrade, and also in yearbooks issued by the institute.

upward pressure but not in the downward direction.  The
effects of easy and tight monetary policy are reflected
in changes in the rates of increase in price level (mainly
between 5 and 10 percent on an annual rate ) rather than
increase vs. decrease or stability of price level.


### Bslance-of-Payments Goals

It is clear that monetary policy goals in this field
refer to improvement in the country's balance of payments.
It is not clear, however, what precise meaning is attached
to the word "improvement."  For instance, according to official declaration of economic policy goals in 1970, "improvement" means significant decrease in balance-of-payments
deficit, including a higher rate of increase in exports
than in imports.[1]  A similar definition is applied to balance-of-payments goals in 1969.  In discussions and in the
first drafts of the Five-Year Plan, however, "improvement"
has been interpreted as balance-of-payments equilibrium
with minor annual fluctuations including both small deficits and small surpluses.  In view of the relatively low
level of development of the Yugoslav economy, balance-of-
payments equilibrium as a monetary policy goal does not
seem very reasonable, and if a policy of optimal economic
growth is pursued it appears inconsistent and unacceptable.
The most reasonable goal in this field may be a balance-
of-payments deficit that stays within the optimal borrowing
capacity of the country.

The mechanism of monetary policy in the field of balance of payments includes influence on demand for goods
and services and influence on price level.  In addition to
general measures, monetary policy may affect balance of
payments through selective measures, such as preferential
conditions for granting credits for exports, for preparation of exports, and the like.  However, in addition to
these very common components of the working mechanism of
monetary policy on balance of payments, there are at least
two significant specific components of this mechanism in
Yugoslavia.

First, there is the dual character of foreign transactions, including transactions with convertible and nonconvertible currency countries.*  The problem comes from the

---

*Exports in convertible currencies accounted for 60
percent of total exports in 1969.  The share of imports in

opposite behavior of exports and imports in these two kinds
of foreign transaction. Exports to nonconvertible currency
countries, of course, are far easier than those to convertible currency countries. The opposite is the case with
imports, where importers strongly prefer imports from convertible currency countries (better assortment and quality
of goods, easy trading facilities, etc.) to imports from
nonconvertible currency countries. In other words, free
foreign trade transactions lead to deficits with convertible currency countries and to surpluses with nonconvertible
currency countries, so that policy measures have to counter-
act deficits in one area and surpluses in other areas of
foreign trade transactions. Thus, monetary policy would
have both restrictive and expansionary effects at the same
time. This is not possible except where monetary measures
are strongly corrected by selective measures. Such a
duality in foreign transactions requires an appropriate
combination of quantitative and qualitative monetary policy
measures to solve the problem of differential effects in
the two fields of foreign transactions.

The second peculiarity is the relatively small number
of foreign capital transactions. This obviously makes the
problem of monetary policy action easier. However, recent
developments show a strong increase in these transactions
and a differentiation of the instruments and channels used
by increasing numbers of borrowers (including socialist
enterprises and banks). Thus, monetary policy has to take
into account the changing role and pattern of foreign capital transactions, which significantly complicates its
task.*

---

convertible currencies was on the order of 67 percent of
total imports. The remaining 40 percent of exports and 33
percent of imports mainly involved Eastern socialist countries.

*In addition to the increased share of decentralized
borrowers (other banks, socialist enterprises) in total
foreign borrowing from a negligible amount in the pre-reform
period to about 80 percent in 1969, there has been a significant change in the purposes of borrowing. Before the reform foreign borrowing was related to the acquisition of
foreign currency for foreign payments. Now there is an increasing amount of borrowing aimed at acquisition of dinars,
especially by banks in periods of monetary restriction (borrowing foreign exchange and then selling it to the central
bank). This is obviously a very significant new phenomenon
for policymakers.

## Other Goals of Monetary Policy

In addition to the above four basic goals, there may be other goals related to monetary policy action. Although defined as separate goals they in fact represent a more detailed specification of the four basic goals. This specification, in practice, is related to some parts of the working mechanism of monetary policy. It happens that monetary policy, for instance, is engaged in promoting the production of export goods, production of some groups of goods and services (e.g., wheat, meat, etc.), higher rate of growth of less-developed regions, and acceleration-deceleration of the rate of growth of investment.[2]

These specific goals play a significant role in Yugoslav monetary policy formation and composition of monetary measures. They determine the use of selective credit policy measures, which are, as will be shown, the essential of monetary policy. New developments, however, are aimed at decreasing the number of specific monetary policy goals.*

## THE ISSUE OF TRADE-OFFS

The widely discussed problem of trade-offs has become very important recently in Yugoslavia. Before the reform the basic monetary policy goals were economic growth and employment, with stabilization and balance-of-payments goals subordinated to them. Since the reform the relative priority of these goals has been fundamentally changed. Stabilization and balance-of-payments goals have been elevated to the same level of significance as employment and

---

*Relatively extensive use of specific goals is largely determined by inefficiencies and rigidities of the market mechanism. This is why many specific goals that are solved by the market mechanisms in developed market economies have to be supported by monetary policy in Yugoslavia. Thus, monetary policy necessarily has longer lists of responsibilities in Yugoslavia than in these economies. It already was explained that the role of monetary policy is broader also in financial markets because of the inefficiencies of these markets. Thus, inefficiencies of both real and financial markets require broader responsibility on the part of monetary policy than in developed market economies, and this is primarily reflected in a larger list of specific goals and selective credit policy measures.

economic growth.  It has become clear that implementation
of economic policy and employment goals is dependent on a
relatively stable price level and more open foreign trade
transactions.  Stabilization of prices and the opening of
the economy to foreign market influence have become an essential precondition for the efficient working of opportunity cost reasoning, imports of modern technology and
entrepreneurship, and the stimulating effects of competition.  Thus, stabilization and balance-of-payments goals
have become essential as intermediary goals preparing favorable conditions for efficient implementation of the
final goals of economic growth and employment.

The second reason for the increased priority of stabilization goals has been the growing need for the development of an efficient financial market.  It is clear that
rapid increases in the price level hamper development of
financial markets, especially if historical experience
justifies expectation of further price increases.  Since
efficient financial markets in Yugoslavia have become an
essential precondition for further economic growth at a
reasonable rate, stabilization goals have been necessarily
added to economic growth goals.  Introduction of stabilization and balance-of-payments goals, in addition to employment and economic goals of the same order of priority,
has made the problem of trade-offs very complicated indeed.
Theoretical solution of the questions of projecting the
optimal type of goals with maximum compatibility and com-
plementarity and minimum conflicting effects has produced
few satisfactory insights.  It is possible, however, to
have a pragmatic solution.  This is the approach we shall
discuss here.

Such an approach may simplify the problem in several
respects.  First, monetary policy goals are necessarily
expressed in rather vague terms.  They are never as exact
as is necessary to measure conflicting effects accurately.
Second, it is very difficult to translate economic goals
into monetary targets, even if it were possible to define
goals in a precise way (e.g., definition of appropriate
changes in monetary indicators).  Difficulties in transforming monetary goals into operational targets of monetary
policy further complicate the problem.  Third, the problem
of conflicting goals is not the problem of absolute con-
flict.  It is rather a problem of degree of individual
goals or, better, the problem of deviation of planned degrees of individual goals from the optimal combination of
degrees of individual goals.  Fourth, monetary policy is
not the only instrument of economic policy.  This is par-

ticularly true for Yugoslavia, where significant direct measures are used in addition to indirect policy measures. Thus, the problem is further complicated by the difficulties of defining which part of policy goals are left to monetary policy action.

In view of these difficulties the problem of conflicting effects of individual goals is solved by using two working principles. First, monetary policy should be ready to discover conflicting effects and readjust monetary targets and measures in a reasonable time. Second, the problem of readjustment should be investigated not only from the point of view of monetary policy but also from the point of view of other policies. How this problem is resolved in practice will be seen in interpreting the mechanism of monetary policy formation.

## TARGETS OF MONETARY POLICY

There is a general consensus that changes in money supply are to be used as targets of monetary policy. This conclusion is based on the prevailing quantity theory approach and on empirical evidence suggesting that there is a close association between changes in the money supply and real developments (investment and other expenditures for goods and services, rate of increase in production, changes in price level, imports, exports).*

Alternative indicators might be monetary base (high-powered money), bank credit, and interest rate. Not all of these indicators can be used under specific Yugoslav conditions. Interest rates cannot be used since they do not reflect correct market conditions. High-powered money can be used as a subsidiary monetary indicator substituting for the money supply. This is possible because of the close association between changes in the monetary base and changes in money supply, at least in the long run.

Similar arguments hold for the choice between the money supply and bank credit. Bank credit has at least two advantages over high-powered money. First, it is related more closely to the money supply, as well as to expenditures for goods and services, than high-powered money. Second, bank credit is conceptually and statistically simpler (at least under Yugoslav conditions). Thus, bank

---

*See the interpretation of the adjustment processes of demand to supply of money in Chapter 9.

credit may be a better substitution for the money supply as a monetary indicator than high-powered money. There is, however, a significant field of monetary action where bank credit serves as an independent indicator. This is the field of selective credit policy goals. In this instance bank credit, classified according to selective credit policy goals, presents the targets of credit policy that have to be implemented in supporting specific economic policy goals.

Declarations of the Federal Assembly on economic policy goals, which define monetary policy goals and targets, include the rate of increase in money supply and in bank short-term credit. Changes in the money supply are considered a primary monetary target, whereas changes in bank credit are treated as a secondary target. Thus, the declaration of the Federal Assembly on economic policy goals in 1970 stipulated that the money supply is to increase up to 12 percent and short-term credit up to 14 percent.[3] In addition, the declaration defined specific goals that are to be supported by selective credit policy measures.

## NOTES

1. Federal Official Gazette, No. 56 (1969), p. 1496.

2. For instance, the declaration of the Federal Assembly on economic policy goals for 1970 includes the following specific goals that should be supported by economic policy measures: production of export goods, especially those made of domestic materials; export of ships and equipment; construction and other works performed by domestic firms abroad; and accumulation of federal government stocks of some goods. Federal Official Gazette, No. 56 (1969).

3. Ibid., p. 1496.

# 12

**TOOLS OF
MONETARY
POLICY**

In addition to an explanation of the pattern of tools used by monetary policy, the aim of this chapter is to investigate these tools and determine their peculiarities.

## THE PATTERN OF TOOLS

Several peculiarities characterize the pattern of tools used by monetary policy in Yugoslavia. A list of these tools presented below shows that monetary policy uses a relatively large number of instruments of monetary regulation. Major parts of these instruments are related to regulation of the supply of credit, so that instruments for regulating the demand for credit are far less significant. Tools related to regulation of the supply of credit are mainly of bilateral type, including central bank and other bank relationships that govern the credit capacity of these banks (discounting reserve requirements). Multilateral tools, such as open market operations, are missing. The discount rate is not a significant instrument of monetary policy, whereas the selective credit policy instruments are used very broadly.

### Monetary Policy Tools

I.  Tools for regulating credit capacity of other banks

    1.  Tools for regulating changes in high-powered money

        a. Discount mechanism
        b. Special central bank credit to other banks
        c. Central bank credit to other banks for
           liquidity purposes

    2. Tools for regulating uses of high-powered
       money (and credit and monetary multipliers)

        a. Changes in reserve requirement ratio
        b. Changes in obligatory liquidity ratio
        c. Other obligatory deposits with central bank

II.  Other tools for regulating the supply of bank credit

    1. Tools regulating use of bank resources
    2. Gentlemen's agreements and moral suasion
    3. Credit ceiling

III. Tools for regulating the demand for credit

    1. Discount rate
    2. Subsidization of interest rates

IV.  Selective credit policy measures

    The controlling factor in these monetary policy tools
is a relatively undifferentiated financial market.  Poor
differentiation of financial instruments, especially in
significant quantities of securities, makes it impossible to
use open market operations as an instrument of monetary
policy.  On the other hand, the inefficient nature of the
financial market requires extensive use of selective instruments aimed at substitution for the absence of market facilities.
    Second, the need for extensive selective intervention
by the central bank, together with narrow and uncertain
borrowing facilities on the market, has induced relatively
large borrowing by other banks from the central bank.  The
high share of borrowings from the central bank in total
bank resources has made discount policy one of the most
significant instruments of monetary regulation.  Thus,
relatively long lists of instruments of monetary policy and
extensive use of selective instruments reflect deficiencies
of financial and real markets and encourage broader responsibilities of monetary policy.  The efforts made to improve
the efficiency of financial and other markets, if successful, will presumably lead to a reduction in the list of

monetary policy tools, particularly in the field of selective intervention.

## TOOLS FOR REGULATING
## HIGH-POWERED MONEY

### The Discounting Mechanism

The discounting mechanism is by and large the most significant tool for regulating changes in high-powered money and one of the country's most significant tools of monetary policy. This is, in the first instance, because of the instrument's flexibility and effectiveness in selective credit policy and, in the second, because of its dominant contribution to changes in high-powered money.*

The discounting mechanism in Yugoslavia has unique features, although its basic nature is similar to that in market economies (other banks borrowing from the central bank on the basis of their credit granted to customers). It will be seen that, in the process of the adaptation of this mechanism to specific needs, it acquired several characteristics.

The discount mechanism in Yugoslavia contains five basic components: purpose of credit granted to customer, documents and procedure, terms of discounting, credit worthiness of the discounting bank, and discount ceiling.**

### Purpose of Credit

Purpose of credit is an essential element in the discount mechanism. As a rule, only credits granted for specific purposes may be discounted. The definition of purposes varies. At times they are broadly defined and at

---

*For instance, in the period 1967-69 discount credits increased by 6.276 billion dinars, which was 74 percent of the total amount of creation of high-powered money (8.439 billion dinars).

**Explanations of these tools and of their changes during the period under investigation will necessarily contain relatively limited details. For further details see annual reports of the National Bank of Yugoslavia and other relevant literature.

others narrowly defined.* Nearly all credits eligible for discounting are "self-liquidating" credits. There may be exceptions, such as discounting of specific consumer credits, including credits for housing. There has been a tendency to increase the number of purposes eligible for discounting, resulting in more and more detailed specification of these purposes. Difficulties caused by this overspecification of purposes and the danger of a pyramidal increase in their number in the future have stimulated efforts to change the system of decision-making in this field. For the moment, the Federal Executive Council (federal government) is responsible for the list of credits eligible for discounting, which results in an overexpansion of these credits.** There are plans to reduce the scope of federal decision-making in this matter to a very narrow group of purposes (for instance, only exports and production and inventories of wheat) and to leave decisions on other purposes to republics within a quota decided by the Federal Assembly. This would simplify the problem from the point of view of monetary policy and at the same time leave room for flexible treatment of predominantly regional interests.

## Documents and Procedure

The Yugoslav discounting mechanism differs significantly from a discounting mechanism in the strict sense of the term. Discounting in Yugoslavia does not involve transfer of discounting documents to the central bank. In practice it consists of the granting of credit to banks on the basis of credit granted by banks to their customers. When applying for discounting, banks issue a statement on the discountable credits (properly classified), and the central bank grants the credit (discounts) on the basis of this

---

*For instance, such broad purposes as credits granted to trade enterprises for buying goods. On the other hand, there are also such specifications as credit for production of wheat, credit for tobacco stocks, etc.

**This is because of the different requirements of the six republics taking part in federal decision-making. Each republic has its own preferred purposes for discounting, so that introduction of one purpose into the list is possible only if it is accompanied by introduction of several other purposes in an attempt to reach a compromise with all the republics.

statement. It is assumed that there are appropriate documents (as prescribed by the central bank)* underlying the credit.

This simplified discounting procedure was introduced to save the enormous work that had to be done if individual documents were discounted. In view of the large number of these documents, the costs of processing would far outweigh the advantages of individual discounting.

The second significant element in the procedure is that other banks have a right to discounting if all conditions are fulfilled (not only the "privileged," as in the United States). This does not mean, however, that banks have an unconditional right to the discounting of eligible credits. As will be seen, there are conditions that restrict this right (e.g., the "credit worthiness" of the bank) consonant with the needs of monetary policy.

Discountable documents are defined in such a way as to enable central bank supervisors to control the real nature of the credit, e.g., the purpose for which it is requested. In addition to such classic discountable documents as bills there may be various other types of documents, such as certificates issued by customs proving that declared exports were really effected, contracts showing that the equipment was ordered and that the essential conditions have been fulfilled, etc.

The basic terms of discounting are discount rate, maturity, and percentage of discounting. In addition to these basic terms there may be some specific terms that are applied exceptionally. Definition of these terms represents a very significant component of discount policy, enabling monetary authorities to regulate changes in the amount of discount crediting.

Discount rate as such is not a significant instrument of discount policy, for reasons already explained. This is why it has not been changed since 1963, when it was established at 6 percent. Development of a financial market and abolishment of rigid regulation of interest rate formation will presumably make the discount rate more influential.

Discount credits are short-term credits. The terms of maturity, however, may vary significantly from three months to one year or in special cases to two years. Changes in the terms of maturity may be a very significant instrument of discount control.

---

*The central bank may check on whether the bank really has the appropriate documents. This is one of the main tasks of the central bank's supervisory activity.

The percentage of discounting of eligible credits is also a very efficient instrument of control. As a rule, credits are discounted only partially so that a bank is obliged to participate in financing of the original credit. Variations of percentages of discounting are used for two purposes: first as an instrument of selective credit policy (higher percentage reflecting higher priority), and second as an instrument for regulating the total amount of discounts. Other terms may be very different: a higher percentage of discounting in the case of exports of equipment, a longer term of maturity in the case of exports to remote countries, and so on.

## Credit Worthiness

Credit worthiness is one of the basic components of discount policy. It may be said that it is related less to credit worthiness proper (ability to repay the credit) and more to credit worthiness as an instrument of expansion of discounting. Recent main components of this instrument have been the obligation of the bank to have at least 50 percent of short-term credit granted up to three months of maturity, to follow all regulations issued by monetary authorities, not to allow its total borrowing from the central bank (discounting or other) to exceed 100 percent of deposits charges with reserve requirements (total short-term deposits, excluding savings deposits),* the appropriate use of special reserve funds, and the holding of a definite amount of liquid reserve money on gyro accounts with the central bank.** Definition of credit worthiness also includes selective components. Thus, some of the above terms are not necessary in the case of some specified discounts, or they are made easier.

## Discount Ceiling

Discount ceiling is primarily the instrument of control of the total amount of discounts. Each bank has its own

---

*This is the present regulation. However, both the percentage and the basis on which it is applied may be changed.

**In practice the effects are similar to reserve requirements.

discount ceiling, calculated by applying the general discount ceiling rate (fixed by the central bank)* to the total amount of short-term deposits excluding savings deposits (the same basis as for calculation of reserve requirements). Thus, the central bank can influence discounting by changing the discount rate. It can also affect discounting by redefining the basis on which the discount ceiling rate is applied.

Although predominantly an instrument of regulation of the total amount of discounts, the discount ceiling may be significant also for selective crediting. The lower the credit ceiling, the more room there is for preferential discount credits, which are granted regardless of the discount ceiling.

Finally, two characteristics of the Yugoslav discount mechanism should be mentioned. First, since it is selective, based primarily on purpose of the discounted credit, there are differential regional effects. Discounting of export credits favors primarily developed regions; discounting of credits for production or stocks of agricultural products favors primarily the agricultural regions. It is for this reason that the discount mechanism has become very complicated, with political implications. There are other factors already mentioned suggesting that selective discounting should be divided into (very limited) federal and (all other) republican responsibility and decision-making. Second, there is no tradition against borrowing from the central bank, as is the case in market economies with the American and British tradition in banking. On the contrary, banks are accustomed to relying primarily on borrowing from the central bank. This makes it possible to use the discount mechanism, which is to be sharply distinguished from the discount rate, as a regular tool of monetary policy.

### Special Central Bank Credit

In addition to discounts there is another central bank credit available to banks--special credit. This special credit, which is far less significant than discount credit, represents consolidated bank debts created in 1967 when

---

*The discount ceiling rate was fixed at 20 percent in 1966. In 1967 it was decreased to 15 percent, then increased to 20 percent in April 1968, and decreased to 15 percent in November 1968. In 1969 it was not changed.

the new credit system was introduced.  At that time the new
discount credit replaced only one part of existing bank
borrowing from the central bank (up to the amount of 20
percent of short-term deposits).  The remaining part, above
the amount of discount credit, was covered by a special
credit granted by the central bank to other banks.  The
central bank was at the same time authorized to require
partial repayment of this credit as a means of withdrawing
high-powered money.  Such repayment could not be required
except at an equal percentage for all banks.  The peculiarity of this type of credit is that it is relatively higher
in the case of banks located in less-developed regions
where bank deposits are a smaller fraction of total bank
resources.  As a result, these banks have a smaller discount
ceiling and consequently a larger noncovered bank debt to
the central bank.  This is significant from the point of
view of the regional effects of a requirement for repayment
of this type of credit, resulting in a relatively higher
amount of withdrawal of high-powered money from banks in
less-developed regions.

When these special credits were introduced in 1967,
they accounted for 71 percent of total central bank credit
to other banks, whereas discount credits shared only 23 percent of these credits.  After several repayments of these
special credits[1] and a substantial increase in discount
credits, the share of the former decreased to 31 percent and
that of the latter increased to 66 percent of total central
bank credit to other banks at the end of 1969.  Special
credits have thus become far less significant an instrument
of monetary regulation.

## Central Bank's Credit
## for Liquidity

The purpose of this credit is to help other banks overcome temporary and unexpected drains of reserve money.
Thus, it is a substitute for the "call money market."

On this basis banks in 1969 were authorized to borrow
from the central bank up to 2 percent of their short-term
deposits (excluding savings deposits) for a period of 10
days in a quarter.*

---

*The amount of borrowing and the number of days were
changed several times.  In 1970 the system of borrowing was
changed by extending the number of days to 10 days monthly,

According to the purpose of this credit, banks are not allowed to use such credit for further expansion. For all practical purposes, however, it does increase the credit capacity of banks by allowing them to hold lower reserves. As a result, this tool is partly an instrument for the creation of high-powered money and partly an instrument for the regulation of the use of high-powered money and the monetary multiplier.

## TOOLS FOR REGULATING THE MONETARY MULTIPLIER

The basic tool in this area is the reserve requirements ratio. The other tools are special reserve funds. There are also instruments that work partly in this direction, such as the obligatory liquidity ratio (as a part of credit worthiness) and the central bank's credit for liquidity.

### Reserve Requirement Ratio

This has been one of the most powerful tools of monetary management and the one with the longest tradition in Yugoslavia. The central bank decides this ratio up to a maximum of 35 percent, which is fixed by the Federal Assembly. The central bank also decides the basis on which the ratio is applied as well as its changes. At the end of 1969 the reserve requirements ratio was 30 percent on short-term deposits (excluding savings deposits). Savings deposits and time deposits were not charged with reserve requirements.*

-----------------------

and the amount was limited to the amount of banks' holdings of federal government securities (the credit was granted on the basis of these securities).

*The reserve requirements ratio was changed three times in 1968 and six times in 1969. Relatively frequent changes in the reserve requirements ratio reflect the significance of this tool for monetary management. The lowest ratio was 25 percent and the highest, 35 percent. The average rate, however, was significantly lower (if savings deposits and time deposits are included), amounting to about one-half of the above ratios. At the end of 1969 reserve requirements amounted to 7.247 billion dinars, or nearly seven times more than reserve money on regular gyro accounts of banks with the central bank.

Although this tool is very close to similar instruments used in market economies, there are special features in the case of its use in Yugoslavia. First, obligatory reserves have to be held in a separate account and cannot be used.* The system of holding obligatory reserves is thus rather rigid. Second, large differences in the pattern of bank resources (a higher share of deposits in developed regions than in less-developed regions in total bank resources) result in a differential effect of changes in reserve requirements. The effects are significantly higher in developed than in less-developed regions. From this point of view changes in the reserve requirements ratio have the same differential effects as changes in the discount ceiling and opposite effects in comparison with the repayment of special credit. Finally, reserve requirements, defined and used in the above way, do not represent an instrument of regulation of the liquidity of the banking system. Primarily they are a tool for regulating the monetary multiplier. They also represent a significant fiscal instrument by forcing banks to borrow from the central bank larger amounts than necessary and pay the discount rate.**

Special Reserve Funds

Banks are obliged to allocate "special" reserve funds" amounting to 0.2 percent of total bank credit up to the amount of 2 percent of total bank credit. These funds must be held in a separate account. They may be used only for liquidity purposes in the case of an unexpected drain of reserve money from the regular gyro accounts of the bank with the central bank. Now, they also may be used for (discountable) federal government securities. At the end of 1969 these funds amounted to 1.006 billion dinars. This is close to the amount of reserve money on regular gyro accounts of the other banks with the central bank (1.129 bil-

---

*Exceptionally, they can be used for buying of central bank papers if it is specifically allowed by monetary authorities.

**Only one part of the interest rate charged by the central bank is used to cover its costs. The remaining part goes to the federal government and represents a significant source of its regular income. Thus, a higher reserve requirements ratio means higher borrowing from the central bank and higher residual for the government.

lion dinars). Thus, special reserve funds have become very significant components of bank liquidity policy.

## Obligatory Deposits with the Central Bank

This is not a strict tool of monetary policy. It is, however, a very powerful "quasi-monetary instrument" for such practices as freezing-defreezing of balances and as a means of countercyclical regulation of expenditures. The frozen balances may be deposited with other banks and with the central bank. In the first case the effect is rather small, resulting in a withdrawal of the money supply while at the same time creating additional bank credit capacity so that withdrawal of money is significantly lower than the amount of frozen balances. The effect in the second case is stronger. In addition to the full amount of withdrawal from the money supply, the same amount of high-powered money is withdrawn so that the total restrictive effect is far higher than the amount of frozen balances (amount of withdrawal of high-powered money minus freeing of reserve requirements, multiplied by monetary multiplier).

## OTHER TOOLS REGULATING SUPPLY OF CREDIT

There are three other tools for regulating the supply of credit: regulations for the use of bank resources, gentlemen's agreements, and credit ceiling.

## Regulations for Use of Bank Resources

The basic instrument in this connection is definition of "investment resources" of other banks, i.e., resources that may be used for investment credits. The basic point, as has been explained, is that investment credits (credits based on investment resources) remain outside monetary regulations related to purpose, borrower, terms, etc., so that investment resources are highly preferred in comparison with other resources.* Legal provisions and central

_____

*We have noted already that the distinction between investment and short-term resources is so important that

164

bank decision, therefore, significantly affect credit supply and particularly the pattern and composition of this supply.

The significance of this instrument is that it is correlated with the scope of use of selective measures, such as, for example, the degree of regulations of short-term credits according to purpose. The more these regulations are applied (and backed by a right of borrowing from the central bank, if the regulations are followed) the more significant become resources that escape these regulations (investment resources). The future of this tool appears to depend on the share of selective credits in total bank credits. The new trend is to decrease selective regulations, which leads to reduction in the significance of and necessity for the regulation in the use of bank resources. There are already suggestions current that this instrument should be eliminated.

## Gentlemen's Agreements and Moral Suasion

This method has not been applied significantly in the period under consideration. There is, however, growing interest in its application. The fact is that the central bank plays a more significant role in monetary regulation in Yugoslavia than in some other economies, owing in part to the absence of a developed financial market.

## Credit Ceiling

This is an extraordinary tool of monetary policy, used in cases where the efficiency and effectiveness of other tools are in doubt. The rationale for its implementation is the desire to provide additional protection against credit expansion. Such a situation may arise when strong exogenous factors bring about a sharp increase in high-powered money and when it is not clear how long their impact will last. If regular restrictive measures are taken

---

banks are considered as split into two separate departments, commercial bank and investment bank departments, with separate balance sheets and policy formation. The basic elements of investment resources are credit funds, time deposits, domestic borrowings, and foreign borrowings.

they may not take effect quickly, so that there must be a protection against overexpansion in the meantime.

Credit ceiling as a tool is rather rigid and its application has many disadvantages, especially in Yugoslavia with its inadequate financial market. This is particularly valid for seasonal and differential regional needs for financing. Credit ceiling prevents banks from efficiently and effectively adjusting their policy to these needs. The fact that there are no other important sources of financing creates serious difficulties in production, trade, and the economy in general. To avoid or at least to mitigate these disadvantages, credit ceiling as a tool is used only for a short period (two to three months) and in cases when its use is unavoidable.*

Credit ceiling is applied only on short-term credit, so that banks are allowed to extend investment credit if they have unused investment resources. This significantly weakens the efficiency of this instrument, so that it may be used efficiently only if parallel measures reducing liquidity of the banking system are taken. The decision on the use of this instrument is made by the central bank, but agreement on the part of the Federal Executive Council is necessary. The credit ceiling may be defined as the obligation not to increase short-term credits, to decrease them at least a definite percentage, or, to increase them not more than a definite percentage of the amount at a definite date.

## TOOLS REGULATING DEMAND
## FOR CREDIT

It is reasonable to expect that under the conditions of Yugoslavia's financial market--rather stronger demand than supply of funds, rigid mechanism of interest rate formation, and relatively low interest-rate elasticity--tools related to demand for credit are of limited influence. An instrument that might be used in this field is the discount rate of the central bank. The discount rate, however, is used more as an instrument of fiscal policy (representing a source of income of the federal government) than as an instrument for the regulation of the demand for credit.

---

*In the period under consideration credit ceiling was used in the second half of 1966 and the first quarter of 1967. It was not used in 1968 and 1969.

This explains why the discount rate (6 percent) has not been changed during the period under consideration. It is expected, however, that the discount rate will play a more significant role in the future when the rigidities surrounding the development of financial markets are substantially reduced.

In addition to the discount rate there is a selective set of instruments for influencing the formation of interest rates, including a system of differential subsidies for specified branches and activities, e.g., agriculture, exports, and tourism. The mechanism operates on the principle that a bank charges the "normal rate" but a borrower pays the reduced rate. The difference is paid by the government body that has decided on the subsidized rate. The aim of subsidization is to stimulate investments in specified branches and activities and to make investors in these fields more competitive.

## Selective Credit Policy Instruments

The strongest selective instruments are related to the discount policy. The nature of the discount policy is basically selective. It involves privileged (or prohibitive) components according to branches, purposes of credit, terms, and credit worthiness. In addition to discount policy, a selective influence on supply of credit is performed by regulations related to the question of who may be granted credit by a bank. Recent regulations forbid short-term bank lending to government bodies, except to the federal government when decided by the Federal Assembly. There are also regulations related to granting credits to individuals. On the demand side selective influence is based on the system of subsidization of interest rates.

## INTERRELATIONSHIPS AMONG THE TOOLS

The rather long list of tools applied in the area of monetary policy raises the question of their interrelationships, particularly their complementary or competitive nature. The above interpretation of individual tools of monetary policy suggests that they have complementary rather than competitive effects. This is because nearly all of them belong to the list of tools affecting the supply of credit. Discount rate influencing demand for credit is the only exception. This tool has not been important thus far. It is not properly applied as a tool of monetary policy. Although numerous in number, tools of monetary policy in Yugoslavia have one-directional effects: they are complementary rather than competitive. This is a very significant property of the monetary tools in Yugoslavia. The dominant complementary nature of these tools makes the problem of projection of an optimal combination of monetary measures easier. It also makes the effects of these tools stronger and more predictable. This does not, however, mean that the problem of projecting the appropriate combination of monetary measures is easy and that it does not involve a significant degree of uncertainty.

NOTE

1. Repayment of special credits has been used frequently as an instrument of withdrawal of excess high-powered money. In the period 1967-69 repayment of these credits was required on six occasions, resulting in the withdrawal of 2.444 billion dinars in 1967, 1.742 billion dinars in 1968, and 559 million dinars in 1969, and reducing the amount of special credits from 9.147 billion dinars in the beginning of 1967 to 4.402 billion dinars at the end of 1969. Annual Report of the National Bank of Yugoslavia, 1967, p. 60, and 1969, p. 42.

There are two basic questions we shall consider:
first, the problem of method of projection and decision-
making on monetary policy targets and of measures for implementation of these targets (monetary planning); second,
the pattern of institutions involved in monetary policy,
their functions and interrelationships.

MONETARY PLANNING

With the increased role of autonomous economic processes, the growing perplexity of interrelationships among
economic phenomena, and increasing responsibility on the
part of monetary policy, the traditional monetary management based on "feelings" has proved less and less suitable.
It was clear that more sophisticated methods of policy
formation were necessary. It became necessary to provide
policymakers with appropriate information on past developments and reliable forecasts of future developments of
relevant phenomena in order to make it possible for them
to reach rational decisions on monetary targets. Implementation of monetary targets also required an appropriate
basis for the projection of monetary measures.

Investigations suggested that the most realistic approach to this problem was to introduce a system of monetary
planning based on flow-of-funds accounts. In addition to
the feasibility of flow-of-funds for this purpose, this ap-

proach had the advantage of nearly one decade of use by the National Bank of Yugoslavia.*

This system of monetary planning includes annual and monthly plans. The annual plan involves projection of a flow-of-funds matrix on the basis of historical trends, functional relationships, economic policy goals, institutional changes, and other significant determinants of relevant developments. The final result of this projection is the estimation of transactions of the sector "monetary system" as residuals in horizontal matrix identities. These estimates contain two strategic amounts: on the liability (sources) side they give the change in money supply, which corresponds to demand for money estimated in individual sectors, and on the assets (uses) side they contain the change in short-term bank credit** necessary to achieve the estimated change in money supply. The projected change in the money supply (equal to the estimated change in demand for money) represents the final outcome of forecasts and estimates of developments in all financial and nonfinancial sectors. It answers the question of what change in the money supply corresponds to the monetary policy goals and thus defines the basic target of monetary policy. The projected change in short-term bank credit shows what monetary policy should do to achieve a similar change in money supply.

The second stage of monetary planning is devoted to decomposition of the estimated monetary system transactions into transactions of two subsectors: the National Bank of Yugoslavia (central bank) and other banks. The estimates of the central bank's transactions provide policymakers with the strategic basis for decision-making on the composition of monetary tools. It shows, first, the amount of change in high-powered money that is consistent with the projected change in short-term credit (and money supply) and, second, the basic sources of this change in high-powered money (discount credit, credit to the federal government, foreign exchange transactions), and its uses (currency

---

*Flow-of-funds accounts produced by the National Bank of Yugoslavia are published in annual reports of this bank.

**Change in short-term bank credit is estimated as a residual item balancing the vertical (sector) identity of the monetary system. Thus, the estimated change in short-term bank credit represents a residual item balancing the whole system of matrix identities of the flow-of-funds accounts (both horizontal and vertical).

in circulation, obligatory reserves of other banks, liquid
reserves, balances of special reserve funds, other bank's
deposits with central bank, float).  This is the final
stage of annual planning.  Estimates reached at this stage
are not, however, suitable for decision-making on the application of monetary tools.  To make them applicable for
practical purposes of monetary policy it is necessary to
translate them from annual to monthly language.  This is
done by transforming annual estimates into seasonally adjusted monthly figures.  Then other relevant determinants
of monthly pattern annual estimates are also taken into
account (institutional, extraordinary determinants, etc.).
This is the basic purpose of monthly planning.  In addition,
monthly planning may include revision of annual estimates,
if in the meantime they have become inconsistent with economic policy goals (e.g., because of change in goals, because of significant deviations of actual developments
from forecasts, etc.).

Finally, on the basis of monthly projections of sources
and uses of high-powered money, monetary authorities decide
on implementation of tools of monetary policy.  Practically,
this means decision on changes of the existing monetary
measures.

Monetary planning was introduced in 1967.  However,
1967 and 1968 may be considered the experimental period of
monetary planning.  In 1969 the above system of monetary
planning was finally accepted as the basis for policy formation by monetary authorities.  This has proved helpful
in many ways.  The extensive quantitative argumentation
proved very useful for policymakers, especially for the
Federal Assembly and the Federal Executive Council.  It
has, for instance, significantly reduced vague verbal argumentation and time-consuming, often useless, discussions.
Thus, it became possible for the central bank to promote a
rational process of decision-making based on advanced professional knowledge of monetary problems and monetary planning.  In view of the always present danger that widely
discussed and seemingly attractive monetary policy topics
may be interpreted very arbitrarily and without appropriate
knowledge and experience, introduction of the aforementioned
scientific elements into the procedure of policy formation
has significantly contributed to its efficiency.

## MONETARY AUTHORITIES

Monetary authorities consist of the Federal Assembly,
the Federal Executive Council, the Secretariat of Finance,

and the National Bank of Yugoslavia. The Federal Assembly
is the highest monetary authority. It decides on basic
goals and targets of monetary policy. It also regulates
the institutional framework of monetary policy (banking
structure, tools of monetary policy) by formulating and
passing relevant legislation and decides on monetary policy
goals and targets in annual declarations on economic policy.[1]

The governor of the National Bank of Yugoslavia is
appointed by the Federal Assembly and is responsible to it
for the implementation of monetary targets and for the performance of other tasks of the National Bank of Yugoslavia.

The Federal Executive Council is responsible for sub-
mitting proposals on monetary policy goals and targets to
the Federal Assembly. It also has decision power on some
tools of monetary policy, while still other tools are sub-
ject to the approval of the council. Selective measures
that have redistributive effects and strong regional impacts are controlled by the council (by vesting the council
with decision power or approval power). Measures of monetary policy that do not have these effects are left to the
National Bank of Yugoslavia. Vesting of the Federal Executive Council with decision power in selective credit policy
reflects the mobility of the National Bank of Yugoslavia
to take responsibility for the possible political consequences of redistributive effects of selective credit policy.

In practice, the National Bank of Yugoslavia stays in
close contact with the Federal Executive Council by taking
part in its meetings, giving information on all measures
the bank is planning to take within its decision-making
powers, preparing reports on relevant developments, and
the like. This makes it possible for the Federal Executive
Council to follow closely operations of the central bank
and to exercise a significant influence on its decision-
making.

As an organizational part of the Federal Executive
Council, the Secretariat of Finance has no power in relation
to the National Bank of Yugoslavia in the field of monetary
management. It controls only the legal aspects of the
bank's operations. It has, however, significant power in
regulating banking structure and bank operations, the payments mechanism, issues, buying and selling of securities,
and operations of other financial institutions. Although
it is not involved in monetary policy directly, it performs
functions that are indirectly very significant for monetary
policy.

The National Bank of Yugoslavia is the central bank
and performs the usual functions of central banks. It is

independent in implementing monetary policy targets, except in applying selective credit policy instruments. It
is not independent in deciding on monetary policy goals
and targets. It is required to pursue policy goals and
targets defined by the Federal Assembly.

NOTE

1. For an example, see Federal Official Gazette, No.
56 (1969).

# 14

**EFFICIENCY
OF MONETARY
POLICY**

The problem of efficiency of monetary policy involves the issues of implementation of monetary targets and achieving the goals of monetary policy.

## EFFICIENCY IN IMPLEMENTING
## MONETARY TARGETS

The question of efficiency in implementing monetary targets is mainly one of consistency between projected and realized changes in the money supply (changes in money supply being the basic target of monetary policy). Thus, the question of the efficiency of monetary policy in achieving its targets should be answered by investigating the empirical evidence on the actual development of money supply as compared with projected changes. This method, however, is fully applicable only for 1969, when the monetary target was defined as the percentage change in the money supply. In other years during this period (1965-68) monetary targets were defined as higher or lower rates of increase in money supply relative to the rate of increase in GNP, so that a precise evaluation is not possible.

Monetary policy targets in 1966-67 were a lower rate of increase in money supply than the rate of increase in GNP, to promote the strongly emphasized stabilization goals; a higher rate of increase in money supply than in GNP in 1968, to stimulate revival of economic activity; an increase in money supply up to 12 percent; and, for the implementation of this target, an increase in short-term credit up to 16 percent in 1969.

TABLE 14.1

Projected and Actual Development of Money Supply
(annual rate, end of year, in percent)

|                                | 1965 | 1966 | 1967 | 1968 | 1969 | 1970 | 1971 |
|--------------------------------|------|------|------|------|------|------|------|
| Actual rate of growth          | 5    | 5    | -2   | 24   | 12   | 12   | 12   |
| Projected rate of growth[a]    | less than 26 | less than 11 | less than 6 | more than 9 | 12 | 18 | 14 |

[a]The rate of growth for 1969 was fixed by monetary authorities. The other rates are calculated approximately on the basis of rates of growth of GNP in real terms plus a 5 percent increase in price level (and, as already noted, the minimum rate of increase in price level under Yugoslav conditions). For 1965 a 25 percent increase in price level was applied, involving effects of price regulations within the reform measures (see Chapter 2).


Table 14.1 suggests that monetary policy was not completely successful during the period under consideration. It was particularly effective in 1969, when it managed to achieve exactly the projected monetary targets. In other years monetary policy succeeded in changing the rate of increase in money supply in the projected direction (i.e., to make it higher or lower than the rate of increase in GNP). As we shall observe, however, actual deviations of the money supply from the rates of growth of GNP were significantly larger than would correspond to economic policy goals. This suggests that monetary policy was effective in changing the rate of increase in the projected direction but not in controlling the intensity of the change.

The excellent results reached in 1969 should not be exaggerated. The less successful results achieved in 1965-68 are more realistic, if the above investigations of the process of creation of money are taken into account.*

---

*See Chapter 7. The higher rate of increase in the money supply for 1970 was the consequence of a substantial increase in high-powered money brought about by the National

These investigations suggest that there are significant degrees of variability in the determinants of changes in money
supply and that monetary policy consequently involves a
considerable degree of uncertainty.  It was shown that a
relatively high degree of uncertainty comes from the erratic
behavior both of high-powered money and of the monetary
multiplier, reflecting in part (unavoidable) mistakes in
projections and in part effects of stochastic variables as
well as extraordinary exogenous impacts.  The variability
of the monetary multiplier also largely reflects time lags
in the effects of changes in high-powered money, particularly sharp changes.

In summary, we may conclude that monetary policy has
been fully efficient in the sense of effectively pursuing
the projected monetary objectives.

Empirical evidence suggests, however, that the degree
of tightness or ease was not efficiently controlled by
monetary policy and that the effects of monetary measures
involved a significant degree of uncertainty in this respect.  The evidence for 1969, on the other hand, shows
that monetary policy may be efficient and effective on occasion.

Efficiency of monetary policy in implementing goals
and targets during the above three periods also may be distinguished:  first, the 1965-67 period featured emphasis
on "stabilization goals"; second, during 1968, employment
and growth received top priorities; and finally, during 1969
and 1970 overall stabilization was emphasized.

The period 1965-67 is dominated by the reform measures,
wherein monetary policy measures were to play one of the
most significant roles.  Monetary policy was used for the
creation of a favorable climate for reform in the first
half of 1965.  Following the first (and most significant)
reform measures taken in July 1965, monetary policy was
used to support a "stabilization program."  Thus, the goals
of promoting stable levels of prices and improvement in the
balance of payments gained higher priority than the previous high-priority goals of increase in production and
economic growth.  The rationale for this change in relative
priorities was the recognition that further economic growth
and improvement in efficiency of the economy were strongly

---

Bank as a result of two disastrous earthquakes (Bosnia and
Dalmatia) and floods in several parts of the country.  It
is for this reason that 1970 should be excluded from further considerations of the efficiency of monetary policy.

hampered by high increases in prices and restricted foreign trade and foreign exchange transactions. Thus, the essential precondition for increase in the rate of economic growth and improvement of efficiency in the economy in the long run was reduction of the rate of price increase to a minimum and the opening of the economy to broader influence by foreign markets. Both of these preconditions however required, at least temporarily, the preference for stabilization over employment and economic growth priorities. More specifically, the goals of monetary policy in this period may be defined as follows: increase in the GNP of about 5 percent in real terms per year; increase in prices of 5 percent a year*; substantial decrease in the foreign trade deficit; and transition from the relatively large deficit to a small surplus in balance of payments.

The second period was rather short and lasted from the second quarter of 1968 to the end of the year. The main feature of this period was modification of the effect of the tight monetary policy in the previous period, which had resulted in strong depressionary effects on economic activity so that employment and growth were substituted for stabilization priorities. Within this framework an increase in GNP was expected at a rate of 0.75 percent (after a 1 percent increase in total GNP and a 1 percent decrease in total nonagricultural production in 1968). The price level was expected to increase at the minimum rate of 5 percent.** Decreases in the foreign trade and balance-of-payments deficits were also considered as basic goals of monetary policy.

Finally, the 1969-70 period represents an attempt to reach an equilibrium in relative priorities in the country's monetary policy goals. Economic policy goals that had to be supported by monetary policy were an increase in GNP at a rate of from 7 to 8 percent (in real terms), a minimum rate of increase in the price level (about 5 percent), and a decrease in the foreign trade and balance-of-payments deficits.

---

*The rates of increase in GNP and price level applied here represent approximate estimates of policy goals made on the basis of verbally expressed goals in official documents (declarations of the Federal Assembly on economic policy goals). These estimates are necessary for comparison with actual developments.

**This is an estimate made on the basis of a rather free interpretation of verbally defined goals in the field of prices.

# EMPIRICAL EVIDENCE

Two aspects of the effectiveness and efficiency of monetary policy will be discussed here: first, the effectiveness and efficiency of monetary policy in implementing individual goals; second, its effectiveness and efficiency in implementing a set of goals in a given period. We have already answered these questions in part. The fact that monetary policy was not fully effective in implementing its targets during the period under investigation suggests the conclusion that it may be only partially effective in implementing its goals. To judge from the results presented, the exaggerated tightness of monetary policy in 1965-67 might be efficient in implementing stabilization goals but not at the same time in implementing employment and economic growth goals. The opposite effects might be expected in the 1968 period of exaggerated ease in monetary policy, presumably causing strong revival effects but at the same time deteriorating price stability and balance of payments. Only 1969 can be used as a suitable period for testing the problem of efficiency of monetary policy, under the assumption that the targets were properly calculated.

Table 14.2 suggests that monetary policy was significantly efficient in implementing higher priority goals but that lower priority goals were not achieved at all. Thus, stabilization goals, which were preferred to employment and growth goals in 1965-67, were to a significant degree achieved. However, monetary policy proved inefficient in achieving stabilization goals in the next period of prevailing employment and economic growth priorities.

The employment and economic growth goals were achieved with a satisfactory degree of efficiency in 1968. Monetary policy, however, was unable to endorse significantly the expected rate of increase in GNP parallel with the successful support of stabilization goals in 1965-67. In 1969, when attempts were made to achieve both stabilization and employment goals, the efficiency of monetary policy in the former was rather poor and in the latter very high. This is consistent with the conclusions relating to the role of money and the effects of changes in money supply.* In the period of very tight monetary policy the effects of the reduced rate of growth (even decrease) in the money supply tended to depress economic activity and improve the balance of payments. The same is true for 1968, when the money

---

*See Chapter 9.

TABLE 14.2

Monetary Goals and Actual Developments Increase
(in percent)

| | 1965 | 1966 | 1967 | 1968 | 1969 | 1970 |
|---|---|---|---|---|---|---|
| Goals of monetary pol-icy | | | | | | |
| GNP in real terms | 5 | 5 | 5 | 3-4 | 7-8 | 7 |
| Price level | 5 | 5 | 5 | 5 | 5 | 5 |
| Foreign trade balance | D | D | D | D | D | D |
| Balance-of-payments deficit | S | S | S | D | D | D |
| | | | | | | |
| Actual developments | | | | | | |
| GNP in real terms | 1 | 6 | 1 | 4 | 10 | 5 |
| Total nonagricultural production | 5 | 2 | -1 | 6 | 11 | 9 |
| Retail prices | 44 | 7 | 5 | 5 | 8 | 10 |
| Producer's prices of industrial goods | 21 | 3 | 1 | 1 | 4 | 12 |
| Exports | 22 | 12 | 3 | 1 | 17 | 14 |
| Imports | -3 | 22 | 8 | 5 | 19 | 35 |
| | | | | | | |
| Foreign trade deficit | | | | | | |
| Millions of dollars | -196 | -355 | -455 | -533 | -660 | -1,195 |
| Change in percent | -54 | 81 | 28 | 17 | 24 | 81 |
| | | | | | | |
| Balance of payment | | | | | | |
| Millions of dollars | +23 | -69 | -116 | -120 | -63 | -348 |
| Change in percent | | | 68 | 3 | -47 | 552 |
| Investment expenditures in real terms | -11 | -1 | -10 | 20 | 9 | 18 |
| Total expenditures in real terms | -2 | 2 | 0 | 13 | 8 | 15 |

D = decrease; S = small surplus.

Sources: Annual Report of the National Bank of Yugoslavia, 1969, p. 8; Index, 1966, 1967, 1968, 1969; Statisticki godisnjak Saveznog zavoda za statistiku, 1969, p. 120, and 1970, p. 113; investment expenditures according to Statisticki bilten Sluzbe drustvenog knjigovodsta, No. 2 (1970), Table 89, deflated by index of prices of investment goods and services; investment expenditures plus expenditures of individuals for goods and services (excluding interindividual transactions) for expenditures of individuals, Statisticki Bilten, No. 2 (1970), Table 44, deflated by consumer price index.

supply increased at a rate of 24 percent. Developments in 1969 do not appear to fit this pattern. The increased rate of GNP is consistent with the policy goals, although not with the radical decrease in the rate of increase in the money supply (24 percent in 1968, 12 percent in 1969). On the other hand, an increased rate of price level and a significant deterioration of the foreign trade balance fully contradicted the hypothesis. The reasonable explanation for this behavior in 1969 may be the lag effects of the extremely high rate of growth in the money supply in 1968, which were only partially and gradually canceled by the monetary equilibrium policy in 1969.

Table 14.2 suggests that the effects of monetary policy on employment are the most consistent with our expectation regarding monetary effects. Effects on the price level are less and on balance of payments the least consistent with our expectations. This is presumably the result of rather extensive regulation of prices, particularly of foreign trade and foreign exchange transactions, and significant changes in these regulations, so that the economic behavior in these transactions is strongly distorted. The evidence summarized in Table 14.2 is consistent with the view that monetary effects appear to influence investment expenditures more than total expenditures and through expenditures (representing demand for goods and services) employment, prices, and balance of payments.

The question of efficiency of monetary policy in implementing the entire set of goals in a given period is far more difficult. Excluding the rare cases of full achievement of all goals or complete failure, the usual case is that individual goals are achieved in different degrees. The evidence presented in Table 14.2 shows that monetary policy was close to a satisfactory degree of efficiency only in 1965.* In other years there was a rather large discrepancy between its efficiency in achievement of stabilization and employment goals, particularly in achievement of balance-of-payments goals. Thus, the empirical evidence suggests that the efficiency of monetary

---

*An increase in price level in 1965 does not contradict this conclusion. Price level (represented here by retail prices) increased after the reform very slightly. The 44 percent increase in retail prices occurred partly before the reform (11 percent) and partly as a result of reform measures--administrative adjustment of relative prices by nearly all of the remaining amount of their increase.

policy in achieving the planned set of goals in a definite period of time is rather weak.

In effect, the problem of efficiency of monetary policy may be summarized as follows:

1. Monetary policy is fully efficient to pursue a tight or easy money policy. However, it is rather inefficient in achieving a definite degree of tightness or ease, so that the rates of changes in money supply may deviate strongly from the planned changes.

2. Partly because of inefficiency in implementing monetary targets (a definite rate of change in money supply), and presumably because of errors in the projection of monetary targets, and partly because of numerous other reasons related to uncertainties in the adjustment processes of demand to supply of money, monetary policy is necessarily rather less efficient in implementing the planned set of policy goals.

PART

IV

**SUMMARY
AND OUTLOOK**

# 15

In concluding this study we may say that development of the Yugoslav economic system and its determinants appears to be consistent with the hypotheses discussed at the outset. Economic growth considerations have required adjustment of institutional infrastructure to accommodate the increased complexity of economic relationships and processes. This adjustment required appropriate adaptation of financial suprastructure to the increased role of financial variables.

Both infrainstitutional and financial adjustments involved three basic fields of adaptation: first, changes in the organizational pattern of decision-making; second, changes in the list of economic problems whose solution was to be delegated to decentralized and free decision-making on the part of individual economic units; third, changes in the role, development, and differentiation of markets. In addition to a hypothetical perfect central planning stage, the whole process of these adjustments may be divided into three basic periods: mixed central planning stage, first stage of decentralization, and advanced stage of decentralization.

The general line of development in both the infrainstitutional and the financial field has involved decentralization of decision-making, building a free market mechanism, and a parallel decrease in role and responsibility in economic affairs on the part of the central government.

The stage of development that has been reached recently is characterized by inconsistency in the development of the basic components of the economic system. First, there are inconsistent solutions in the field of such institutional infrastructure as foreign trade and foreign exchange transactions, pricing of capital, pricing of goods (a significant part of which is still under heavy government regulations, far more than is consistent with free decision-making in production), income distribution, saving and investment. Second, development and differentiation of the financial system is lagging significantly behind the process of decentralization in the infrainstitutional field. This is especially true of the differentiation of financial instruments and financial institutions. The functioning of the financial structure is particularly hampered by numerous external obstacles, so that its efficiency in financial intermediation (both in stimulating saving and financial investment and in economic allocation) does not satisfy the growing needs for financing. This leads to the conclusion that the system is not yet complete and that further adjustments are to come. It is according to the logic of past developments and of the proclaimed general lines of development of the Yugoslav economic system to expect corrections. New, significant adjustments may be expected in the foreign trade and foreign exchange system in the sense of further liberalization of foreign trade, reduction of foreign exchange restrictions, and making the dinar a convertible currency.

In the financial field further differentiation of financial institutions and instruments may be expected as an essential precondition for the efficient functioning of the country's economic system. The increasing role of financial variables, the growing complexity of monetary and other financial processes, and the increasing need for an efficient functioning of financial markets will necessarily require further growth and diversification of the financial structure. It was shown that development and efficiency of the financial system have been lagging behind the need for financing (particularly after the reform) and that inefficiency of financial structure has hampered a more efficient functioning of the whole economic system. Thus, further development of the economic system in the direction proclaimed two decades ago will require not only adjustments to the new needs for financing but also adaptations to fill the present gap in the development and differentiation of the financial system.

If prediction of the general line of development of the financial system is possible, foreseeing the details of this development is difficult. The Yugoslav economic system has been developed in a pragmatic way. It does not have a theoretical structure per se. It does have, however, a very clear concept of general lines of development. The pragmatic approach will presumably dominate future development. It is difficult to say how much this development will draw upon the experiences of the relatively free market financial instruments and financial organization and how much will be drawn from the country's own experiences. Very rapid institutional developments in the Yugoslav economic system can be expected. Recent developments and growing discussion on financial topics show that significant new adjustments in the financial field are indeed very near.

In the field of monetary theory and monetary policy, investigations justify the adherence of Yugoslav academic and applied economists to a monetarist approach. The country's experience during the period under investigations is consistent with the key propositions of monetarism:

1. There is an observable interrelationship between changes in the rate of growth in the money supply on the one hand and rate of increase in expenditures, production, employment, foreign trade, and prices on the other. The transmission mechanism and effects of changes in the rate of growth of money supply in Yugoslavia obviously deviate from those in a developed market economy, particularly the United States. First, the transmission mechanism is based mainly on money-real goods portfolio adjustments of individual balance sheets, excluding financial assets as a significant choice for holding assets instead of money. Second, as a result of these peculiarities of the transmission mechanism, effects of changes in money supply are shorter-lagged and more directly related to changes in expenditures for goods and services--expenditures for investments in fixed assets and then expenditures for consumption. These peculiarities are consistent with the monetarist view. They present the effects of changes in money supply under specific conditions of an undifferentiated financial structure and a rigid system of interest-rate formation.

2. The above process of adjustments of demand to the supply of money contains also peculiarities in the demand function and supply function of money, as a result of institutional peculiarities. Demand for money depends mainly on income, the interest rate being a rather insignificant variable. Because of a changing pattern of income distribution by sector (especially an increasing share of individuals in income distribution), demand for money appears at first hand as rather unstable, which may contradict the monetarist view in this respect. This is, however, consistent with the monetarist approach if the stability of demand

for money is interpreted as stability of a demand function
for money under stable institutional conditions.  As for
the supply function of money, it too appears unstable in
the short run owing to a changing institutional framework
and a strong pressure for government borrowing from the
central bank.  In the long run, however, it does show that
changes in high-powered money are the dominant determinant
of the money supply.

3.  Under these conditions monetary policy traditionally has been the main instrument of indirect economic
policy intervention.  Empirical evidence shows that monetary policy may be efficient in implementing monetary policy targets (changes in money supply being the main target
of monetary policy) if strong government pressure is excluded.  Thus, the question of whether creation of money
is under control of monetary authorities (whether it is an
exogenous variable on the monetary model) or cannot be
controlled by these authorities (it is an endogenous variable) has a promonetarist answer.

4.  The problem of efficiency of monetary policy in
implementing economic policy goals is more complicated.
Empirical evidence suggests that the efficiency of monetary
policy in this field is less than in implementing targets.
This is, however, mainly because policy measures always
have been taken too late and therefore necessarily have
been too strong.  In addition, under changing institutional
conditions monetary measures usually have not been followed
by the appropriate adjustments in other economic policy
measures.  For all these reasons, monetary policy usually
has had overshooting effects upward or downward, which suggests that monetary policy may be fairly efficient if
properly used, not that it is an inefficient instrument of
economic policy.

5.  There are two widely discussed questions related
to monetary policy that deserve investigation in a specific
Yugoslav framework:  rules vs. discretion in policy formation and fiscal vs. monetary policy in implementing economic policy goals.  Discretion has been traditionally preferred to the rule in policy formation in Yugoslavia.  The
adherence of Yugoslav monetary authorities to discretion
seems to be a logical consequence of the highly changing
institutional structure of the Yugoslav economic system.
The rules approach lacks the essential precondition of
stable institutional and other relevant relationships.
The question of fiscal vs. monetary policy has had a traditionally promonetary policy answer.  Fiscal policy has
been neglected in part as a result of the central planning

stage and in part because strict Keynesian theory never has been dominant in Yugoslavia.

6. Future development may be expected to follow past trends: a further increase in the role of money, finance, and monetary policy; growth in the role of individual decision-making in all fields of economic activity; growth in the role of autonomous processes; and greater reliance on market forces. Under these conditions further adjustments and improvement of efficiency of financial markets and monetary policy will represent the essential precondition for further increase in efficiency of the economic system and for promoting economic growth.

Past experience, however, shows that this process will not go smoothly. Future institutional adjustments presumably will create new disturbances in demand and supply functions of money and adjustment processes of demand to supply of money, requiring appropriate accommodations in the field of monetary policy formation and the instruments for the implementation of monetary policy targets.

**POPULATION, GNP,
INDUSTRIAL OUTPUT,
AND TOTAL
NONAGRICULTURAL
OUTPUT**

TABLE A.1

Population
(in thousands)

|                                                              | 1948   | 1953   | 1961   | 1971   |
|--------------------------------------------------------------|--------|--------|--------|--------|
| Total                                                        | 15,772 | 16,937 | 18,549 | 20,335 |
| Active population, total                                     | 7,740  | 7,849  | 8,340  | 8,816  |
| In agriculture                                               | 5,627  | 5,360  | 4,692  | 3,859  |
| In nonagricultural activities                                | 2,113  | 2,489  | 3,648  | 4,957  |
| Active population according to status                        |        |        |        |        |
| Employed                                                     | --     | --     | 3,653  | 4,376  |
| Private firms and farms, no hired labor                      | --     | --     | 2,190  | 1,944  |
| Private firms and farms hiring labor                         | --     | --     | 30     | 32     |
| Active family members of owners of private firms and farms   | --     | --     | 2,442  | 1,877  |
| Employed abroad                                              | --     | --     | --     | 577    |
| Unclassified                                                 | --     | --     | 25     | 10     |

Sources:  Statisticki godisnjak Saveznog zavoda za
statistiku, 1972, Tables 103-5, 103-7, 103-8, and 1963,
Table 103-4.

## TABLE A.2

### GNP at Constant Prices, 1966
### (billions of dinars)

| Year | Socialist Sector | Private Sector | Total | GNP According to Activities | | | | | | | | | |
|---|---|---|---|---|---|---|---|---|---|---|---|---|---|
| | | | | Indus-try and Mining | Agriculture | | | Con-struc-tion | For-est-ry | Trans-porta-tion | Trade and Catering | Ar-ti-san |
| | | | | | Social-ist Sector | Private Sector | Total | | | | | |
| 1953 | 22.9 | 15.1 | 38.0 | 8.0 | 1.9 | 13.3 | 15.2 | 3.7 | 1.0 | 2.3 | 5.3 | 2.5 |
| 1954 | 24.3 | 14.2 | 38.5 | 8.9 | 1.1 | 12.1 | 13.2 | 4.3 | 1.0 | 2.4 | 5.8 | 2.9 |
| 1955 | 27.2 | 17.0 | 44.2 | 10.4 | 1.1 | 15.0 | 16.1 | 4.1 | 1.1 | 2.9 | 6.6 | 3.0 |
| 1956 | 27.2 | 14.3 | 41.5 | 11.3 | 1.0 | 12.4 | 13.4 | 3.0 | 1.1 | 3.0 | 6.6 | 3.1 |
| 1957 | 32.1 | 19.4 | 51.5 | 13.3 | 1.6 | 17.5 | 19.1 | 3.4 | 1.1 | 3.4 | 7.9 | 3.3 |
| 1958 | 35.0 | 17.3 | 52.3 | 14.7 | 1.7 | 15.4 | 17.1 | 3.7 | 1.1 | 3.8 | 8.5 | 3.4 |
| 1959 | 40.4 | 21.1 | 61.5 | 16.8 | 2.7 | 19.4 | 22.1 | 4.2 | 1.2 | 4.2 | 9.5 | 3.5 |
| 1960 | 46.2 | 18.9 | 65.1 | 19.2 | 2.8 | 17.2 | 20.0 | 5.2 | 1.2 | 5.0 | 10.9 | 3.6 |
| 1961 | 50.3 | 18.5 | 68.8 | 20.4 | 2.9 | 16.7 | 19.6 | 6.3 | 1.2 | 5.2 | 11.8 | 3.9 |
| 1962 | 53.4 | 18.3 | 71.7 | 22.2 | 3.4 | 16.4 | 19.8 | 6.4 | 1.3 | 5.5 | 12.2 | 3.8 |
| 1963 | 61.1 | 19.5 | 80.6 | 25.9 | 3.8 | 17.7 | 21.5 | 7.4 | 1.5 | 5.9 | 13.9 | 3.9 |
| 1964 | 69.3 | 20.5 | 89.8 | 30.3 | 4.3 | 18.3 | 22.6 | 8.5 | 1.4 | 6.3 | 15.9 | 4.4 |
| 1965 | 71.9 | 19.3 | 91.2 | 32.5 | 4.1 | 16.6 | 20.7 | 8.1 | 1.5 | 6.7 | 16.5 | 4.8 |
| 1966 | 76.2 | 22.8 | 99.0 | 34.1 | 5.1 | 19.6 | 24.7 | 8.6 | 1.4 | 7.1 | 17.6 | 5.0 |
| 1967 | 78.3 | 23.3 | 101.6 | 34.3 | 5.4 | 19.4 | 24.8 | 9.3 | 1.4 | 7.7 | 18.5 | 5.2 |
| 1968 | 82.9 | 22.8 | 105.7 | 36.7 | 5.4 | 18.5 | 23.9 | 10.0 | 1.4 | 8.2 | 19.6 | 5.4 |
| 1969 | 91.4 | 25.2 | 116.6 | 41.0 | 5.7 | 20.6 | 26.3 | 10.9 | 1.4 | 8.8 | 21.9 | 5.8 |
| 1970 | 99.3 | 24.4 | 123.7 | 45.1 | 5.4 | 19.4 | 24.8 | 11.8 | 1.5 | 9.6 | 24.1 | 6.1 |
| 1971 | 108.7 | 25.5 | 134.2 | 49.6 | 6.5 | 20.3 | 26.8 | 12.1 | 1.5 | 10.5 | 26.7 | 6.5 |

Note: Some less significant activities are not presented, so that the sum of individual activities is not always equal to total amount of GNP.

Source: Statisticki godisnjak Saveznog zavoda za statistiku, 1972, Table 105-1.

193

## TABLE A.3

### Industrial Production, 1952–71
### (indexes 1952 = 100)

|      | I   | II  | III | IV  | V   | VI  |
|------|-----|-----|-----|-----|-----|-----|
| 1952 | 86  | 84  | 102 | 101 | 100 | 101 |
| 1953 | 88  | 91  | 106 | 107 | 103 | 114 |
| 1954 | 94  | 90  | 123 | 126 | 123 | 128 |
| 1955 | 127 | 130 | 143 | 143 | 141 | 153 |
| 1956 | 135 | 121 | 152 | 148 | 153 | 166 |
| 1957 | 157 | 163 | 167 | 182 | 184 | 190 |
| 1958 | 184 | 186 | 203 | 203 | 201 | 213 |
| 1959 | 193 | 205 | 233 | 224 | 229 | 250 |
| 1960 | 221 | 243 | 279 | 271 | 267 | 290 |
| 1961 | 250 | 262 | 303 | 291 | 294 | 303 |
| 1962 | 271 | 271 | 309 | 294 | 309 | 324 |
| 1963 | 282 | 300 | 354 | 354 | 354 | 361 |
| 1964 | 339 | 368 | 404 | 411 | 407 | 429 |
| 1965 | 391 | 405 | 473 | 468 | 432 | 468 |
| 1966 | 405 | 432 | 500 | 482 | 459 | 495 |
| 1967 | 419 | 443 | 505 | 467 | 476 | 490 |
| 1968 | 429 | 452 | 500 | 505 | 510 | 514 |
| 1969 | 467 | 483 | 556 | 556 | 561 | 578 |
| 1970 | 517 | 550 | 611 | 606 | 600 | 628 |
| 1971 | 581 | 631 | 706 | 706 | 688 | 731 |

| VII | VIII | IX | X | XI | XII | Ø |
|-----|------|-----|-----|-----|-----|-----|
| 96 | 100 | 103 | 114 | 105 | 111 | 100 |
| 107 | 111 | 118 | 128 | 123 | 138 | 111 |
| 121 | 130 | 143 | 148 | 140 | 153 | 127 |
| 137 | 147 | 153 | 164 | 156 | 171 | 147 |
| 153 | 168 | 174 | 192 | 181 | 190 | 161 |
| 180 | 194 | 201 | 213 | 209 | 226 | 190 |
| 191 | 205 | 224 | 235 | 226 | 254 | 211 |
| 217 | 233 | 264 | 264 | 252 | 293 | 238 |
| 250 | 269 | 290 | 302 | 283 | 326 | 274 |
| 262 | 297 | 309 | 318 | 309 | 329 | 294 |
| 285 | 318 | 329 | 356 | 341 | 359 | 315 |
| 339 | 361 | 379 | 414 | 386 | 407 | 357 |
| 389 | 404 | 439 | 457 | 439 | 482 | 414 |
| 405 | 445 | 486 | 491 | 464 | 532 | 455 |
| 423 | 472 | 505 | 500 | 482 | 545 | 473 |
| 424 | 471 | 500 | 519 | 486 | 514 | 476 |
| 471 | 505 | 524 | 571 | 538 | 571 | 505 |
| 528 | 550 | 600 | 628 | 572 | 583 | 556 |
| 561 | 589 | 638 | 667 | 644 | 672 | 606 |
| 631 | 669 | 725 | 744 | 706 | 781 | 688 |

Sources: Index, No. 1 (1954), No. 3 (1955), No. 2 (1956), No. 6 (1957), No. 2 (1959), No. 2 (1961), No. 2 (1963), No. 2 (1965), No. 2 (1967), No. 2 (1969), No. 1 (1971), and No. 2 (1972).

TABLE A.4

Total Nonagricultural Production
(indexes 1952 = 100)

| | I | II | III | IV | V | VI | VII | VIII | IX | X | XI | XII | Ø |
|---|---|---|---|---|---|---|---|---|---|---|---|---|---|
| 1952 | | | | | | | | | | | | | 100 |
| 1953 | 82 | 85 | 102 | 108 | 110 | 119 | 114 | 119 | 127 | 133 | 126 | 136 | 100 |
| 1954 | 84 | 82 | 117 | 125 | 126 | 133 | 131 | 142 | 151 | 153 | 144 | 151 | 129 |
| 1955 | 119 | 123 | 135 | 139 | 141 | 156 | 142 | 151 | 155 | 158 | 148 | 157 | 145 |
| 1956 | 120 | 107 | 133 | 134 | 142 | 155 | 146 | 163 | 169 | 182 | 167 | 172 | 149 |
| 1957 | 136 | 142 | 161 | 167 | 170 | 176 | 169 | 182 | 187 | 196 | 191 | 200 | 173 |
| 1958 | 160 | 162 | 179 | 183 | 183 | 195 | 181 | 193 | 207 | 216 | 205 | 221 | 190 |
| 1959 | 165 | 176 | 203 | 201 | 208 | 227 | 203 | 216 | 242 | 242 | 229 | 257 | 214 |
| 1960 | 189 | 206 | 241 | 243 | 243 | 263 | 233 | 253 | 268 | 273 | 256 | 283 | 245 |
| 1961 | 213 | 226 | 268 | 262 | 265 | 273 | 239 | 268 | 275 | 278 | 268 | 281 | 260 |
| 1962 | 224 | 227 | 259 | 254 | 270 | 284 | 254 | 281 | 289 | 308 | 292 | 300 | 270 |
| 1963 | 226 | 242 | 291 | 306 | 309 | 318 | 300 | 318 | 330 | 358 | 336 | 343 | 306 |
| 1964 | 277 | 305 | 337 | 351 | 351 | 372 | 340 | 354 | 375 | 386 | 368 | 393 | 351 |
| 1965 | 310 | 321 | 380 | 384 | 358 | 384 | 339 | 369 | 399 | 399 | 373 | 421 | 369 |
| 1966 | 308 | 335 | 391 | 387 | 368 | 398 | 346 | 383 | 402 | 395 | 380 | 417 | 376 |
| 1967 | 309 | 335 | 387 | 368 | 380 | 387 | 342 | 376 | 394 | 406 | 383 | 395 | 372 |
| 1968 | 311 | 342 | 385 | 397 | 401 | 405 | 378 | 401 | 413 | 444 | 417 | 433 | 393 |
| 1969 | 343 | 361 | 422 | 435 | 448 | 465 | 430 | 448 | 478 | 496 | 448 | 439 | 435 |
| 1970 | 378 | 409 | 457 | 470 | 470 | 500 | 452 | 474 | 504 | 517 | 500 | 513 | 470 |
| 1971 | 410 | 448 | 510 | 529 | 524 | 557 | 495 | 519 | 552 | 557 | 523 | 562 | 514 |

Sources: Index, No. 4 (1954), No. 4 (1955), No. 4 (1956), No. 4 (1957), No. 3 (1958),
No. 3 (1959), No. 3 (1960), No. 3 (1961), No. 3 (1962), No. 3 (1963), No. 3 (1964), No. 3
(1965), No. 3 (1966), No. 4 (1967), No. 3 (1968), No. 3 (1969), No. 3 (1970), No. 1 (1971),
and No. 2 (1972).

# B

This section includes tables presenting total transactions and financial assets and liabilities of domestic nonfinancial sectors, according to flow-of-funds accounts of the National Bank of Yugoslavia.

Columns "U" include uses and columns "S" sources of individual sectors.

Source: Annual Report of the National Bank of Yugoslavia, 1971.

Households
(millions of dinars)

| | 1963 | | 1964 | |
|---|---|---|---|---|
| | U | S | U | S |
| **Nonfinancial Transactions** | | | | |
| Current transactions | | | | |
| Current receipts and expenditures | 22,056 | 4,745 | 27,942 | 5,535 |
| On account of distribution of social product | | 17,239 | | 22,694 |
| Nonfinancial transfers | 32 | 309 | 50 | 432 |
| Unclassified, errors and omissions | | 1,615 | | 1,872 |
| Gross savings | | 1,820 | | 2,541 |
| Investment | 1,660 | | 2,090 | |
| Fixed assets | 1,280 | | 1,670 | |
| Change in stocks | 380 | | 420 | |
| Financial saving | | 160 | | 451 |
| **Financial Transactions** | | | | |
| Financial saving | | 160 | | 451 |
| Money | 879 | | 923 | |
| Currency | 728 | | 973 | |
| Deposit money | 151 | | −50 | |
| Other liquid assets | 406 | | 544 | |
| Nonliquid assets | 395 | | 186 | |
| Time deposits for over 12 months | 245 | | 66 | |
| Bonds | 150 | | 120 | |
| Short-term bank credits | | 1,370 | | 1,067 |
| Investment credits | | 150 | | 198 |
| Direct credits | | | | |
| Foreign exchange transactions | | | 63 | |
| Gold and foreign exchange | | | | |
| Domestic foreign exchange accounts | | | 63 | |
| Increase in financial assets or liabilities | 1,680 | 1,520 | 1,716 | 1,265 |
| **End-of-Year Position** | | | | |
| Money | 3,677 | | 4,600 | |
| Currency | 3,446 | | 4,419 | |
| Deposit money | 231 | | 181 | |
| Other liquid assets | 2,122 | | 2,666 | |
| Nonliquid assets | 395 | | 581 | |
| Time deposits for over 12 months | 245 | | 311 | |
| Bonds | 150 | | 270 | |
| Short-term bank credits | | 3,146 | | 4,213 |
| Investment credits | | 950 | | 1,148 |
| Direct credits | | | | |
| Foreign exchange transactions | 7 | | 70 | |
| Gold and foreign exchange | | | | |
| Domestic foreign exchange accounts | 7 | | 70 | |
| Total | 6,201 | 4,096 | 7,917 | 5,361 |

| 1965 | | 1966 | | 1967 | | 1968 | | 1969 | |
| U | S | U | S | U | S | U | S | U | S |
|---|---|---|---|---|---|---|---|---|---|
| 37,470 | 6,846 | 47,820 | 9,395 | 51,222 | 11,051 | 59,373 | 13,041 | 70,042 | 14,835 |
| | 31,551 | | 42,213 | 4,125 | 49,041 | 4,224 | 54,130 | 4,917 | 64,504 |
| 143 | 844 | 175 | 1,190 | | 404 | | 500 | | 566 |
| | 1,671 | | 3,912 | | 4,577 | | 6,284 | | 9,124 |
| | 3,299 | | 8,715 | | 9,726 | | 10,358 | | 14,070 |
| 2,300 | | 3,105 | | 6,300 | | 8,585 | | 9,800 | |
| 1,810 | | 2,443 | | 5,500 | | 7,200 | | 8,200 | |
| 490 | | 662 | | 800 | | 1,385 | | 1,600 | |
| | 999 | | 5,610 | | 3,426 | | 1,773 | | 4,270 |
| | 999 | | 5,610 | | 3,426 | | 1,773 | | 4,270 |
| 446 | | 1,743 | | 956 | | 1,596 | | 2,391 | |
| 485 | | 1,734 | | 936 | | 1,560 | | 2,271 | |
| -39 | | 9 | | 20 | | 36 | | 120 | |
| 316 | | 1,834 | | 1,027 | | 1,348 | | 2,213 | |
| 180 | | 1,595 | | 774 | | 788 | | 1,113 | |
| 220 | | 1,548 | | 784 | | 813 | | 1,140 | |
| -40 | | 47 | | -10 | | -25 | | -27 | |
| | -300 | | -555 | | -613 | | 247 | | 178 |
| | 369 | | 368 | | 532 | | 1,125 | | 956 |
| | | | | 386 | | 200 | 2,093 | 126 | 2,000 |
| 126 | | 251 | | 974 | | 1,306 | | 1,561 | |
| | | | | 735 | | 900 | | 400 | |
| 126 | | 251 | | 239 | | 406 | | 1,161 | |
| 1,068 | 69 | 5,423 | -187 | 3,731 | 305 | 5,238 | 3,465 | 7,404 | 3,134 |
| 5,046 | | 6,789 | | 7,745 | | 9,341 | | 11,732 | |
| 4,903 | | 6,638 | | 7,574 | | 9,134 | | 11,405 | |
| 142 | | 151 | | 171 | | 207 | | 327 | |
| 2,982 | | 4,816 | | 5,843 | | 7,193 | | 9,406 | |
| 761 | | 2,356 | | 2,566 | | 3,357 | | 4,470 | |
| 531 | | 2,079 | | 2,299 | | 3,115 | | 4,255 | |
| 230 | | 277 | | 267 | | 242 | | 215 | |
| | 3,913 | | 3,358 | | 2,627 | | 2,236 | | 2,466 |
| | 1,517 | | 1,885 | | 2,417 | | 3,542 | | 4,498 |
| | | | | | 685 | 200 | 2,778 | 326 | 4,778 |
| 196 | | 447 | | 2,326 | | 3,659 | | 5,220 | |
| | | | | 1,640 | | 2,540 | | 2,940 | |
| 196 | | 447 | | 686 | | 1,119 | | 2,280 | |
| 8,985 | 5,430 | 14,408 | 5,243 | 18,480 | 5,729 | 23,750 | 8,556 | 31,154 | 11,742 |

(continued)

| | 1970 | | 1971 | |
|---|---|---|---|---|
| | U | S | U | S |
| **Nonfinancial Transactions** | | | | |
| Current transactions | | | | |
|   Current receipts and expenditures | 87,649 | 18,262 | 112,040 | 20,912 |
|   On account of distribution of social product | 6,311 | 81,424 | 8,982 | 106,169 |
|   Nonfinancial transfers | | 760 | | 968 |
|   Unclassified, errors and omissions | | 9,505 | | 16,730 |
|   Gross savings | | 15,991 | | 23,757 |
| Investment | 11,368 | | 13,300 | |
|   Fixed assets | 9,543 | | 11,000 | |
|   Change in stocks | 1,825 | | 2,300 | |
|   Financial saving | | 4,623 | | 10,457 |
| **Financial Transactions** | | | | |
| Financial saving | | 4,623 | | 10,457 |
| Money | 3,067 | | 3,097 | |
|   Currency | 2,927 | | 3,208 | |
|   Deposit money | 140 | | −111 | |
| Other liquid assets | 2,301 | | 2,361 | |
| Nonliquid assets | 1,762 | | 1,977 | |
|   Time deposits for over 12 months | 1,664 | | 1,750 | |
|   Bonds | 98 | | 227 | |
| Short-term bank credits | | 1,525 | | −537 |
| Investment credits | | 2,490 | | 2,924 |
| Direct credits | 54 | 1,075 | −102 | 1,500 |
| Foreign exchange transactions | 2,529 | | 7,011 | |
|   Gold and foreign exchange | 900 | | 1,000 | |
|   Domestic foreign exchange accounts | 1,629 | | 6,011 | |
| Increase in financial assets or liabilities | 9,713 | 5,090 | 14,344 | 3,887 |
| **End-of-Year Position** | | | | |
| Money | 14,799 | | 17,896 | |
|   Currency | 14,332 | | 17,540 | |
|   Deposit money | 467 | | 356 | |
| Other liquid assets | 11,707 | | 14,068 | |
| Nonliquid assets | 6,232 | | 8,209 | |
|   Time deposits for over 12 months | 5,919 | | 7,669 | |
|   Bonds | 313 | | 540 | |
| Short-term bank credits | | 3,991 | | 3,454 |
| Investment credits | | 6,988 | | 9,912 |
| Direct credits | 380 | 5,853 | 278 | 7,353 |
| Foreign exchange transactions | 7,749 | | 14,760 | |
|   Gold and foreign exchange | 3,840 | | 4,840 | |
|   Domestic foreign exchange accounts | 3,909 | | 9,920 | |
|   Total | 40,867 | 16,832 | 55,211 | 20,719 |

Socialist Enterprises
(millions of dinars)

| | 1963 | | 1964 | |
|---|---|---|---|---|
| | U | S | U | S |
| **Nonfinancial Transactions** | | | | |
| Current transactions | | | | |
| Current receipts and expenditures | 88,316 | 125,107 | 106,985 | 157,459 |
| On account of distribution of social product | 28,920 | | 37,133 | |
| Nonfinancial transfers | | 2,025 | | 2,789 |
| Unclassified, errors and omissions | 3,126 | | 5,276 | |
| Gross savings | | 6,770 | | 10,854 |
| Investment | 14,590 | | 21,597 | |
| Fixed assets | 10,903 | | 14,551 | |
| Change in stocks | 3,687 | | 7,046 | |
| Financial saving | 7,820 | | 10,743 | |
| **Financial Transactions** | | | | |
| Financial saving | 7,820 | | 10,743 | |
| Money | 907 | | 1,241 | |
| Currency | 30 | | 30 | |
| Deposit money | 454 | | 1,002 | |
| Float | 423 | | 209 | |
| Other liquid assets | 190 | | −224 | |
| Nonliquid assets | 587 | | 838 | |
| Time deposits | 477 | | 638 | |
| Bonds | 110 | | 200 | |
| Contribution to credit funds of banks | | | | |
| Short-term bank credits | | 3,048 | | 1,610 |
| Investment credits | | 6,530 | | 10,507 |
| Direct credits | 2,403 | 1,767 | 3,063 | 2,974 |
| Foreign exchange transactions | −609 | −47 | 155 | 725 |
| Domestic foreign exchange accounts | −609 | | 155 | |
| Short-term foreign credits | | −47 | | 327 |
| Long-term foreign credits | | | | 398 |
| Repayment of long-term foreign credits | | | | |
| Other liabilities and assets | | | | |
| Increase in financial assets or liabilities | 3,478 | 11,298 | 5,073 | 15,816 |
| **End-of-Year Position** | | | | |
| Money | 7,305 | | 8,546 | |
| Currency | 150 | | 180 | |
| Deposit money | 5,581 | | 6,583 | |
| Float | 1,574 | | 1,783 | |
| Other liquid assets | 4,964 | | 4,740 | |
| Nonliquid assets | 587 | | 1,425 | |
| Time deposits for over 12 months | 477 | | 1,115 | |
| Bonds | 110 | | 310 | |
| Contribution to credit funds of banks | | | | |
| Short-term bank credits | | 19,904 | | 21,514 |
| Investment credits | | 35,947 | | 46,454 |
| Direct credits | 14,925 | 11,732 | 17,988 | 14,706 |
| Foreign exchange transactions | 284 | 2,967 | 439 | 3,692 |
| Domestic foreign exchange accounts | 284 | | 439 | |
| Short-term foreign credits | | 2,967 | | 3,294 |
| Long-term foreign credits | | | | 39Ɛ |
| Other liabilities and assets | | | | |
| Total | 28,065 | 70,550 | 33,138 | 86,366 |

(continued)

| | 1965 | | 1966 | |
|---|---|---|---|---|
| | U | S | U | S |
| **Nonfinancial Transactions** | | | | |
| Current transactions | | | | |
| Current receipts and expenditures | 129,001 | 194,658 | 157,079 | 243,607 |
| On account of distribution of social product | 45,121 | | 55,980 | |
| Nonfinancial transfers | 785 | 3,068 | | 1,737 |
| Unclassified, errors and omissions | 3,819 | | 13,420 | |
| Gross savings | | 19,000 | | 18,865 |
| Investment | 22,609 | | 27,394 | |
| Fixed assets | 14,552 | | 16,804 | |
| Change in stocks | 8,057 | | 10,590 | |
| Financial saving | 3,609 | | 8,529 | |
| **Financial Transactions** | | | | |
| Financial saving | 3,609 | | 8,529 | |
| Money | 1,873 | | -643 | |
| Currency | 60 | | 70 | |
| Deposit money | 1,423 | | -532 | |
| Float | 390 | | -181 | |
| Other liquid assets | 2,562 | | 717 | |
| Nonliquid assets | 327 | | 2,801 | |
| Time deposits | 307 | | 1,982 | |
| Bonds | 20 | | 271 | |
| Contribution to credit funds of banks | | | 548 | |
| Short-term bank credits | | 2,680 | | 2,548 |
| Investment credits | | 7,769 | | 8,335 |
| Direct credits | 8,290 | 5,453 | 9,227 | 8,433 |
| Foreign exchange transactions | 432 | 1,191 | 297 | 1,612 |
| Domestic foreign exchange accounts | 432 | | 297 | |
| Short-term foreign credits | | 921 | | 1,622 |
| Long-term foreign credits | | 310 | | 30 |
| Repayment of long-term foreign credits | | -40 | | -40 |
| Other liabilities and assets | | | | |
| Increase in financial assets or liabilities | 13,484 | 17,093 | 12,399 | 20,928 |
| **End-of-Year Position** | | | | |
| Money | 10,419 | | 9,776 | |
| Currency | 240 | | 310 | |
| Deposit money | 8,006 | | 7,474 | |
| Float | 2,173 | | 1,992 | |
| Other liquid assets | 7,302 | | 8,019 | |
| Nonliquid assets | 1,752 | | 9,477 | |
| Time deposits for over 12 months | 1,422 | | 3,404 | |
| Bonds | 330 | | 601 | |
| Contribution to credit funds of banks | | | 5,472 | |
| Short-term bank credits | | 24,194 | | 26,742 |
| Investment credits | | 54,223 | | 62,558 |
| Direct credits | 26,278 | 20,159 | 35,505 | 28,592 |
| Foreign exchange transactions | 871 | 4,883 | 1,168 | 6,495 |
| Domestic foreign exchange accounts | 871 | | 1,168 | |
| Short-term foreign credits | | 4,215 | | 5,837 |
| Long-term foreign credits | | 668 | | 658 |
| Other liabilities and assets | | | | |
| Total | 46,622 | 103,459 | 63,945 | 124,387 |

| 1967 | | 1968 | | 1969 | | 1970 | | 1971 | |
|---|---|---|---|---|---|---|---|---|---|
| U | S | U | S | U | S | U | S | U | S |
| 173,466 | 264,448 | 186,361 | 272,496 | 215,400 | 324,276 | 271,603 | 403,737 | 358,678 | 531,510 |
| 58,353 | | 65,081 | | 78,902 | | 95,080 | | 115,605 | |
| | 1,573 | | 1,758 | | 2,035 | | 2,702 | | 2,284 |
| 16,047 | | 2,396 | | 11,372 | | 13,519 | | 20,193 | |
| | 18,155 | | 20,416 | | 20,637 | | 26.237 | | 39,318 |
| 29,242 | | 28,479 | | 33,087 | | 45,291 | | 54,074 | |
| 16,412 | | 20,953 | | 24,087 | | 31,359 | | 33,185 | |
| 12,830 | | 7,526 | | 9,000 | | 13,932 | | 20,889 | |
| 11,087 | | 8,063 | | 12,450 | | 19,054 | | 14,756 | |
| 11,087 | | 8,063 | | 12,450 | | 19,054 | | 14,756 | |
| -2,508 | | 2,300 | | -296 | | 795 | | 396 | |
| 70 | | 70 | | 80 | | 80 | | 200 | |
| -1,969 | | 1,293 | | -332 | | 717 | | 655 | |
| -609 | | 937 | | -44 | | -2 | | -459 | |
| -252 | | 2,419 | | 3,187 | | 2,442 | | 1,168 | |
| 2,869 | | 2,875 | | 3,538 | | 4,266 | | 510 | |
| 2,489 | | 2,477 | | 2,960 | | 3,267 | | 550 | |
| -127 | | -87 | | 29 | | 636 | | -358 | |
| 507 | | 485 | | 549 | | 363 | | 318 | |
| | 4,157 | | 5,378 | | 7,437 | | 5,074 | | 8,146 |
| | 7,914 | | 11,971 | | 13,858 | | 17,697 | | 12,633 |
| 12,567 | 11,888 | 14,688 | 10,496 | 18,258 | 14,162 | 25,463 | 23,764 | 49,126 | 44,017 |
| 1,470 | 2,623 | 830 | 6,380 | -192 | 3,386 | 587 | 6,072 | 2,918 | 4,078 |
| 1,470 | | 830 | | -192 | | 587 | | 2,918 | |
| | 875 | | 4,605 | | 1,232 | | 1,862 | | 699 |
| | 3,131 | | 3,788 | | 4,162 | | 6,332 | | 7,044 |
| | -1,383 | | -2,013 | | -2,008 | | -2,122 | | -3,665 |
| 1,349 | | 3,050 | | 1,898 | | | | | |
| 15,495 | 26,582 | 26,162 | 34,225 | 26,393 | 38,843 | 33,553 | 52,607 | 54,118 | 68,874 |
| 7,787 | | 9,847 | | 9,551 | | 10,346 | | 10,742 | |
| 380 | | 450 | | 530 | | 610 | | 810 | |
| 6,024 | | 7,077 | | 6,745 | | 7,462 | | 8,117 | |
| 1,383 | | 2,320 | | 2,276 | | 2,274 | | 1,815 | |
| 7,592 | | 10,339 | | 13,526 | | 15,968 | | 17,136 | |
| 14,004 | | 17,120 | | 20,658 | | 23,892 | | 24,402 | |
| 7,295 | | 10,014 | | 12,974 | | 15,511 | | 16,061 | |
| 730 | | 642 | | 671 | | 1,005 | | 647 | |
| 5,979 | | 6,464 | | 7,013 | | 7,376 | | 7,694 | |
| | 30,899 | | 37,165 | | 44,550 | | 49,624 | | 61,458 |
| | 70,182 | | 81,899 | | 95,757 | | 113,454 | | 127,957 |
| 48,641 | 42,609 | 63,329 | 53,105 | 81,607 | 67,267 | 107,070 | 91,031 | 156,196 | 135,048 |
| 2,813 | 12,875 | 3,659 | 19,191 | 3,467 | 22,577 | 4,054 | | 6,972 | |
| 2,813 | | 3,659 | | 3,467 | | 4,054 | | 6,972 | |
| | 5,266 | | 9,313 | | 10,545 | | 12,407 | | 2,942 |
| | 7,609 | | 9,878 | | 12,032 | | 16,342 | | 20,053 |
| 1,349 | | 4,399 | | 6,297 | | | | | |
| 82,186 | 156,565 | 108,693 | 191,360 | 135,106 | 230,151 | 161,330 | 282,858 | 215,448 | 437,458 |

Federal Government
(millions of dinars)

| | 1963 | |
| --- | --- | --- |
| | U | S |
| **Nonfinancial Transactions** | | |
| Current transactions | | |
|   Current receipts and expenditures | 3,960 | |
|   On account of distribution of social product | 204 | 6,231 |
|   Nonfinancial transfers | 1,483 | |
|   Unclassified, errors and omissions | 551 | |
|   Gross savings | | 33 |
| Investment | 831 | |
|   Fixed assets | 831 | |
|   Financial saving | 798 | |
| | | |
| **Financial Transactions** | | |
| Financial saving | 798 | |
| Money | 616 | |
|   Deposit money | 616 | |
| Other liquid assets | 219 | |
| Nonliquid assets | | 200 |
|   Time deposits for over 12 months | | |
|   Bonds | | 200 |
| Short-term bank credits | | 261 |
| Investment credits | | |
| Direct credits | | 100 |
| Financial transfers | | 418 |
| Foreign exchange transactions | | 659 |
|   Long-term foreign credits | | 1,041 |
|   Repayment of long-term foreign credits | | -382 |
| Increase in financial assets or liabilities | 840 | 1,638 |
| | | |
| **End-of-Year Position** | | |
| Money | 1,166 | |
|   Deposit money | 1,166 | |
| Other liquid assets | 386 | |
| Nonliquid assets | | 200 |
|   Time deposits for over 12 months | | |
|   Bonds | | 200 |
| Short-term bank credits | | 6,671 |
| Investment credits | | |
| Direct credits | | 800 |
| Foreign exchange transactions | | 5,823 |
|   Long-term foreign credits | | 5,823 |
| Other liabilities and assets | 900 | |
| Total | 2,452 | 13,494 |

| 1964 | | 1965 | | 1966 | | 1967 | |
| U | S | U | S | U | S | U | S |
|---|---|---|---|---|---|---|---|
| 4,553 | | 6,329 | | 6,801 | | 7,944 | |
| 242 | 7,763 | 259 | 7,734 | 349 | 7,910 | 286 | 9,345 |
| 1,951 | | 2,592 | 350 | 886 | | 763 | |
| 1,234 | | 4,562 | | 2,140 | | | 203 |
| 217 | | 5,658 | | 2,266 | | | 555 |
| 246 | | 175 | | 226 | | 250 | |
| 246 | | 175 | | 226 | | 250 | |
| 463 | | 5,833 | | 2,492 | | | 305 |
| | | | | | | | |
| 463 | | 5,833 | | 2,492 | | | 305 |
| −58 | | −510 | | −129 | | −61 | |
| −58 | | −510 | | −129 | | −61 | |
| 927 | | −544 | | −346 | | 361 | |
| | 210 | | −50 | | 61 | | −16 |
| | | | | | | | |
| | 210 | | −50 | | 61 | | −16 |
| | 460 | | 3,266 | | 410 | | −236 |
| | 334 | | 460 | | 899 | | −106 |
| | −200 | | 387 | | 173 | | |
| 6 | 534 | 522 | 1,238 | 281 | 755 | 172 | 525 |
| | 1,403 | | 2,964 | | 2,406 | | 2,031 |
| | −869 | | −1,726 | | −1,650 | | −1,506 |
| 875 | 1,338 | −532 | 5,301 | −194 | 2,298 | 472 | 167 |
| | | | | | | | |
| 1,108 | | 598 | | 469 | | 408 | |
| 1,108 | | 598 | | 469 | | 408 | |
| 1,313 | | 769 | | 423 | | 784 | |
| | 410 | | 360 | | 421 | | 405 |
| | | | | | | | |
| | 410 | | 360 | | 421 | | 405 |
| | 7,131 | | 10,397 | | 10,807 | | 10,571 |
| | 334 | | 794 | | 1,693 | | 1,587 |
| | 600 | | 987 | | 1,160 | | 700 |
| | 6,357 | | 11,038 | | 11,793 | | 13,899 |
| | 6,357 | | 11,038 | | 11,793 | | 13,899 |
| 900 | | 1,500 | | 1,875 | | 1,875 | |
| 3,321 | 14,832 | 2,867 | 13,576 | 2,767 | 25,874 | 3,067 | 26,164 |

(continued)

| | 1968 | |
|---|---|---|
| | U | S |
| **Nonfinancial Transactions** | | |
| Current transactions | | |
|   Current receipts and expenditures | 8,972 | |
|   On account of distribution of social product | 384 | 10,139 |
|   Nonfinancial transfers | 622 | |
|   Unclassified, errors and omissions | 809 | 768 |
|   Gross savings | | 929 |
| Investment | 147 | |
|   Fixed assets | 147 | |
|   Financial saving | | 782 |
| | | |
| **Financial Transactions** | | |
| Financial saving | | 782 |
| Money | 441 | |
|   Deposit money | 441 | |
| Other liquid assets | -955 | |
| Nonliquid assets | | -42 |
|   Time deposits for over 12 months | | |
|   Bonds | | -42 |
| Short-term bank credits | | -602 |
| Investment credits | | -1 |
| Direct credits | | |
| Financial transfers | 392 | |
| Foreign exchange transactions | | -259 |
|   Long-term foreign credits | | 1,123 |
|   Repayment of long-term foreign credits | | -1,382 |
| Increase in financial assets or liabilities | -122 | -904 |
| | | |
| **End-of-Year Position** | | |
| Money | 860 | |
|   Deposit money | 860 | |
| Other liquid assets | 969 | |
| Nonliquid assets | | 363 |
|   Time deposits for over 12 months | | |
|   Bonds | | 363 |
| Short-term bank credits | | 9,969 |
| Investment credits | | 1,586 |
| Direct credits | | 700 |
| Foreign exchange transactions | | 12,537 |
|   Long-term foreign credits | | 12,537 |
| Other liabilities and assets | 1,875 | |
| Total | 3,704 | 25,155 |

| 1969 | | 1970 | | 1971 | |
|---|---|---|---|---|---|
| U | S | U | S | U | S |
| 9,691 | | 12,827 | | 13,037 | |
| 429 | 10,753 | 483 | 14,170 | 496 | 15,591 |
| 520 | | 2,617 | | 1,712 | 595 |
| | 20 | 808 | 1,130 | 3,465 | |
| | 133 | 1,435 | | 2,524 | |
| 135 | | 140 | | 177 | |
| 135 | | 140 | | 177 | |
| 2 | | 1,575 | | 2,701 | |
| 2 | | 1,575 | | 2,701 | |
| −281 | | 685 | | −237 | |
| −281 | | 685 | | −237 | |
| −234 | | −210 | | −155 | |
| 679 | −42 | 955 | 1,186 | 192 | −1,000 |
| 679 | | 955 | | 192 | |
| | −42 | | 1,186 | | −1,000 |
| | −137 | | 2,440 | | 2,450 |
| | 42 | | −50 | | 987 |
| 400 | | 803 | | 785 | |
| | 703 | | 232 | | 849 |
| | 2,120 | | 1,874 | | 2,219 |
| | −1,417 | | −1,642 | | −1,370 |
| 564 | 566 | 2,233 | 3,808 | 585 | 3,286 |
| 579 | | 1,264 | | 1,027 | |
| 579 | | 1,264 | | 1,027 | |
| 735 | | 525 | | 370 | |
| 679 | 321 | 1,634 | 1,507 | 1,826 | 507 |
| 679 | | 1,634 | | 1,826 | |
| | 321 | | 1,507 | | 507 |
| | 9,832 | | 12,272 | | 13,922 |
| | 1,628 | | 511 | | 1,498 |
| | 700 | | 700 | | 700 |
| | 13,240 | | 13,472 | | 16,367 |
| | 13,240 | | 13,472 | | 16,367 |
| 1,875 | | 2,587 | | 3,825 | |
| 3,868 | 25,721 | 6,010 | 28,462 | 7,048 | 32,994 |

Other Governments
(millions of dinars)

| | 1963 | | 1964 | |
|---|---|---|---|---|
| | U | S | U | S |
| **Nonfinancial Transactions** | | | | |
| Current transactions | | | | |
| Current receipts and expenditures | 4,303 | | 5,578 | |
| On account of distribution of social product | 2,243 | 6,567 | 2,658 | 8,459 |
| Nonfinancial transfers | 82 | | 178 | |
| Unclassified, errors and omissions | | 2,103 | | 2,235 |
| Gross savings | | 2,042 | | 2,280 |
| Investment | 1,706 | | 2,551 | |
| Fixed assets | 1,706 | | 2,551 | |
| Financial saving | | 336 | | 271 |
| **Financial Transactions** | | | | |
| Financial saving | | 336 | 271 | |
| Money | 232 | | −52 | |
| Deposit money | 232 | | −52 | |
| Other liquid assets | 143 | | 118 | |
| Nonliquid assets | 33 | | 51 | |
| Time deposits for over 12 months | 33 | | 51 | |
| Bonds | | | | |
| Short-term bank credits | | −15 | | 243 |
| Investment credits | | 81 | | 103 |
| Direct credits | | 6 | | −194 |
| Increase in financial assets or liabilities | 408 | 72 | −119 | 152 |
| **End-of-Year Position** | | | | |
| Money | 604 | | 552 | |
| Deposit money | 604 | | 552 | |
| Other liquid assets | 569 | | 451 | |
| Nonliquid assets | 33 | | 84 | |
| Time deposits for over 12 months | 33 | | 84 | |
| Bonds | | | | |
| Short-term bank credits | | 122 | | 365 |
| Investment credits | | 481 | | 584 |
| Direct credits | | 1,093 | | 899 |
| Total | 1,206 | 1,696 | 1,087 | 1,848 |

| 1965 | | 1966 | | 1967 | | 1968 | | 1969 | |
| --- | --- | --- | --- | --- | --- | --- | --- | --- | --- |
| U | S | U | S | U | S | U | S | U | S |
| 6,698 | | 7,437 | | 5,025 | | 5,411 | | 6,728 | |
| 4,264 | 12,168 | 5,231 | 14,212 | 5,522 | 12,025 | 6,429 | 13,665 | 7,587 | 16,417 |
| 340 | | 511 | | 310 | | 336 | | 415 | |
| | 1,252 | | 2,137 | | 372 | | 263 | | 508 |
| | 2,118 | | 3,370 | | 1,540 | | 1,752 | | 2,195 |
| 2,505 | | 2,604 | | 1,524 | | 1,561 | | 1,647 | |
| 2,505 | | 2,604 | | 1,524 | | 1,561 | | 1,647 | |
| 387 | | | 766 | | 16 | | 191 | | 548 |
| 387 | | | 766 | | 16 | | 191 | | 548 |
| -11 | | 337 | | -72 | | 697 | | 760 | |
| -11 | | 337 | | -72 | | 697 | | 760 | |
| -37 | | 12 | | 13 | | -17 | | 21 | |
| 9 | | 216 | | 274 | | -289 | | 345 | |
| 9 | | 216 | | 274 | | 272 | | 358 | |
| | | | | | | -17 | | -13 | |
| | -162 | | -188 | | -12 | | 8 | | 114 |
| | 214 | | -282 | | 211 | | 192 | | 264 |
| | 300 | | 269 | | | | | | 200 |
| -39 | 348 | 565 | -201 | 215 | 196 | 391 | 200 | 1,126 | 578 |
| 541 | | 878 | | 992 | | 2,123 | | 2,883 | |
| 541 | | 878 | | 992 | | 2,123 | | 2,883 | |
| 414 | | 426 | | 439 | | 422 | | 443 | |
| 93 | | 309 | | 803 | | 664 | | 1,009 | |
| 93 | | 309 | | 803 | | 531 | | 889 | |
| | | | | | | 133 | | 120 | |
| | 203 | | 15 | | 3 | | 11 | | 125 |
| | 794 | | 512 | | 913 | | 1,162 | | 1,426 |
| | 1,199 | | 1,468 | | 800 | | 800 | | 1,000 |
| 1,048 | 2,196 | 1,613 | 1,995 | 2,234 | 1,716 | 3,209 | 1,973 | 4,335 | 2,551 |

(continued)

| | 1970 | | 1971 | |
|---|---|---|---|---|
| | U | S | U | S |
| **Nonfinancial Transactions** | | | | |
| Current transactions | | | | |
| Current receipts and expenditures | 8,189 | | 13,193 | |
| On account of distribution of social product | 8,978 | 19,867 | 10,958 | 27,710 |
| Nonfinancial transfers | 555 | | 424 | |
| Unclassified, errors and omissions | | 2,161 | | 1,576 |
| Investment | 2,501 | | 2,549 | |
| Fixed assets | 2,501 | | 2,549 | |
| Financial saving | 340 | | 973 | |
| **Financial Transactions** | | | | |
| Financial saving | 340 | | 973 | |
| Money | 484 | | 496 | |
| Deposit money | 484 | | 496 | |
| Other liquid assets | 347 | | −20 | |
| Nonliquid assets | −28 | | 298 | |
| Time deposits for over 12 months | −29 | | 298 | |
| Bonds | 1 | | | |
| Short-term bank credits | | 454 | | 428 |
| Investment credits | | 689 | | 1,019 |
| Direct credits | | | | 300 |
| Increase in financial assets or liabilities | 803 | 1,143 | 774 | 1,747 |
| **End-of-Year Position** | | | | |
| Money | 3,367 | | 3,863 | |
| Deposit money | 3,367 | | 3,863 | |
| Other liquid assets | 790 | | 770 | |
| Nonliquid assets | 863 | | 1,161 | |
| Time deposits for over 12 months | 860 | | 1,158 | |
| Bonds | 3 | | 3 | |
| Short-term bank credits | | 579 | | 1,007 |
| Investment credits | | 2,115 | | 3,134 |
| Direct credits | | 1,000 | | 1,300 |
| Total | 5,020 | 3,694 | 5,794 | 5,441 |

# C

**BALANCE SHEETS
OF FINANCIAL
INSTITUTIONS**

## TABLE C.1

### Balance Sheet of Investment Loan Funds
(millions of dinars)

| | 1962 | 1963 | 1964 | 1965 | 1966 | 1967 | 1968 | 1969 | 1970 | 1971 |
|---|---|---|---|---|---|---|---|---|---|---|
| **Assets** | | | | | | | | | | |
| Credit to socialist enterprises | 28,513 | 32,098 | 13,760 | 5,124 | 7,089 | 6,142 | 7,722 | 26,585 | 27,362 | 27,149 |
| For fixed assets | 23,208 | 26,751 | 12,575 | 4,855 | 6,831 | 6,030 | 7,441 | 21,917 | 22,730 | 22,699 |
| For working assets | 5,305 | 5,347 | 1,185 | 269 | 258 | 112 | 281 | 4,668 | 4,632 | 4,450 |
| Credit to other organizations | 3,080 | 3,553 | 4,137 | 5,390 | 68 | 50 | 136 | 1,881 | 1,167 | 2,315 |
| Credit to other financial institutions | 5,342 | 1,121 | 2,398 | 2,120 | 30,654 | 37,582 | 39,754 | 30,918 | 44,024 | 42,008 |
| Monetary balances | 1,065 | 1,590 | 2,120 | 842 | 336 | 261 | 392 | 499 | 784 | 1,353 |
| Other assets | 4,529 | 1,229 | 1,629 | 2,177 | 509 | 590 | 519 | 693 | 1,444 | 845 |
| Total | 33,471 | 39,591 | 24,044 | 15,653 | 38,656 | 44,625 | 48,523 | 60,576 | 74,781 | 73,670 |
| **Liabilities** | | | | | | | | | | |
| Federal funds | 20,056 | 21,869 | 2,460 | 1,500 | 26,070 | 28,538 | 30,964 | 41,812 | 53,296 | 44,248 |
| Investment accounts | -- | -- | 301 | 568 | 23,881 | 25,170 | 25,794 | 34,202 | 42,596 | 34,528 |
| Investment loan funds | 20,056 | 21,869 | 2,159 | 932 | 2,189 | 3,368 | 5,170 | 7,610 | 10,700 | 9,720 |
| Funds of other governments | 13,415 | 17,722 | 21,584 | 14,153 | 12,586 | 16,087 | 17,559 | 18,764 | 21,485 | 29,422 |
| Investment accounts | -- | -- | -- | 5 | 7,305 | 9,760 | 10,542 | 10,264 | 10,876 | 17,463 |
| Investment loan funds | 13,415 | 17,722 | 21,584 | 14,148 | 5,281 | 6,327 | 7,017 | 8,500 | 10,609 | 11,959 |

Source: Statisticki bilten Sluzbe drustvenog knjigovodsta, No. 2 (1972), Table 9.

212

## TABLE C.2

### Balance Sheet of Business Banks, Short-Term Operations
(millions of dinars)

| | 1962 | 1963 | 1964 | 1965 | 1966 | 1967 | 1968 | 1969 | 1970 | 1971 |
|---|---|---|---|---|---|---|---|---|---|---|
| **Assets** | | | | | | | | | | |
| Foreign assets | 244 | 293 | 392 | 464 | 893 | 835 | 1,091 | 1,621 | 1,714 | 247 |
| Credit | 17,222 | 20,296 | 21,563 | 23,953 | 25,786 | 29,176 | 35,019 | 10,490 | 45,806 | 53,742 |
| Consumer credit | 1,700 | 3,023 | 4,074 | 3,790 | 3,225 | 2,465 | 3,923 | 4,482 | 6,409 | 5,923 |
| Foreign exchange credit to domestic residents | 655 | 473 | 715 | 1,162 | 1,572 | 2,070 | 1,137 | 810 | 1,109 | 11,142 |
| Use of short-term sources for investment credit | -- | -- | 1,164 | 1,197 | 408 | -- | 1,976 | 2,708 | 4,198 | 22,814 |
| Credit to other banks | 9,630 | 1,804 | 497 | 416 | 2,108 | 1,772 | 1,904 | 2,225 | 2,312 | 3,118 |
| Deposits with the National Bank of Yugoslavia | 6,586 | 7,452 | 7,601 | 10,152 | 9,218 | 8,964 | 10,381 | 12,570 | 13,173 | 12,933 |
| Gyro accounts | 1,703 | 1,995 | 2,305 | 1,851 | 2,060 | 1,276 | 1,517 | 1,129 | 1,147 | 1,276 |
| Obligatory reserves | 4,255 | 4,570 | 4,447 | 5,887 | 7,157 | 7,025 | 6,481 | 7,247 | 8,735 | 10,457 |
| Other deposits | 628 | 887 | 849 | 2,414 | 1 | 663 | 2,383 | 4,194 | 3,291 | 4,200 |
| Other assets | 197 | 364 | 1,153 | 598 | 1,343 | 1,592 | 675 | 788 | 1,808 | 8,520 |
| Total | 36,234 | 33,705 | 37,159 | 41,732 | 44,553 | 46,874 | 56,106 | 65,694 | 76,529 | 94,269 |
| **Liabilities** | | | | | | | | | | |
| Foreign liabilities | 187 | 191 | 444 | 1,242 | 1,158 | 1,118 | 2,073 | 2,918 | 3,664 | 5,764 |
| Foreign exchange deposits by domestic residents | 298 | 293 | 480 | 754 | 2,600 | 4,900 | 5,278 | 6,567 | 8,091 | 13,350 |
| Deposits | 14,498 | 17,956 | 20,626 | 23,881 | 25,743 | 26,117 | 31,323 | 37,334 | 40,686 | 45,344 |
| Gyro and similar accounts | 8,054 | 10,908 | 13,853 | 14,022 | 13,705 | 13,173 | 15,827 | 17,191 | 19,366 | 22,093 |
| Other sight deposits | 3,409 | 2,890 | 3,742 | 4,254 | 5,680 | 6,245 | 8,085 | 10,284 | 12,059 | 12,851 |
| Restricted deposits | 3,035 | 4,158 | 3,031 | 5,605 | 6,358 | 6,699 | 7,411 | 9,859 | 9,261 | 10,300 |
| Borrowings from the National Bank of Yugoslavia | 10,965 | 13,524 | 14,678 | 14,739 | 11,901 | 12,272 | 13,562 | 14,840 | 19,986 | 24,630 |
| Borrowings from other banks | 10,286 | 1,678 | 576 | 704 | 1,194 | 2,333 | 2,581 | 2,610 | 2,476 | 2,796 |
| In dinars | 10,136 | 1,537 | 436 | 461 | 542 | 1,598 | 1,704 | 2,178 | 2,153 | 2,476 |
| In foreign exchange | 150 | 141 | 140 | 243 | 652 | 735 | 877 | 432 | 323 | 320 |
| Other liabilities | -- | 63 | 355 | 412 | 957 | 134 | 289 | 1,425 | 1,626 | 385 |

Source: Statisticki bilten Sluzbe drustvenog knjigovodsta, No. 2 (1972), Table 6.

## TABLE C.3

### Balance Sheet of Business Banks, Investment Financing
### (millions of dinars)

| | 1963 | 1964 |
|---|---|---|
| **Assets** | | |
| Foreign assets | -- | -- |
| Credit for investment | 2,496 | 30,933 |
| Credit for housing and communal investments | -- | -- |
| Credit in foreign exchange to domestic investors | -- | -- |
| Credit to other financial institutions | 625 | 3,685 |
| In dinars | 625 | 3,685 |
| In foreign exchange | -- | -- |
| Unused resources | 675 | 2,065 |
| Other assets | -- | 193 |
| Total | 3,796 | 36,876 |
| **Liabilities** | | |
| Foreign liabilities | -- | 1,883 |
| Own funds | 577 | 23,791 |
| Foreign exchange deposits by domestic residents | -- | -- |
| Deposits | 1,407 | 3,233 |
| Time deposits | 1,365 | 2,804 |
| Restricted deposits | 42 | 429 |
| Bonds | 139 | 392 |
| Borrowings from other financial institutions | 1,643 | 5,725 |
| In dinars | 1,643 | 5,725 |
| In foreign exchange | -- | -- |
| Sources for housing financing | -- | -- |
| Other liabilities | 30 | 1,852 |
| Total | 3,796 | 36,876 |

TABLE C.3 (continued)

| 1965 | 1966 | 1967 | 1968 | 1969 | 1970 | 1971 |
|---|---|---|---|---|---|---|
| -- | -- | -- | 233 | 173 | 334 | 519 |
| 47,571 | 52,381 | 61,468 | 71,292 | 66,470 | 85,372 | 99,414 |
| -- | 12,463 | 12,796 | 14,732 | 17,259 | 21,905 | 26,086 |
| | | | | | | |
| -- | -- | -- | 1,638 | 2,051 | 2,862 | 5,614 |
| 8,229 | 10,373 | 15,689 | 17,361 | 11,096 | 8,524 | 9,347 |
| 8,229 | 10,373 | 15,689 | 16,977 | 10,912 | 8,267 | 8,907 |
| -- | -- | -- | 384 | 184 | 257 | 440 |
| 973 | 706 | 1,596 | 3,123 | 4,089 | 3,658 | 3,011 |
| 256 | 395 | 338 | 648 | 511 | 547 | 1,630 |
| | | | | | | |
| 57,029 | 76,318 | 91,877 | 109,027 | 101,679 | 123,202 | 145,621 |
| | | | | | | |
| 3,179 | 3,518 | 3,791 | 5,453 | 2,568 | 5,058 | 9,181 |
| 35,145 | 8,928 | 9,465 | 12,758 | 13,792 | 14,398 | 14,259 |
| | | | | | | |
| -- | -- | -- | 709 | 1,640 | 2,521 | 5,872 |
| 4,070 | 8,824 | 13,238 | 17,726 | 23,424 | 30,641 | 34,521 |
| 3,346 | 7,377 | 11,682 | 15,465 | 20,100 | 25,942 | 28,460 |
| 724 | 1,447 | 1,556 | 2,261 | 3,324 | 4,699 | 6,061 |
| 458 | 976 | 814 | 696 | 350 | 567 | 1,099 |
| | | | | | | |
| 12,297 | 40,266 | 48,908 | 53,655 | 37,924 | 42,374 | 48,344 |
| 12,297 | 40,266 | 48,908 | 53,193 | 37,512 | 41,875 | 47,654 |
| -- | -- | -- | 462 | 412 | 499 | 690 |
| -- | 12,482 | 13,004 | 15,252 | 18,172 | 21,694 | 25,329 |
| 1,880 | 1,324 | 2,667 | 2,778 | 3,779 | 5,949 | 7,016 |
| | | | | | | |
| 57,029 | 76,318 | 91,887 | 109,027 | 101,679 | 123,202 | 145,621 |

Source:  Statisticki bilten Sluzbe drustvenog knjigovodsta, No. 2 (1972), Table 7.

## TABLE C.4

Combined Balance Sheet of the National Bank of Yugoslavia

(millions of dinars)

| | 1962 | 1963 | 1964 | 1965 | 1966 | 1967 | 1968 | 1969 | 1970 | 1971 |
|---|---|---|---|---|---|---|---|---|---|---|
| **Assets** | | | | | | | | | | |
| <u>Foreign assets</u> | 1,157 | 1,284 | 984 | 2,428 | 2,913 | 3,586 | 4,151 | 5,209 | 3,394 | 5,636 |
| Gold and foreign exchange | 673 | 879 | 720 | 1,577 | 1,815 | 1,654 | 2,030 | 3,550 | 2,243 | 4,236 |
| Other | 484 | 405 | 264 | 851 | 1,098 | 1,932 | 2,121 | 1,659 | 1,151 | 1,400 |
| Credit to other banks | 11,185 | 14,288 | 15,545 | 16,075 | 14,494 | 14,134 | 16,838 | 18,539 | 25,763 | 29,914 |
| Discount and other credit | 11,035 | 14,150 | 15,415 | 15,848 | 13,833 | 13,391 | 16,119 | 17,623 | 24,820 | 28,949 |
| Credit in foreign exchange | 150 | 138 | 130 | 227 | 661 | 743 | 719 | 916 | 943 | 965 |
| Credit to the federal government and other direct credit | 6,657 | 6,730 | 7,518 | 10,229 | 11,006 | 11,866 | 12,248 | 13,939 | 15,973 | 18,885 |
| Other assets | 1,123 | 826 | 892 | 1,486 | 1,693 | 1,607 | 1,725 | 1,714 | 2,407 | 5,107 |
| Total | 20,122 | 23,128 | 24,939 | 30,218 | 30,106 | 31,193 | 34,962 | 39,401 | 47,537 | 59,542 |
| | | | | | | | | | | |
| **Liabilities** | | | | | | | | | | |
| Foreign liabilities | 597 | 677 | 1,251 | 2,053 | 1,557 | 2,498 | 1,695 | 2,728 | 3,854 | 7,554 |
| Foreign exchange deposits by domestic residents | 602 | 303 | 312 | 769 | 1,324 | 580 | 565 | 114 | 172 | 704 |
| Deposits | 8,781 | 9,246 | 9,298 | 9,862 | 8,989 | 8,995 | 9,263 | 8,752 | 12,076 | 14,482 |
| Currency in circulation | 2,838 | 3,596 | 4,599 | 5,144 | 6,948 | 7,954 | 9,584 | 11,935 | 14,942 | 18,350 |
| Float | 1,151 | 1,574 | 1,783 | 2,173 | 1,992 | 1,383 | 2,320 | 2,276 | 2,274 | 1,815 |
| Bank deposits | 6,140 | 7,654 | 7,696 | 10,217 | 9,206 | 8,985 | 10,359 | 12,479 | 13,106 | 15,843 |
| Gyro accounts | 1,773 | 2,208 | 2,355 | 1,892 | 2,053 | 1,327 | 1,519 | 1,144 | 1,143 | 1,302 |
| Obligatory reserves | 3,742 | 4,567 | 4,446 | 5,886 | 7,153 | 7,025 | 6,492 | 7,245 | 8,857 | 10,450 |
| Other deposits | 625 | 879 | 895 | 2,439 | -- | 633 | 2,348 | 4,090 | 3,106 | 4,091 |
| Other liabilities | 13 | 78 | -- | -- | 90 | 798 | 1,176 | 1,117 | 1,113 | 794 |

Source: Statisticki bilten Sluzbe drustvenog knijgovodsta, No. 2 (1972), Table 5.

Balance of Payments
(millions of dollars)

| Items | 1966 | | 1967 | |
|---|---|---|---|---|
| | I | O | I | O |
| Goods and Services | 1,731 | 1,844 | 1,831 | 1,988 |
| Exchange of goods (exports fob; imports cif) | 1,223 | 1,576 | 1,252 | 1,707 |
| Freight and insurance | 178 | | 187 | 2 |
| Other transportation | 48 | 86 | 52 | 92 |
| Tourism | 117 | 35 | 151 | 56 |
| Interest | 6 | 76 | 8 | 82 |
| Other (including workers' remittances) | 159 | 71 | 181 | 49 |
| Trade balance of goods and services | | -113 | | -157 |
| Transfers | 78 | 4 | 89 | 7 |
| Private | 67 | 4 | 77 | 7 |
| Intergovernment | 11 | | 12 | |
| Balance of current transactions (goods and services plus transfers) | | -39 | | -75 |
| Financial Transactions (net changes) | 140 | | 47 | |
| Nonmonetary sectors | 495 | 302 | 490 | 338 |
| Foreign borrowing | 386 | 210 | 393 | 233 |
| Foreign lending | 36 | 75 | 46 | 78 |
| Short-term credits or transitional items | 73 | 17 | 51 | 27 |
| Monetary sector | | 53 | 22 | 127 |
| Business banks | | 14 | | 33 |
| Short-term credits | | 9 | | 27 |
| Other | | 5 | | 6 |
| Central bank | | 39 | 22 | 94 |
| Clearing accounts | | 28 | | 94 |
| Short-term credits | | 8 | 21 | |
| Other | | 3 | 1 | |
| Allocations of SDR | | | | |
| Official Foreign Reserves and IMF Position | 2 | | 39 | |
| Borrowings from IMF | | 10 | 33 | |
| Other | 22 | | | |
| Foreign exchange reserves | | 10 | 6 | |
| Errors and omissions (net) | -- | 103 | -- | 11 |

| 1968 | | 1969 | | 1970 | | 1971 | |
|---|---|---|---|---|---|---|---|
| I | O | I | O | I | O | I | O |
| 1,934 | 2,109 | 2,350 | 2,493 | 2,911 | 3,363 | 3,389 | 3,882 |
| 1,264 | 1,797 | 1,474 | 2,134 | 1,679 | 2,874 | 1,814 | 3,252 |
| 197 | 2 | 219 | 3 | 272 | 3 | 279 | 6 |
| 54 | 103 | 69 | 114 | 90 | 148 | 121 | 168 |
| 189 | 53 | 243 | 75 | 276 | 132 | 367 | 220 |
| 8 | 88 | 12 | 102 | 18 | 137 | 16 | 156 |
| 222 | 66 | 333 | 65 | 576 | 69 | 798 | 80 |
| | -175 | | -143 | | -452 | | -493 |
| 90 | 10 | 93 | 73 | 126 | 22 | 170 | 34 |
| 77 | 8 | 89 | 11 | 123 | 20 | 169 | 33 |
| 13 | 2 | 4 | 2 | 3 | 2 | 1 | 1 |
| | -95 | | -63 | | -348 | | -357 |
| 338 | | 247 | | 191 | | 545 | |
| 631 | 390 | 676 | 508 | 831 | 631 | 791 | 447 |
| 407 | 257 | 520 | 281 | 641 | 379 | 640 | 368 |
| 59 | 107 | 45 | 139 | 47 | 86 | 71 | 55 |
| 165 | 26 | 111 | 88 | 143 | 166 | 80 | 24 |
| 129 | 32 | 123 | 44 | 73 | 82 | 201 | |
| 81 | 14 | 40 | 42 | | 74 | 162 | |
| 81 | | 40 | | | 30 | 99 | |
| | 14 | | 42 | | 44 | 63 | |
| 48 | 18 | 83 | 2 | 73 | 8 | 39 | |
| 48 | | 63 | | 71 | | -- | -- |
| | 16 | 20 | | | 8 | 39 | |
| | 2 | | 2 | 2 | | 22 | |
| | | | | 25 | | 22 | |
| | 51 | | 154 | 53 | | 22 | |
| | 18 | | 38 | | 55 | 93 | |
| | | 1 | | | 10 | | |
| | 33 | | 117 | 118 | | | 77 |
| -- | 192 | -- | 30 | 79 | -- | -- | 232 |

Note: Compiled according to the International Monetary Fund's methodology: I = inflow; O = outflow. In the case of foreign exchange reserves and clearing accounts: I = decrease; O = increase.

Source: Bilten Narodne banke Jugoslavije, No. 2 (1972).

TABLE D.2

Imports
(millions of dollars)

| | I | II | III | IV | V | VI |
|------|-------|-------|-------|-------|-------|-------|
| 1953 | 40.2 | 33.0 | 35.2 | 37.0 | 37.3 | 45.0 |
| 1954 | 24.7 | 20.6 | 25.7 | 34.3 | 31.8 | 31.6 |
| 1955 | 35.0 | 40.9 | 42.1 | 49.9 | 28.9 | 31.9 |
| 1956 | 39.8 | 33.9 | 40.5 | 33.3 | 48.4 | 56.5 |
| 1957 | 29.8 | 42.7 | 62.7 | 71.3 | 62.4 | 63.2 |
| 1958 | 53.0 | 51.8 | 59.5 | 64.2 | 59.5 | 64.9 |
| 1959 | 53.0 | 42.0 | 55.4 | 64.0 | 58.3 | 69.7 |
| 1960 | 64.6 | 75.7 | 76.3 | 74.3 | 70.6 | 63.8 |
| 1961 | 69.6 | 62.7 | 65.8 | 65.8 | 84.1 | 70.3 |
| 1962 | 75.0 | 59.8 | 79.0 | 79.2 | 83.5 | 69.4 |
| 1963 | 72.7 | 68.2 | 91.0 | 97.3 | 100.3 | 97.4 |
| 1964 | 108.8 | 90.7 | 111.1 | 111.9 | 117.0 | 120.6 |
| 1965 | 98.4 | 81.7 | 93.8 | 108.5 | 125.2 | 113.8 |
| 1966 | 121.0 | 125.7 | 120.1 | 125.4 | 135.8 | 136.5 |
| 1967 | 135.4 | 136.0 | 125.2 | 148.2 | 131.4 | 159.1 |
| 1968 | 126.0 | 123.0 | 124.4 | 155.7 | 158.6 | 150.0 |
| 1969 | 177.2 | 139.7 | 177.1 | 174.8 | 181.6 | 189.1 |
| 1970 | 174.4 | 164.1 | 188.8 | 227.7 | 216.3 | 285.9 |
| 1971 | 317.6 | 183.3 | 264.6 | 274.3 | 280.3 | 326.7 |

| VII | VIII | IX | X | XI | XII | I–XII |
|------|------|------|------|------|------|--------|
| 36.7 | 28.4 | 25.1 | 26.6 | 22.6 | 28.2 | 395.3 |
| 30.0 | 26.2 | 19.7 | 28.8 | 26.6 | 39.5 | 339.5 |
| 45.3 | 42.8 | 35.1 | 28.3 | 28.3 | 32.5 | 441.0 |
| 34.5 | 34.7 | 34.8 | 39.9 | 37.4 | 40.5 | 474.2 |
| 68.2 | 63.0 | 42.9 | 55.6 | 42.2 | 57.4 | 661.4 |
| 63.7 | 63.7 | 50.2 | 51.8 | 48.2 | 54.6 | 685.7 |
| 57.0 | 59.4 | 54.3 | 56.0 | 53.3 | 64.6 | 687.0 |
| 59.4 | 62.3 | 61.4 | 67.7 | 55.0 | 95.0 | 826.1 |
| 74.2 | 81.5 | 75.6 | 93.7 | 81.6 | 85.4 | 910.3 |
| 89.6 | 75.6 | 69.9 | 62.0 | 65.8 | 79.0 | 887.8 |
| 92.4 | 96.0 | 75.2 | 86.2 | 84.2 | 95.8 | 1,056.7 |
| 127.0 | 118.6 | 116.6 | 95.5 | 91.7 | 113.8 | 1,323.3 |
| 138.0 | 103.8 | 101.0 | 110.7 | 94.8 | 118.2 | 1,287.9 |
| 135.3 | 136.8 | 116.2 | 128.5 | 126.5 | 167.6 | 1,575.4 |
| 145.4 | 134.6 | 149.7 | 144.0 | 150.0 | 148.4 | 1,707.4 |
| 151.2 | 170.5 | 171.1 | 150.6 | 161.5 | 184.2 | 1,796.8 |
| 205.3 | 169.5 | 165.8 | 183.9 | 163.4 | 206.4 | 2,133.8 |
| 308.0 | 260.6 | 245.1 | 288.9 | 246.9 | 287.3 | 2,874.0 |
| 304.7 | 280.1 | 250.3 | 258.7 | 238.0 | 273.4 | 3,252.0 |

Source: Index, No. 4 (1954), No. 6 (1955), No. 1 (1957), No. 1 (1958), No. 1 (1959), No. 2 (1960), No. 1 (1961), Nos. 1, 8 (1962), No. 12 (1963), No. 1 (1965), No. 1 (1966), No. 2 (1967), No. 3 (1968), No. 3 (1969), No. 4 (1970), No. 2 (1971), and No. 2 (1972).

## TABLE D.3

### Exports
### (millions of dollars)

| | I | II | III | IV | V | VI | VII | VIII | IX | X | XI | XII | I-XLI |
|---|---|---|---|---|---|---|---|---|---|---|---|---|---|
| 1953 | 12.2 | 10.9 | 16.9 | 14.4 | 15.3 | 16.2 | 13.1 | 12.2 | 16.5 | 15.0 | 20.4 | 23.0 | 186.1 |
| 1954 | 16.2 | 12.2 | 19.3 | 18.5 | 21.0 | 20.8 | 18.6 | 21.0 | 21.4 | 23.6 | 23.2 | 24.6 | 240.4 |
| 1955 | 15.3 | 14.2 | 19.2 | 18.8 | 17.4 | 23.3 | 20.0 | 22.5 | 21.5 | 22.4 | 23.4 | 38.6 | 256.6 |
| 1956 | 17.5 | 19.7 | 28.2 | 25.9 | 26.9 | 26.7 | 26.2 | 25.8 | 28.5 | 29.0 | 28.8 | 40.2 | 323.4 |
| 1957 | 24.4 | 29.5 | 31.4 | 29.4 | 29.2 | 29.0 | 35.2 | 34.3 | 36.2 | 39.4 | 36.1 | 41.0 | 395.1 |
| 1958 | 27.9 | 31.9 | 35.3 | 34.0 | 37.8 | 37.5 | 36.4 | 36.8 | 31.9 | 36.5 | 41.8 | 53.7 | 441.5 |
| 1959 | 23.3 | 37.7 | 38.6 | 34.0 | 46.0 | 41.0 | 32.0 | 40.0 | 42.6 | 39.0 | 48.3 | 54.2 | 476.7 |
| 1960 | 31.4 | 39.0 | 47.4 | 48.0 | 41.4 | 53.4 | 44.6 | 43.7 | 46.6 | 50.3 | 52.0 | 68.0 | 565.8 |
| 1961 | 38.4 | 40.7 | 49.0 | 42.8 | 48.7 | 58.4 | 46.0 | 43.4 | 41.9 | 45.0 | 51.7 | 62.9 | 568.9 |
| 1962 | 44.6 | 43.2 | 47.1 | 41.7 | 54.2 | 56.9 | 57.5 | 60.2 | 68.1 | 70.5 | 70.2 | 76.4 | 690.6 |
| 1963 | 54.7 | 51.0 | 64.3 | 62.2 | 63.6 | 66.6 | 69.8 | 66.6 | 62.2 | 71.7 | 74.5 | 83.2 | 790.4 |
| 1964 | 74.2 | 64.1 | 66.8 | 71.8 | 70.2 | 70.1 | 73.4 | 73.2 | 65.4 | 78.4 | 81.1 | 104.6 | 893.3 |
| 1965 | 77.0 | 63.5 | 83.8 | 80.1 | 88.1 | 88.5 | 100.8 | 77.8 | 94.1 | 105.0 | 95.5 | 137.4 | 1,091.6 |
| 1966 | 85.2 | 80.5 | 100.0 | 102.6 | 86.0 | 108.1 | 100.8 | 96.6 | 100.6 | 107.8 | 95.3 | 156.1 | 1,220.1 |
| 1967 | 78.6 | 84.0 | 110.3 | 104.7 | 98.0 | 123.0 | 98.1 | 92.3 | 109.1 | 112.4 | 112.2 | 129.0 | 1,251.7 |
| 1968 | 93.2 | 72.1 | 91.0 | 104.0 | 101.1 | 100.1 | 123.1 | 105.6 | 100.7 | 117.8 | 107.5 | 147.5 | 1,263.7 |
| 1969 | 99.5 | 86.1 | 100.0 | 127.2 | 109.5 | 119.0 | 149.8 | 126.8 | 117.6 | 145.5 | 136.1 | 157.4 | 1,474.5 |
| 1970 | 130.6 | 128.5 | 122.7 | 145.1 | 122.3 | 147.6 | 179.0 | 112.5 | 153.3 | 138.3 | 137.7 | 191.3 | 1,678.9 |
| 1971 | 143.1 | 108.4 | 131.0 | 126.0 | 130.5 | 152.4 | 187.7 | 150.0 | 158.8 | 153.7 | 153.3 | 219.5 | 1,814.4 |

Source: _Index_, No. 4 (1954), No. 6 (1955), No. 1 (1957), No. 1 (1958), No. 1 (1959), No. 2 (1960),
No. 1 (1961), Nos. 1, 8 (1962), No. 12 (1963), No. 1 (1965), No. 1 (1966), No. 2 (1967), No. 3 (1968),
No. 3 (1969), No. 4 (1970), No. 2 (1971), and No. 2 (1972).

TABLE E.1

Goods and Services Sold by Socialist Enterprises
(millions of dinars)

| | I | II | III | IV | V | VI |
|------|--------|--------|--------|--------|--------|--------|
| 1953 | 1,792 | 1,619 | 1,814 | 1,976 | 1,990 | 2,069 |
| 1954 | 1,617 | 1,881 | 2,325 | 2,133 | 2,500 | 2,467 |
| 1955 | 2,747 | 2,554 | 2,812 | 2,859 | 2,814 | 3,005 |
| 1956 | 2,716 | 2,578 | 2,664 | 2,705 | 3,072 | 3,045 |
| 1957 | 3,355 | 3,138 | 3,427 | 3,902 | 3,762 | 3,860 |
| 1958 | 4,542 | 3,551 | 4,367 | 4,617 | 4,627 | 4,576 |
| 1959 | 4,712 | 3,965 | 4,742 | 5,144 | 5,211 | 5,809 |
| 1960 | 5,703 | 5,100 | 5,814 | 6,620 | 5,970 | 6,746 |
| 1961 | 7,045 | 5,716 | 6,574 | 6,892 | 7,163 | 7,700 |
| 1962 | 9,493 | 5,958 | 6,423 | 8.962 | 9,511 | 8,662 |
| 1963 | 7,488 | 6,048 | 8,150 | 9,938 | 10,272 | 10,778 |
| 1964 | 9,707 | 8,555 | 11,147 | 13,083 | 11,990 | 13,721 |
| 1965 | 11,498 | 10,748 | 14,612 | 14,350 | 12,739 | 16,234 |
| 1966 | 14,308 | 13,356 | 19,423 | 20,459 | 17,748 | 20,719 |
| 1967 | 15,898 | 17,048 | 21,492 | 21,861 | 23,122 | 22,603 |
| 1968 | 15,616 | 14,223 | 17,419 | 18,670 | 27,360 | 21,886 |
| 1969 | 19,517 | 17,977 | 22,164 | 26,224 | 26,064 | 26,452 |
| 1970 | 24,735 | 25,147 | 30,014 | 32,072 | 33,561 | 35,424 |
| 1971 | 38,872 | 32,385 | 38,407 | 43,948 | 41,645 | 46,022 |

| VII | VIII | IX | X | XI | XII | I-XII |
|---|---|---|---|---|---|---|
| 2,152 | 1,920 | 2,106 | 2,451 | 2,270 | 3,110 | 25,269 |
| 2,507 | 2,594 | 2,909 | 3,045 | 2,962 | 3,728 | 30,668 |
| 2,859 | 3,277 | 3,174 | 3,182 | 3,015 | 3,826 | 36,124 |
| 2,846 | 3,403 | 3,174 | 3,730 | 3,502 | 4,390 | 37,825 |
| 3,901 | 4,219 | 4,075 | 4,488 | 4,307 | 5,599 | 48,033 |
| 4,935 | 4,867 | 4,841 | 5,419 | 4,975 | 6,398 | 57,715 |
| 5,502 | 5,839 | 6,061 | 6,643 | 6,299 | 8,094 | 68,021 |
| 6,373 | 7,208 | 7,090 | 7,386 | 6,811 | 9,429 | 80,200 |
| 7,675 | 8,332 | 8,391 | 8,459 | 8,507 | 10,485 | 92,939 |
| 8,112 | 9,474 | 8,934 | 10,162 | 9,059 | 14,056 | 108,806 |
| 10,264 | 11,011 | 10,868 | 12,061 | 11,402 | 16,827 | 125,107 |
| 12,951 | 13,136 | 14,039 | 15,414 | 13,770 | 19,946 | 157,459 |
| 15,811 | 15,292 | 17,966 | 19,161 | 18,859 | 27,388 | 194,658 |
| 20,048 | 22,088 | 22,380 | 22,613 | 21,067 | 29,398 | 243,607 |
| 21,498 | 24,095 | 21,373 | 22,679 | 18,758 | 31,804 | 262,231 |
| 23,837 | 24,811 | 24,131 | 25,775 | 23,833 | 34,935 | 272,496 |
| 26,702 | 28,891 | 29,439 | 30,313 | 30,535 | 40,534 | 324,812 |
| 33,870 | 32,323 | 36,404 | 35,864 | 36,154 | 48,169 | 403,737 |
| 44,767 | 48,534 | 45,626 | 47,624 | 47,901 | 63,779 | 539,510 |

Note: 1953-61 = cash plus credit plus accounts receivable; 1962-68 = cash receipts; 1969-70 = cash plus credit plus accounts receivable.

Sources: For 1953-54, unpublished materials; for 1955-71, Statisticki bilten Sluzbe drustvenog knjigovodsta.

## TABLE E.2

Money Receipts of Individuals from Socialist Enterprises, Governments, And Other Organizations
(millions of dinars)

| | I | II | III | IV | V | VI | VII | VIII | IX | X | XI | XII | Ukupno |
|---|---|---|---|---|---|---|---|---|---|---|---|---|---|
| 1949 | | | | | | | | | | | | | 1,663 |
| 1950 | | | | | | | | | | | | | 1,842 |
| 1951 | | | | | | | | | | | | | 2,165 |
| 1952 | | | | | | | | | | | | | 3,186 |
| 1953 | 309 | 339 | 357 | 426 | 371 | 426 | 429 | 451 | 441 | 480 | 452 | 521 | 4,995 |
| 1954 | 335 | 348 | 338 | 468 | 404 | 466 | 504 | 514 | 558 | 578 | 581 | 661 | 5,805 |
| 1955 | 441 | 459 | 488 | 572 | 473 | 571 | 571 | 603 | 614 | 634 | 651 | 732 | 6,809 |
| 1956 | 453 | 485 | 528 | 617 | 496 | 637 | 613 | 660 | 662 | 727 | 758 | 831 | 7,469 |
| 1957 | 529 | 600 | 675 | 831 | 649 | 746 | 786 | 882 | 843 | 902 | 983 | 1,033 | 9,461 |
| 1958 | 621 | 721 | 769 | 949 | 695 | 838 | 871 | 908 | 921 | 978 | 1,069 | 1,198 | 10,537 |
| 1959 | 710 | 810 | 856 | 1,086 | 802 | 1,017 | 1,084 | 1,122 | 1,103 | 1,180 | 1,298 | 1,300 | 12,451 |
| 1960 | 793 | 1,003 | 1,090 | 1,368 | 975 | 1,228 | 1,261 | 1,302 | 1,289 | 1,320 | 1,511 | 1,793 | 14,933 |
| 1961 | 1,034 | 1,189 | 1,337 | 1,645 | 1,180 | 1,533 | 1,497 | 1,581 | 1,601 | 1,666 | 1,834 | 2,083 | 18,180 |
| 1962 | 1,232 | 1,400 | 1,492 | 1,770 | 1,325 | 1,627 | 1,643 | 1,686 | 1,690 | 1,841 | 2,026 | 2,248 | 19,980 |
| 1963 | 1,392 | 1,562 | 1,678 | 2,084 | 1,575 | 1,910 | 2,047 | 2,092 | 2,015 | 2,152 | 2,481 | 2,789 | 23,777 |
| 1964 | 1,817 | 2,022 | 2,049 | 2,559 | 1,958 | 2,445 | 2,649 | 2,679 | 2,736 | 2,978 | 2,382 | 3,650 | 30,824 |
| 1965 | 2,282 | 2,667 | 2,902 | 3,508 | 2,632 | 3,351 | 3,587 | 3,757 | 3,823 | 4,110 | 4,599 | 5,062 | 42,280 |
| 1966 | 3,002 | 3,956 | 4,259 | 4,988 | 3,698 | 4,906 | 5,222 | 5,085 | 4,899 | 5,288 | 5,841 | 5,819 | 57,023 |
| 1967 | 3,698 | 4,574 | 4,863 | 5,524 | 4,267 | 5,658 | 5,532 | 5,720 | 5,490 | 5,334 | 6,060 | 6,189 | 62,912 |
| 1968 | 4,031 | 4,827 | 4,909 | 6,074 | 4,821 | 5,952 | 6,552 | 6,406 | 5,978 | 6,201 | 6,899 | 7,094 | 69,744 |
| 1969 | 5,077 | 5,684 | 5,824 | 7,338 | 5,894 | 7,186 | 7,823 | 7,549 | 7,455 | 7,773 | 8,227 | 8,977 | 84,238 |
| 1970 | 6,306 | 6,886 | 7,484 | 9,132 | 7,222 | 8,947 | 10,025 | 9,090 | 9,227 | 10,025 | 10,490 | 11,173 | 106,037 |
| 1971 | 7,668 | 8,715 | 9,736 | 11,827 | 9,987 | 12,186 | 13,455 | 12,068 | 12,067 | 11,972 | 13,310 | 15,410 | 138,401 |

Note: Interpayments are not included.

Sources: For 1949-55, internal materials; for 1956-71, Statisticki bilten Sluzbe drustvenog knjigovodsta; Statisticki godisnjak Saveznog zavoda za statistiku.

226

## TABLE E.3

Personal Incomes Received by Individuals from Socialist Enterprises, Governments, And Other Organizations
(millions of dinars)

| | I | II | III | IV | V | VI | VII | VIII | IX | X | XI | XII | Ukupno |
|---|---|---|---|---|---|---|---|---|---|---|---|---|---|
| 1949 | | | | | | | | | | | | | 941 |
| 1950 | | | | | | | | | | | | | 1,842 |
| 1951 | | | | | | | | | | | | | 2,165 |
| 1952 | | | | | | | | | | | | | 3,186 |
| 1953 | 154 | 172 | 173 | 218 | 161 | 189 | 198 | 202 | 198 | 210 | 216 | 249 | 2,339 |
| 1954 | 154 | 173 | 175 | 244 | 179 | 217 | 245 | 237 | 243 | 256 | 282 | 323 | 2,728 |
| 1955 | 196 | 224 | 234 | 296 | 206 | 256 | 275 | 280 | 282 | 281 | 318 | 357 | 3,206 |
| 1956 | 204 | 249 | 249 | 330 | 199 | 296 | 288 | 301 | 295 | 306 | 380 | 391 | 3,488 |
| 1957 | 210 | 283 | 311 | 439 | 255 | 347 | 361 | 390 | 376 | 386 | 492 | 505 | 4,355 |
| 1958 | 258 | 345 | 373 | 519 | 297 | 396 | 430 | 442 | 445 | 467 | 587 | 643 | 5,202 |
| 1959 | 337 | 433 | 432 | 615 | 369 | 513 | 587 | 583 | 550 | 563 | 704 | 732 | 6,418 |
| 1960 | 371 | 518 | 554 | 772 | 450 | 619 | 659 | 652 | 639 | 648 | 829 | 958 | 7,669 |
| 1961 | 476 | 627 | 674 | 942 | 539 | 774 | 786 | 799 | 799 | 804 | 987 | 1,142 | 9,349 |
| 1962 | 587 | 757 | 791 | 1,004 | 617 | 854 | 836 | 833 | 860 | 874 | 1,106 | 1,236 | 10,355 |
| 1963 | 627 | 835 | 866 | 1,163 | 728 | 987 | 1,031 | 1,059 | 1,008 | 1,056 | 1,371 | 1,509 | 12,240 |
| 1964 | 781 | 1,109 | 1,106 | 1,467 | 939 | 1,290 | 1,430 | 1,429 | 1,423 | 1,550 | 1,868 | 2,055 | 16,447 |
| 1965 | 1,109 | 1,567 | 1,625 | 2,110 | 1,340 | 1,782 | 1,948 | 1,964 | 2,022 | 2,175 | 2,721 | 2,841 | 23,202 |
| 1966 | 1,491 | 2,275 | 2,372 | 2,889 | 1,829 | 2,569 | 2,730 | 2,598 | 2,679 | 2,862 | 3,446 | 3,188 | 30,960 |
| 1967 | 2,001 | 2,742 | 2,817 | 3,467 | 2,179 | 3,141 | 3,002 | 2,995 | 3,099 | 2,974 | 3,702 | 3,442 | 35,561 |
| 1968 | 2,196 | 2,939 | 2,916 | 3,729 | 2,585 | 3,157 | 3,403 | 3,384 | 3,139 | 3,435 | 4,127 | 3,924 | 38,934 |
| 1969 | 2,687 | 3,384 | 3,325 | 4,297 | 3,041 | 3,777 | 4,115 | 3,834 | 3,941 | 4,313 | 4,728 | 4,677 | 46,119 |
| 1970 | 3,179 | 3,910 | 4,046 | 5,119 | 3,569 | 4,647 | 5,151 | 4,452 | 4,597 | 5,331 | 5,786 | 5,813 | 55,591 |
| 1971 | 3,969 | 4,573 | 5,171 | 6,457 | 4,640 | 6,097 | 6,439 | 5,560 | 5,935 | 6,146 | 7,387 | 8,049 | 70,423 |

Note: Interpayments are not included.

Sources: For 1949-55, internal materials; for 1956-71, Statisticki bilten Sluzbe drustvenog knjigovodsta; Statisticki godisnjak Saveznog zavoda za statistiku.

## TABLE E.4

### Budget Receipts
(millions of dinars)

| | I | II | III | IV | V | VI | VII | VIII | IX | X | XI | XII | I–XII |
|---|---|---|---|---|---|---|---|---|---|---|---|---|---|
| 1952 | | | | | | | | | | | | | 2,490 |
| 1953 | | | | | | | | | | | | | 3,177 |
| 1954 | | | | | | | | | | | | | 4,506 |
| 1955 | | | | | | | | | | | | | 3,669 |
| 1956 | 90 | 96 | 16 | 1 | 369 | 571 | 369 | 311 | 268 | 321 | 346 | 358 | 3,116 |
| 1957 | 230 | 258 | 251 | 384 | 325 | 321 | 285 | 243 | 398 | 366 | 370 | 431 | 3,862 |
| 1958 | 239 | 230 | 426 | 366 | 332 | 354 | 337 | 382 | 500 | 431 | 457 | 578 | 4,632 |
| 1959 | 272 | 422 | 455 | 497 | 503 | 475 | 460 | 531 | 527 | 501 | 610 | 644 | 5,897 |
| 1960 | 70 | 552 | 1,012 | 669 | 606 | 600 | 571 | 838 | 738 | 690 | 749 | 886 | 7,981 |
| 1961 | 241 | 1,080 | 788 | 716 | 740 | 771 | 755 | 657 | 814 | 819 | 876 | 982 | 9,239 |
| 1962 | 250 | 980 | 642 | 750 | 820 | 895 | 890 | 800 | 889 | 850 | 870 | 828 | 9,464 |
| 1963 | 442 | 1,031 | 1,112 | 759 | 955 | 928 | 1,014 | 1,132 | 973 | 1,107 | 1,106 | 1,279 | 11,838 |
| 1964 | 537 | 1,200 | 1,189 | 1,182 | 1,221 | 1,266 | 1,285 | 1,272 | 991 | 1,165 | 1,131 | 1,687 | 14,126 |
| 1965 | 696 | 1,208 | 1,668 | 1,445 | 1,458 | 1,536 | 1,607 | 1,428 | 1,272 | 1,302 | 1,232 | 1,952 | 16,804 |
| 1966 | 542 | 1,017 | 1,280 | 1,248 | 1,394 | 1,275 | 1,467 | 1,415 | 1,479 | 1,532 | 1,462 | 2,282 | 16,393 |
| 1967 | 576 | 1,351 | 1,342 | 1,178 | 1,445 | 1,453 | 1,370 | 1,420 | 1,353 | 1,527 | 1,647 | 2,016 | 16,678 |
| 1968 | 630 | 1,268 | 1,403 | 1,487 | 1,469 | 1,537 | 1,551 | 1,759 | 1,700 | 1,807 | 1,852 | 2,486 | 18,949 |
| 1969 | 788 | 1,521 | 1,609 | 1,800 | 1,681 | 1,725 | 2,147 | 1,823 | 1,939 | 2,168 | 2,007 | 2,594 | 21,802 |
| 1970 | 965 | 1,790 | 2,284 | 2,186 | 2,293 | 2,331 | 2,679 | 2,581 | 2,600 | 2,939 | 2,810 | 3,520 | 29,028 |
| 1971 | 1,250 | 2,268 | 2,836 | 2,606 | 2,526 | 2,692 | 2,840 | 2,861 | 2,746 | 3,134 | 2,837 | 4,225 | 32,821 |

Sources: Statisticki bilten Sluzbe drustvenog knjigovodsta, No. 3 (1958), Table 32, No. 2 (1960), Table 33, No. 2 (1961), Table 33, No. 2 (1962), Table 33, No. 2 (1965), Table 25, No. 2 (1965), Table 25, No. 2 (1966), Table 25, No. 2 (1967), Table 29, No. 2 (1969), Table 29, No. 1 (1971), Table 29, and No. 2 (1972), Table 29.

# F

**EXPENDITURES**

## TABLE F.1

### Total Investment Expenditures for Fixed Assets
(millions of dinars)

|  | I | II | III | IV | V | VI | VII | VIII | IX | X | XI | XII | Ukupno |
|---|---|---|---|---|---|---|---|---|---|---|---|---|---|
| 1952 | | | | | | | | | | | | | 2,486 |
| 1953 | 72 | 75 | 145 | 208 | 205 | 278 | 258 | 245 | 305 | 328 | 315 | 860 | 3,294 |
| 1954 | 127 | 55 | 105 | 257 | 245 | 336 | 357 | 359 | 368 | 422 | 395 | 985 | 4,011 |
| 1955 | 163 | 155 | 260 | 295 | 380 | 435 | 394 | 395 | 350 | 360 | 350 | 752 | 4,289 |
| 1956 | 341 | 344 | 191 | 260 | 216 | 289 | 361 | 379 | 311 | 441 | 468 | 726 | 4,327 |
| 1957 | 390 | 254 | 243 | 365 | 340 | 432 | 430 | 407 | 424 | 515 | 456 | 1,157 | 5,413 |
| 1958 | 216 | 224 | 363 | 461 | 372 | 435 | 535 | 435 | 461 | 542 | 502 | 894 | 5,440 |
| 1959 | 282 | 276 | 333 | 503 | 453 | 603 | 621 | 571 | 592 | 726 | 657 | 1,403 | 7,020 |
| 1960 | 352 | 340 | 477 | 661 | 640 | 817 | 869 | 804 | 735 | 781 | 702 | 1,617 | 8,795 |
| 1961 | 449 | 514 | 608 | 867 | 693 | 909 | 953 | 1,035 | 787 | 876 | 904 | 2,173 | 10,768 |
| 1962 | 500 | 533 | 727 | 817 | 864 | 1,119 | 1,018 | 1,185 | 964 | 1,150 | 1,133 | 2,296 | 12,306 |
| 1963 | 378 | 475 | 768 | 969 | 1,011 | 1,410 | 1,106 | 1,240 | 1,257 | 1,397 | 1,324 | 3,301 | 14,636 |
| 1964 | 528 | 831 | 1,089 | 1,543 | 1,411 | 1,849 | 1,574 | 1,501 | 1,727 | 1,817 | 1,469 | 3,489 | 18,828 |
| 1965 | 668 | 986 | 1,490 | 1,623 | 1,151 | 1,954 | 1,565 | 1,393 | 1,586 | 1,643 | 1,652 | 3,439 | 19,150 |
| 1966 | 501 | 998 | 1,591 | 1,720 | 1,732 | 2,402 | 1,749 | 1,973 | 1,906 | 1,881 | 1,741 | 3,268 | 21,162 |
| 1967 | 894 | 1,176 | 1,418 | 1,668 | 1,615 | 2,122 | 1,323 | 1,755 | 1,655 | 1,505 | 1,649 | 3,118 | 19,898 |
| 1968 | 1,028 | 1,107 | 1,513 | 1,890 | 2,380 | 2,438 | 2,039 | 2,092 | 2,135 | 2,414 | 2,134 | 4,072 | 25,242 |
| 1969 | 1,283 | 1,323 | 1,782 | 2,284 | 2,101 | 2,873 | 2,412 | 2,466 | 2,537 | 2,467 | 2,437 | 5,095 | 29,060 |
| 1970 | 1,833 | 2,289 | 2,686 | 3,006 | 2,923 | 3,695 | 3,214 | 3,156 | 3,273 | 3,438 | 3,107 | 5,844 | 38,464 |
| 1971 | 2,324 | 2,686 | 3,037 | 3,484 | 3,429 | 3,698 | 3,529 | 3,510 | 3,201 | 3,226 | 3,515 | 5,809 | 41,438 |

Sources:  Statisticki bilten Sluzbe drustvenog knjigovodsta, No. 2 (1960), Table 17, No. 7 (1954), Table 49, No. 2 (1961), Table 31, No. 10 (1956), Table 27, No. 3 (1958), Table 16, No. 2 (1959), Table 17, No. 2 (1961), Table 17, No. 2 (1962), Table 17, No. 2 (1963), Table 27, No. 2 (1964), Table 36, No. 2 (1965), Table 41, No. 2 (1966), Table 43, No. 2 (1967), Table 40, No. 2 (1968), Table 37, No. 2 (1969), Table 37, No. 2 (1970), Table 39, No. 1 (1971), Table 39, and No. 2 (1972), Table 39.

## TABLE F.2

### Expenditures of Socialist Enterprises
(millions of dinars)

| | I | II | III | IV | V | VI | VII | VIII | IX | X | XI | XII | I-XII |
|---|---|---|---|---|---|---|---|---|---|---|---|---|---|
| 1953 | 1,816 | 1,724 | 1,831 | 2,113 | 1,963 | 2,195 | 2,184 | 1,879 | 2,157 | 2,553 | 2,297 | 2,994 | 25,706 |
| 1954 | 1,530 | 1,986 | 2,420 | 2,294 | 2,687 | 2,685 | 2,651 | 2,783 | 3,003 | 3,097 | 3,077 | 3,743 | 31,956 |
| 1955 | 2,557 | 2,630 | 2,957 | 2,855 | 2,803 | 3,151 | 2,855 | 3,392 | 3,294 | 3,263 | 3,228 | 4,024 | 37,009 |
| 1956 | 2,710 | 2,728 | 2,775 | 2,999 | 3,146 | 3,441 | 3,080 | 3,694 | 3,282 | 3,808 | 3,747 | 4,515 | 39,928 |
| 1957 | 3,371 | 3,223 | 3,765 | 4,164 | 3,899 | 4,117 | 3,944 | 4,225 | 4,044 | 4,458 | 4,417 | 5,707 | 49,337 |
| 1958 | 4,392 | 3,731 | 4,701 | 5,152 | 4,662 | 4,675 | 4,844 | 4,976 | 4,950 | 5,326 | 5,207 | 6,478 | 59,067 |
| 1959 | 4,408 | 4,101 | 5,004 | 5,815 | 5,276 | 6,106 | 5,617 | 6,229 | 6,126 | 6,721 | 6,617 | 7,846 | 69,866 |
| 1960 | 5,578 | 5,526 | 6,523 | 7,531 | 6,015 | 6,938 | 6,420 | 7,586 | 7,251 | 7,363 | 7,351 | 9,677 | 83,759 |
| 1961 | 6,751 | 6,046 | 7,303 | 7,643 | 7,279 | 8,314 | 7,651 | 9,048 | 8,900 | 8,675 | 8,868 | 10,851 | 97,329 |
| 1962 | 8,919 | 6,970 | 8,871 | 9,274 | 9,778 | 9,073 | 8,596 | 9,904 | 9,228 | 10,546 | 10,019 | 13,387 | 114,565 |
| 1963 | 9,025 | 8,286 | 10,932 | 12,519 | 11,855 | 12,592 | 13,304 | 13,263 | 12,704 | 14,991 | 14,213 | 19,277 | 152,961 |
| 1964 | 11,918 | 12,784 | 15,111 | 17,263 | 15,082 | 17,133 | 17,630 | 16,755 | 17,495 | 20,015 | 17,929 | 23,564 | 202,679 |
| 1965 | 15,082 | 16,029 | 19,826 | 18,891 | 16,107 | 20,705 | 21,346 | 20,229 | 22,660 | 25,834 | 24,893 | 33,298 | 254,897 |
| 1966 | 18,206 | 20,169 | 26,487 | 26,809 | 22,284 | 25,489 | 28,593 | 27,547 | 26,229 | 29,530 | 26,163 | 34,281 | 311,787 |
| 1967 | 19,903 | 21,178 | 24,373 | 24,072 | 24,437 | 25,453 | 23,792 | 26,672 | 26,120 | 25,862 | 26,688 | 37,701 | 305,141 |
| 1968 | 19,033 | 20,012 | 21,670 | 23,127 | 34,122 | 25,537 | 28,389 | 28,979 | 27,720 | 30,352 | 28,787 | 39,105 | 326,827 |
| 1969 | 23,535 | 24,671 | 27,110 | 32,548 | 30,341 | 31,504 | 31,584 | 34,358 | 34,464 | 35,456 | 36,074 | 45,720 | 387,368 |
| 1970 | 29,767 | 32,543 | 37,928 | 39,399 | 38,672 | 41,865 | 39,950 | 38,079 | 42,455 | 41,807 | 42,540 | 53,989 | 478,994 |
| 1971 | 35,735 | 37,848 | 46,875 | 50,227 | 46,635 | 52,309 | 50,493 | 53,875 | 50,682 | 53,984 | 54,236 | 70,231 | 603,130 |

Sources: Statisticki bilten Sluzbe drustvenog knjigovodsta, No. 12 (1954), Table 2, No. 12 (1955), Table 7/1, No. 1 (1957), Table 6, No. 1 (1958), Table A/1, No. 2 (1959), Table A/1, No. 2 (1960), Table A/1, No. 3 (1961), Table A/1, No. 3 (1962), Table 9, No. 3 (1963), Table 10, No. 3 (1964), Table 11, No. 3 (1965), Table 11, No. 3 (1966), Table 11, No. 3 (1967), Table 12, No. 3 (1968), Table 12, No. 3 (1969), Table 14, No. 3 (1970), Table 14, No. 1 (1971), Table 14, and No. 2 (1971), Table 14.

## TABLE F.3

### Expenditures of Socialist Enterprises for Materials
### (millions of dinars)

|       | I      | II     | III    | IV     | V      | VI     |
|-------|--------|--------|--------|--------|--------|--------|
| 1953  | 1,263  | 1,224  | 1,394  | 1,575  | 1,448  | 1,516  |
| 1954  | 1,068  | 1,413  | 1,740  | 1,597  | 1,987  | 1,762  |
| 1955  | 1,956  | 1,869  | 2,230  | 2,173  | 2,092  | 2,272  |
| 1956  | 2,013  | 1,921  | 1,997  | 2,176  | 2,477  | 2,423  |
| 1957  | 2,610  | 2,406  | 2,689  | 3,042  | 3,045  | 3,053  |
| 1958  | 3,584  | 2,893  | 3,457  | 3,651  | 3,730  | 3,584  |
| 1959  | 3,536  | 3,141  | 3,819  | 3,930  | 4,211  | 4,682  |
| 1960* | 4,498  | 4,289  | 4,829  | 5,253  | 4,646  | 5,258  |
| 1961* | 5,386  | 4,604  | 5,180  | 5,276  | 5,702  | 6,285  |
| 1962* | 7,082  | 5,164  | 6,238  | 6,238  | 7,720  | 6,687  |
| 1963* | 5,797  | 4,671  | 6,675  | 7,932  | 8,128  | 8,424  |
| 1964  | 7,138  | 6,469  | 8,692  | 10,178 | 9,141  | 10,164 |
| 1965  | 8,364  | 7,845  | 10,849 | 10,115 | 8,913  | 11,791 |
| 1966  | 9,982  | 9,330  | 14,462 | 14,621 | 12,787 | 14,562 |
| 1967  | 11,647 | 10,753 | 15,048 | 14,598 | 16,535 | 16,926 |
| 1968  | 10,606 | 9,009  | 11,528 | 12,294 | 23,146 | 15,117 |
| 1969  | 13,417 | 11,682 | 15,230 | 18,645 | 18,553 | 18,898 |
| 1970  | 17,176 | 17,982 | 21,354 | 23,025 | 24,780 | 25,945 |
| 1971  | 21,180 | 22,533 | 27,126 | 31,947 | 30,721 | 34,058 |

| VII | VIII | IX | X | XI | XII | I-XII |
|---|---|---|---|---|---|---|
| 1,634 | 1,364 | 1,463 | 1,832 | 1,597 | 2,113 | 18,423 |
| 1,780 | 2,010 | 2,239 | 2,328 | 2,205 | 2,673 | 22,802 |
| 2,050 | 2,468 | 2,478 | 2,404 | 2,310 | 2,939 | 27,241 |
| 2,181 | 2,704 | 2,479 | 2,839 | 2,659 | 3,228 | 29,097 |
| 2,988 | 3,193 | 3,073 | 3,422 | 3,309 | 4,282 | 37,112 |
| 3,797 | 3,713 | 3,661 | 4,154 | 3,829 | 4,959 | 45,012 |
| 4,204 | 4,582 | 4,736 | 5,186 | 4,917 | 6,100 | 53,044 |
| 4,617 | 5,600 | 5,627 | 5,620 | 5,349 | 7,349 | 62,935 |
| 5,433 | 6,374 | 6,788 | 6,545 | 6,546 | 8,547 | 72,666 |
| 5,960 | 7,138 | 6,979 | 7,970 | 7,055 | 10,277 | 84,508 |
| 7,847 | 8,337 | 8,304 | 9,348 | 8,725 | 12,454 | 96,642 |
| 9,374 | 9,576 | 10,423 | 11,246 | 10,037 | 14,006 | 116,444 |
| 10,940 | 11,310 | 13,512 | 14,542 | 13,943 | 20,149 | 142,273 |
| 13,332 | 15,086 | 16,024 | 15,559 | 14,547 | 21,089 | 171,381 |
| 14,910 | 17,245 | 16,776 | 16,172 | 13,294 | 23,518 | 187,422 |
| 16,247 | 17,437 | 17,114 | 18,504 | 16,691 | 24,550 | 192,243 |
| 18,060 | 20,510 | 21,125 | 21,274 | 21,184 | 28,145 | 226,723 |
| 22,891 | 22,790 | 26,534 | 24,668 | 25,700 | 33,763 | 286,608 |
| 30,742 | 35,354 | 33,177 | 34,749 | 34,391 | 47,481 | 384,089 |

*Annual figures corrected after publication without correcting monthly figures.

Sources: Statisticki bilten Sluzbe drustvenog knjigovodsta, No. 12 (1954), Table 2, No. 12 (1955), Table 7/1, No. 1 (1957), Table 6, No. 1 (1958), Table A/1, No. 2 (1959), Table A/1, No. 2 (1960), Table A/1, No. 3 (1961), Table A/1, No. 3 (1962), Table 9, No. 3 (1963), Table 10, No. 3 (1964), Table 11, No. 3 (1965), Table 11, No. 3 (1966), Table 11, No. 3 (1967), Table 12, No. 3 (1968), Table 12, No. 3 (1969), Table 14, No. 3 (1970), Table 14, No. 1 (1971), Table 14, and No. 2 (1971), Table 14.

## TABLE F.4

### Expenditures by Individuals on Goods and Services
### (millions of dinars)

| | I | II | III | IV | V | VI | VII | VIII | IX | X | XI | XII | Ukupno |
|---|---|---|---|---|---|---|---|---|---|---|---|---|---|
| 1949 | | | | | | | | | | | | | 985 |
| 1950 | | | | | | | | | | | | | 1,091 |
| 1951 | | | | | | | | | | | | | 1,327 |
| 1952 | | | | | | | | | | | | | 2,023 |
| 1953 | 209 | 220 | 274 | 281 | 277 | 288 | 280 | 288 | 295 | 346 | 329 | 378 | 3,455 |
| 1954 | 244 | 238 | 290 | 330 | 308 | 328 | 339 | 347 | 369 | 412 | 397 | 489 | 4,094 |
| 1955 | 328 | 319 | 367 | 395 | 390 | 399 | 401 | 431 | 447 | 467 | 445 | 543 | 4,933 |
| 1956 | 346 | 325 | 385 | 385 | 424 | 435 | 434 | 453 | 465 | 540 | 522 | 642 | 5,356 |
| 1957 | 413 | 429 | 504 | 566 | 520 | 533 | 558 | 563 | 582 | 637 | 640 | 773 | 6,722 |
| 1958 | 478 | 455 | 511 | 602 | 561 | 565 | 585 | 586 | 642 | 709 | 693 | 875 | 7,262 |
| 1959 | 551 | 548 | 642 | 706 | 633 | 706 | 706 | 734 | 786 | 843 | 831 | 983 | 8,675 |
| 1960 | 633 | 690 | 748 | 838 | 739 | 785 | 781 | 843 | 891 | 927 | 894 | 1,293 | 10,062 |
| 1961 | 741 | 712 | 890 | 908 | 909 | 946 | 930 | 977 | 1,017 | 1,101 | 1,098 | 1,330 | 11,559 |
| 1962 | 933 | 828 | 955 | 1,076 | 1,098 | 1,084 | 1,069 | 1,096 | 1,104 | 1,279 | 1,213 | 1,472 | 13,217 |
| 1963 | 990 | 916 | 1,103 | 1,356 | 1,337 | 1,358 | 1,405 | 1,368 | 1,369 | 1,569 | 1,529 | 1,855 | 16,154 |
| 1964 | 1,281 | 1,259 | 1,431 | 1,648 | 1,538 | 1,639 | 1,680 | 1,713 | 1,905 | 2,110 | 2,010 | 2,407 | 20,621 |
| 1965 | 1,593 | 1,565 | 1,957 | 2,139 | 1,886 | 2,297 | 2,442 | 2,316 | 2,505 | 2,726 | 2,965 | 3,741 | 28,132 |
| 1966 | 2,065 | 2,268 | 2,816 | 3,036 | 2,677 | 2,911 | 3,058 | 3,145 | 3,030 | 3,311 | 3,341 | 4,031 | 35,689 |
| 1967 | 2,589 | 2,726 | 3,270 | 3,177 | 3,313 | 3,410 | 3,337 | 3,576 | 3,572 | 3,591 | 3,597 | 4,307 | 40,475 |
| 1968 | 2,899 | 2,940 | 3,324 | 3,804 | 3,536 | 3,953 | 4,177 | 4,158 | 4,175 | 4,371 | 4,185 | 5,181 | 46,693 |
| 1969 | 3,684 | 3,287 | 3,994 | 4,319 | 4,256 | 4,406 | 4,558 | 4,597 | 4,822 | 5,142 | 4,810 | 6,148 | 54,033 |
| 1970 | 4,202 | 4,115 | 5,130 | 5,385 | 5,235 | 5,737 | 5,657 | 5,764 | 6,166 | 6,520 | 6,343 | 7,835 | 68,089 |
| 1971 | 5,468 | 5,872 | 6,343 | 6,729 | 6,891 | 7,469 | 7,312 | 7,418 | 7,682 | 7,533 | 7,864 | 9,368 | 86,449 |

Sources: Statisticki bilten Sluzbe drustvenog knjigovodsta, No. 3 (1958), Table 45, No. 3 (1960), Table 46, No. 3 (1961), Table 45, No. 3 (1962), Table 34, No. 3 (1964), Table 48, No. 3 (1966), Table 47, No. 3 (1968), Table 42, No. 3 (1969), Table 42, No. 3 (1970), Table 44, No. 1 (1971), Table 11, and No. 2 (1972), Table 11; unpublished materials.

234

TABLE F.5

Budget Expenditures for Goods
(millions of dinars)

| | I | II | III | IV | V | VI | VII | VIII | IX | X | XI | XII | I-XII |
|---|---|---|---|---|---|---|---|---|---|---|---|---|---|
| 1952 | | | | | | | | | | | | | 2,561 |
| 1953 | | | | | | | | | | | | | 2,669 |
| 1954 | | | | | | | | | | | | | 2,109 |
| 1955 | | | | | | | | | | | | | 2,990 |
| 1956 | 226 | 272 | 151 | 182 | 202 | 191 | 187 | 180 | 186 | 236 | 207 | 365 | 2,585 |
| 1957 | 209 | 218 | 181 | 211 | 188 | 206 | 235 | 199 | 202 | 238 | 214 | 361 | 2,662 |
| 1958 | 280 | 207 | 224 | 305 | 253 | 260 | 319 | 281 | 278 | 299 | 273 | 485 | 3,464 |
| 1959 | 347 | 252 | 254 | 329 | 268 | 296 | 342 | 288 | 267 | 326 | 350 | 539 | 3,858 |
| 1960 | 478 | 241 | 331 | 366 | 369 | 393 | 427 | 364 | 380 | 501 | 280 | 767 | 4,897 |
| 1961 | 310 | 546 | 371 | 454 | 388 | 476 | 533 | 483 | 460 | 456 | 404 | 685 | 5,566 |
| 1962 | 281 | 304 | 481 | 412 | 536 | 438 | 663 | 510 | 563 | 621 | 450 | 944 | 6,203 |
| 1963 | 203 | 424 | 450 | 502 | 499 | 534 | 539 | 563 | 419 | 577 | 482 | 948 | 6,140 |
| 1964 | 274 | 453 | 512 | 708 | 601 | 648 | 738 | 557 | 558 | 596 | 647 | 1,232 | 7,524 |
| 1965 | 293 | 425 | 514 | 556 | 604 | 661 | 482 | 464 | 549 | 569 | 519 | 1,191 | 6,827 |
| 1966 | 299 | 343 | 416 | 548 | 414 | 526 | 533 | 533 | 599 | 609 | 639 | 917 | 6,376 |
| 1967 | 588 | 725 | 824 | 755 | 690 | 769 | 797 | 698 | 447 | 598 | 829 | 1,008 | 8,728 |
| 1968 | 845 | 647 | 671 | 954 | 786 | 699 | 813 | 928 | 832 | 865 | 884 | 1,374 | 10,298 |
| 1969 | 1,000 | 675 | 883 | 881 | 674 | 806 | 849 | 798 | 868 | 929 | 936 | 1,261 | 10,560 |
| 1970 | 1,011 | 968 | 942 | 1,390 | 947 | 1,087 | 1,301 | 1,009 | 1,260 | 1,440 | 1,164 | 1,902 | 14,420 |
| 1971 | 1,069 | 945 | 1,489 | 1,861 | 1,087 | 1,328 | 1,674 | 1,586 | 1,318 | 2,262 | 2,089 | 3,267 | 19,975 |

Source: Statisticki bilten Sluzbe drustvenog knjigovodsta, No. 2 (1963), Table 19, No. 1 (1958), Table 33, No. 2 (1959), Table 34, No. 2 (1960), Table 34, No. 2 (1961), Table 34, No. 2 (1963), Table 39, No. 2 (1965), Table 26, No. 2 (1966), Table 32, No. 2 (1967), Table 32, No. 2 (1968), Table 31, No. 2 (1969), Table 33, No. 3 (1970), Table 33, No. 1 (1971), Table 33, and No. 2 (1972), Table 33.

## TABLE F.6

### Total Budget Expenditures
(millions of dinars)

| | I | II | III | IV | V | VI | VII | VIII | IX | X | XI | XII | I-XII |
|---|---|---|---|---|---|---|---|---|---|---|---|---|---|
| 1952 | | | | | | | | | | | | | 3,047 |
| 1953 | | | | | | | | | | | | | 2,931 |
| 1954 | | | | | | | | | | | | | 3,637 |
| 1955 | | | | | | | | | | | | | 4,129 |
| 1956 | 293 | 347 | 243 | 265 | 283 | 275 | 265 | 271 | 274 | 356 | 293 | 486 | 3,641 |
| 1957 | 293 | 296 | 307 | 339 | 288 | 317 | 359 | 294 | 287 | 369 | 320 | 492 | 3,961 |
| 1958 | 394 | 300 | 336 | 456 | 367 | 376 | 476 | 402 | 404 | 450 | 423 | 664 | 5,048 |
| 1959 | 479 | 389 | 388 | 489 | 406 | 448 | 504 | 428 | 409 | 498 | 507 | 744 | 5,689 |
| 1960 | 612 | 401 | 514 | 611 | 546 | 578 | 637 | 532 | 555 | 703 | 475 | 990 | 7,154 |
| 1961 | 525 | 778 | 569 | 728 | 587 | 693 | 744 | 687 | 675 | 702 | 637 | 1,016 | 8,341 |
| 1962 | 495 | 498 | 680 | 620 | 731 | 676 | 901 | 727 | 781 | 860 | 681 | 1,283 | 8,931 |
| 1963 | 413 | 602 | 626 | 727 | 698 | 748 | 785 | 779 | 630 | 824 | 703 | 1,302 | 8,837 |
| 1964 | 488 | 627 | 731 | 967 | 823 | 882 | 1,027 | 789 | 799 | 924 | 912 | 1,620 | 10,584 |
| 1965 | 442 | 605 | 759 | 1,003 | 976 | 1,088 | 994 | 935 | 818 | 632 | 774 | 1,789 | 11,015 |
| 1966 | 482 | 507 | 607 | 875 | 658 | 786 | 810 | 781 | 847 | 937 | 963 | 1,226 | 9,479 |
| 1967 | 794 | 923 | 1,033 | 1,016 | 867 | 998 | 1,051 | 891 | 674 | 833 | 1,076 | 1,268 | 11,434 |
| 1968 | 1,084 | 897 | 913 | 1,277 | 1,025 | 977 | 1,114 | 1,173 | 1,069 | 1,169 | 1,194 | 1,691 | 13,583 |
| 1969 | 1,282 | 966 | 1,171 | 1,249 | 942 | 1,207 | 1,196 | 1,063 | 1,160 | 1,282 | 1,261 | 1,651 | 14,350 |
| 1970 | 1,410 | 1,261 | 1,254 | 1,778 | 1,238 | 1,455 | 1,730 | 1,296 | 1,590 | 1,842 | 1,554 | 2,353 | 18,660 |
| 1971 | 1,422 | 1,255 | 1,898 | 2,330 | 1,451 | 1,785 | 2,138 | 1,947 | 1,713 | 2,677 | 2,576 | 3,826 | 25,027 |

Sources: Statisticki bilten Sluzbe drustvenog knjigovodsta, No. 3 (1958), Table 31, No. 2 (1959),
Table 32, No. 3 (1961), Table 32, No. 3 (1963), Table 18, No. 3 (1965), Table 26, No. 3 (1966), Table 31,
No. 2 (1967), Table 32, No. 2 (1968), Table 31, Table 33, No. 3 (1969), Table 33, No. 3 (1970), Table 33, No. 2
(1971), Table 33, and No. 2 (1972), Table 33.

TABLE G.1

Retail Trade Index
(average level Ø 1952 = 100)

| | I | II | III | IV | V | VI | VII | VIII | IX | X | XI | XII | Ø |
|---|---|---|---|---|---|---|---|---|---|---|---|---|---|
| 1952 | 97 | 99 | 99 | 100 | 100 | 100 | 100 | 97 | 99 | 100 | 101 | 104 | 100 |
| 1953 | 107 | 107 | 113 | 124 | 129 | 124 | 114 | 105 | 101 | 100 | 96 | 96 | 110 |
| 1954 | 102 | 103 | 105 | 105 | 106 | 107 | 106 | 107 | 109 | 111 | 112 | 112 | 108 |
| 1955 | 114 | 115 | 116 | 118 | 122 | 120 | 122 | 124 | 123 | 124 | 124 | 124 | 121 |
| 1956 | 123 | 124 | 126 | 126 | 127 | 127 | 126 | 126 | 126 | 126 | 127 | 127 | 126 |
| 1957 | 127 | 127 | 127 | 127 | 128 | 128 | 128 | 127 | 127 | 128 | 127 | 131 | 127 |
| 1958 | 128 | 128 | 128 | 128 | 131 | 134 | 131 | 128 | 132 | 134 | 134 | 134 | 129 |
| 1959 | 130 | 130 | 130 | 130 | 131 | 130 | 130 | 127 | 128 | 132 | 132 | 132 | 130 |
| 1960 | 137 | 137 | 137 | 137 | 139 | 139 | 142 | 139 | 139 | 142 | 141 | 142 | 139 |
| 1961 | 144 | 147 | 147 | 148 | 150 | 150 | 150 | 150 | 150 | 151 | 155 | 156 | 150 |
| 1962 | 158 | 160 | 163 | 164 | 164 | 164 | 160 | 158 | 157 | 160 | 160 | 164 | 160 |
| 1963 | 165 | 166 | 166 | 166 | 166 | 166 | 166 | 166 | 166 | 168 | 170 | 170 | 166 |
| 1964 | 171 | 173 | 173 | 174 | 178 | 179 | 184 | 184 | 186 | 191 | 193 | 193 | 181 |
| 1965 | 197 | 201 | 204 | 206 | 210 | 214 | 214 | 268 | 270 | 271 | 275 | 277 | 233 |
| 1966 | 282 | 284 | 284 | 287 | 289 | 287 | 289 | 284 | 287 | 291 | 296 | 296 | 287 |
| 1967 | 304 | 307 | 307 | 307 | 313 | 313 | 310 | 307 | 304 | 307 | 310 | 310 | 307 |
| 1968 | 315 | 315 | 318 | 321 | 324 | 324 | 321 | 321 | 321 | 324 | 327 | 331 | 319 |
| 1969 | 331 | 333 | 337 | 340 | 343 | 346 | 343 | 340 | 343 | 349 | 356 | 359 | 341 |
| 1970 | 358 | 361 | 364 | 368 | 375 | 375 | 378 | 378 | 378 | 388 | 395 | 395 | 375 |
| 1971 | 401 | 405 | 412 | 420 | 427 | 439 | 435 | 439 | 450 | 457 | 465 | 468 | 431 |

Source: Index.

238

## TABLE G.2

### Producers' Prices, Industrial Products.
### (average level Ø 1952 = 100)

| | I | II | III | IV | V | VI | VII | VIII | IX | X | XI | XII | Ø |
|---|---|---|---|---|---|---|---|---|---|---|---|---|---|
| 1952 | 100 | 100 | 100 | 102 | 101 | 101 | 101 | 99 | 98 | 100 | 99 | 99 | 100 |
| 1953 | 99 | 99 | 100 | 101 | 101 | 100 | 101 | 101 | 99 | 98 | 97 | 96 | 99 |
| 1954 | 97 | 98 | 99 | 100 | 100 | 102 | 102 | 102 | 102 | 102 | 102 | 102 | 101 |
| 1955 | 103 | 104 | 104 | 104 | 104 | 104 | 106 | 106 | 108 | 108 | 108 | 108 | 106 |
| 1956 | 108 | 109 | 110 | 110 | 110 | 110 | 109 | 107 | 107 | 107 | 106 | 106 | 108 |
| 1957 | 107 | 107 | 107 | 107 | 107 | 107 | 107 | 107 | 107 | 107 | 107 | 107 | 107 |
| 1958 | 108 | 108 | 108 | 108 | 108 | 109 | 109 | 109 | 109 | 109 | 109 | 109 | 108 |
| 1959 | 109 | 108 | 108 | 108 | 108 | 108 | 108 | 108 | 108 | 108 | 108 | 108 | 108 |
| 1960 | 108 | 108 | 109 | 109 | 110 | 110 | 110 | 111 | 111 | 112 | 112 | 112 | 110 |
| 1961 | 113 | 113 | 114 | 114 | 114 | 114 | 114 | 114 | 114 | 114 | 114 | 116 | 114 |
| 1962 | 114 | 114 | 114 | 114 | 114 | 114 | 114 | 114 | 114 | 115 | 116 | 116 | 114 |
| 1963 | 114 | 114 | 114 | 114 | 114 | 114 | 115 | 115 | 115 | 115 | 115 | 115 | 115 |
| 1964 | 116 | 116 | 118 | 118 | 118 | 119 | 119 | 121 | 122 | 122 | 123 | 123 | 120 |
| 1965 | 127 | 128 | 129 | 131 | 131 | 131 | 131 | 148 | 148 | 150 | 150 | 150 | 138 |
| 1966 | 152 | 152 | 152 | 152 | 152 | 152 | 153 | 153 | 155 | 155 | 155 | 155 | 153 |
| 1967 | 156 | 156 | 156 | 156 | 156 | 156 | 156 | 156 | 156 | 156 | 156 | 156 | 156 |
| 1968 | 156 | 156 | 156 | 156 | 156 | 156 | 156 | 157 | 157 | 157 | 157 | 157 | 156 |
| 1969 | 157 | 159 | 159 | 159 | 159 | 159 | 161 | 161 | 162 | 164 | 164 | 165 | 161 |
| 1970 | 167 | 169 | 171 | 172 | 174 | 175 | 175 | 177 | 178 | 183 | 185 | 185 | 175 |
| 1971 | 184 | 187 | 191 | 194 | 198 | 201 | 203 | 205 | 207 | 208 | 210 | 213 | 200 |

Source: <u>Index.</u>

239

## TABLE G.3

## Producers' Prices, Agricultural Products
### (average level Ø 1952 = 100)

| | I | II | III | IV | V | VI | VII | VIII | IX | X | XI | XII | Ø |
|---|---|---|---|---|---|---|---|---|---|---|---|---|---|
| 1952 | 100 | 100 | 100 | 101 | 101 | 103 | 99 | 95 | 97 | 99 | 102 | 103 | 100 |
| 1953 | 102 | 106 | 111 | 115 | 122 | 121 | 112 | 107 | 103 | 100 | 100 | 105 | 109 |
| 1954 | 110 | 115 | 115 | 115 | 117 | 120 | 123 | 123 | 127 | 129 | 127 | 128 | 121 |
| 1955 | 131 | 132 | 133 | 134 | 138 | 138 | 144 | 141 | 141 | 141 | 140 | 137 | 138 |
| 1956 | 138 | 138 | 141 | 143 | 144 | 145 | 145 | 142 | 142 | 144 | 145 | 145 | 143 |
| 1957 | 146 | 152 | 152 | 156 | 160 | 156 | 156 | 159 | 160 | 160 | 160 | 163 | 157 |
| 1958 | 146 | 147 | 146 | 144 | 143 | 135 | 128 | 132 | 135 | 130 | 133 | 136 | 138 |
| 1959 | 138 | 138 | 147 | 147 | 146 | 153 | 143 | 138 | 139 | 138 | 145 | 146 | 143 |
| 1960 | 147 | 151 | 154 | 157 | 164 | 167 | 161 | 151 | 150 | 155 | 158 | 161 | 156 |
| 1961 | 167 | 175 | 178 | 181 | 192 | 181 | 172 | 167 | 169 | 173 | 168 | 184 | 176 |
| 1962 | 195 | 202 | 209 | 212 | 212 | 214 | 120 | 202 | 204 | 209 | 212 | 214 | 208 |
| 1963 | 220 | 226 | 231 | 231 | 231 | 231 | 228 | 228 | 228 | 231 | 228 | 228 | 228 |
| 1964 | 245 | 254 | 257 | 266 | 277 | 279 | 307 | 307 | 300 | 302 | 302 | 304 | 283 |
| 1965 | 339 | 362 | 382 | 391 | 393 | 382 | 399 | 435 | 441 | 444 | 447 | 449 | 405 |
| 1966 | 460 | 477 | 497 | 497 | 509 | 501 | 509 | 456 | 444 | 448 | 469 | 473 | 478 |
| 1967 | 497 | 497 | 501 | 492 | 478 | 458 | 501 | 539 | 434 | 434 | 430 | 415 | 464 |
| 1968 | 444 | 454 | 454 | 444 | 444 | 444 | 458 | 449 | 444 | 435 | 430 | 435 | 445 |
| 1969 | 467 | 471 | 467 | 471 | 480 | 485 | 493 | 485 | 489 | 489 | 511 | 516 | 485 |
| 1970 | 528 | 538 | 548 | 557 | 562 | 562 | 562 | 572 | 577 | 582 | 586 | 597 | 564 |
| 1971 | 620 | 637 | 649 | 660 | 671 | 688 | 699 | 705 | 733 | 739 | 739 | 750 | 691 |

Source: Index.

240

## DEFINITIONS OF MONETARY AGGREGATES

Since 1945 monetary authorities have used two definitions of monetary aggregates. During the central planning period (up to 1952) the definition of money included only currency in circulation (notes and coins outside banks and post offices). During the first stage of decentralization (up to 1965) a broader definition of money supply was used, including both currency in circulation and deposit money. Deposit money was defined in a broader sense, involving all sight deposits, both those that were used for payments (balances on gyro and current accounts) and those that were not (e.g., sight savings deposits). Deposit money also included bank checks and similar payment instruments, and float.*

In 1966 the definition of money supply was revised again. The 1953 definition of money supply was replaced by three new definitions of monetary aggregates for different purposes:

(1) $M_1$ = Money supply in the narrow sense, comprising only payment instruments;

(2) $M_2$ = $M_1$ plus quasi-money;

(3) $M_3$ = $M_2$ plus other liquid assets = total liquid assets.

Money supply ($M_1$), defined as the sum of payment instruments, comprises currency in circulation (outside banks and post offices), gyro and similar bank deposits that are used as payment instruments, bank checks and similar instruments, and money float.

Quasi-money includes sight deposits that are not used as payment instruments (mainly sight savings deposits).

---

*Money float in the Yugoslav case (gyro payment system) represents an additional item to gyro accounts balances. In a checking system (e.g., in the United States) it is a subtracting item.

Other liquid assets include restricted deposits,* time deposits, and bonds with maturities of up to one year.

The first definition (up to 1952) is comparable with the data on currency in circulation within the two more recent definitions of money supply. The 1953 definition of money supply is comparable with $M_2$ within the 1966 definitions of monetary aggregates. However, the actual figures may deviate from this rule because of reclassifications of some deposits in the 1966 definitions, mainly in order to correct some misclassifications in the 1953 definition of money supply (some balances in the 1953 definition of money supply were erroneously interpreted as sight deposits or vice versa).

Finally, the definitions of monetary aggregates were changed again in 1972. The main change was related to $M_1$, excluding the "unused investment resources" of banks from the concept of deposit money. The basic concepts have, however, remained unchanged.

---

*Restricted deposits include deposits the use of which is restricted in purpose, time, etc. (e.g., balances of reserve funds, which may be used only temporarily for specific purposes; guarantee deposits by investors; compulsory deposits by importers, etc.).

## TABLE H.1

### Money Supply (M$_1$), 1966 Definition
#### (millions of dinars)

| | I | II | III | IV | V | VI | VII | VIII | IX | X | XI | XII |
|---|---|---|---|---|---|---|---|---|---|---|---|---|
| 1952 | | | | | | | | | | | | 3,271 |
| 1953 | | | | | | | | | | | | 3,300 |
| 1954 | | | | | | | | | | | | 4,547 |
| 1955 | | | | | | | | | | | | 4,457 |
| 1956 | | | | | | | | | | | | 5,290 |
| 1957 | | | | | | | | | | | | 5,967 |
| 1958 | | | 5,511 | | | 5,289 | | | 5,144 | | | 6,362 |
| 1959 | | | 5,390 | | | 5,776 | | | 6,115 | | | 7,480 |
| 1960 | | | 7,854 | | | 7,316 | | | 7,844 | | | 8,993 |
| 1961 | | | 8,669 | | | 9,661 | | | 9,312 | | | 10,577 |
| 1962 | | | 11,846 | | | 10,505 | | | 12,332 | | | 14,284 |
| 1963 | 15,021 | 14,453 | 15,472 | 15,817 | 16,390 | 16,714 | 17,150 | 17,449 | 17,910 | 17,763 | 18,183 | 18,421 |
| 1964 | 17,772 | 20,733 | 22,022 | 22,139 | 20,831 | 20,621 | 21,434 | 21,772 | 22,215 | 21,831 | 21,805 | 21,936 |
| 1965 | 21,321 | 21,887 | 22,898 | 22,380 | 21,996 | 21,589 | 20,878 | 21,660 | 20,748 | 20,779 | 21,581 | 22,854 |
| 1966 | 22,815 | 23,603 | 24,500 | 24,082 | 23,425 | 24,373 | 23,841 | 24,133 | 24,608 | 23,883 | 24,167 | 23,893 |
| 1967 | 24,048 | 23,578 | 22,988 | 23,513 | 23,566 | 23,187 | 23,619 | 23,825 | 23,667 | 23,554 | 23,516 | 23,482 |
| 1968 | 23,334 | 23,725 | 23,138 | 23,541 | 23,814 | 24,842 | 26,468 | 27,526 | 28,680 | 28,800 | 29,236 | 29,093 |
| 1969 | 29,155 | 29,798 | 29,941 | 30,712 | 30,404 | 30,162 | 30,924 | 31,304 | 30,877 | 31,326 | 31,961 | 32,608 |
| 1970 | 33,319 | 33,409 | 34,354 | 36,562 | 36,160 | 32,200 | 36,484 | 37,327 | 37,278 | 38,242 | 37,767 | 38,454 |
| 1971 | 38,357 | 38,707 | 37,966 | 40,136 | 41,121 | 39,727 | 41,719 | 42,417 | 41,423 | 42,338 | 43,399 | 43,883 |

Sources: Statisticki bilten Sluzbe drustvenog knjigovodsta, No. 2 (1967), No. 2 (1969), No. 9 (1969), No. 2 (1971), and No. 2 (1972); unpublished materials.

243

TABLE H.2

Money Supply (M₁), 1972 Definition

Money Supply ($M_1$), 1972 Definition
(millions of dinars)

| | I | II | III | IV | V | VI | VII | VIII | IX | X | XI | XII |
|---|---|---|---|---|---|---|---|---|---|---|---|---|
| 1966 | 21,161 | 21,753 | 22,654 | 22,256 | 21,623 | 22,595 | 22,302 | 22,797 | 23,537 | 22,840 | 23,319 | 23,893 |
| 1967 | 23,641 | 23,106 | 22,325 | 22,780 | 22,575 | 21,978 | 22,309 | 22,745 | 22,613 | 22,549 | 22,492 | 22,353 |
| 1968 | 22,370 | 22,428 | 22,514 | 23,095 | 22,814 | 22,482 | 24,064 | 24,801 | 25,920 | 25,886 | 26,245 | 27,605 |
| 1969 | 26,219 | 26,726 | 26,483 | 27,020 | 26,832 | 26,728 | 27,324 | 27,913 | 28,187 | 28,904 | 29,728 | 30,828 |
| 1970 | 31,032 | 31,457 | 31,619 | 33,253 | 33,045 | 33,516 | 34,056 | 35,487 | 35,467 | 36,364 | 36,025 | 37,029 |
| 1971 | 36,636 | 37,151 | 36,202 | 38,512 | 39,153 | 38,068 | 39,721 | 40,999 | 39,843 | 40,999 | 41,885 | 42,546 |
| 1972 | 43,774 | 44,920 | 45,965 | 46,861 | 47,638 | 48,340 | 51,790 | 53,233 | | | | |

Sources: Bilten Narodne banke Jugoslavije, No. 2 (1972); unpublished materials.

TABLE H.3

Money Supply, 1953 Definition
(millions of dinars)

| | I | II | III | IV | V | VI | VII | VIII | IX | X | XI | XII |
|---|---|---|---|---|---|---|---|---|---|---|---|---|
| 1952 | | | | | | | | | | | | 3,200 |
| 1953 | | | 2,890 | | | 2,940 | | | 2,640 | | | 3,170 |
| 1954 | | | 2,860 | | | 3,680 | | | 4,140 | | | 4,120 |
| 1955 | 4,210 | 4,100 | 4,130 | 3,970 | 3,930 | 3,800 | 3,820 | 3,920 | 3,910 | 3,940 | 3,960 | 4,100 |
| 1956 | 3,920 | 3,850 | 3,820 | 4,040 | 4,160 | 4,350 | 4,680 | 4,920 | 5,250 | 5,310 | 5,400 | 5,530 |
| 1957 | 5,420 | 5,750 | 5,840 | 6,070 | 6,070 | 6,170 | 6,340 | 6,300 | 6,450 | 6,590 | 6,640 | 6,930 |
| 1958 | 7,130 | 7,000 | 6,890 | 7,170 | 6,970 | 6,850 | 6,930 | 6,870 | 6,590 | 6,540 | 6,900 | 7,210 |
| 1959 | 7,750 | 7,590 | 7,790 | 7,960 | 7,860 | 7,820 | 7,880 | 8,110 | 8,040 | 8,250 | 8,380 | 8,730 |
| 1960 | 9,690 | 9,840 | 9,760 | 10,210 | 10,010 | 9,830 | 9,950 | 9,970 | 10,110 | 10,130 | 10,410 | 11,050 |
| 1961 | 11,450 | 11,210 | 11,480 | 11,250 | 12,120 | 12,140 | 12,190 | 11,810 | 11,560 | 11,580 | 11,500 | 12,160 |
| 1962 | 13,600 | 13,420 | 13,400 | 14,100 | 13,620 | 13,670 | 13,460 | 13,600 | 14,250 | 14,310 | 14,410 | 15,880 |
| 1963 | 15,710 | 16,920 | 19,120 | 19,210 | 19,990 | 20,090 | 20,130 | 20,240 | 20,610 | 20,460 | 21,040 | 21,570 |
| 1964 | 20,990 | 22,310 | 23,130 | 23,460 | 24,100 | 23,860 | 23,760 | 24,020 | 24,970 | 25,510 | 25,610 | 25,590 |
| 1965 | 24,500 | 25,520 | 26,650 | 25,900 | 25,720 | 25,180 | 24,950 | 25,340 | 25,560 | 25,360 | 25,990 | 27,430 |

Sources: Statisticki bilten Sluzbe drustvenog knjigovodsta, No. 2 (1959), No. 2 (1960), No. 2 (1961), No. 2 (1962), No. 2 (1963), No. 5 (1965), and No. 2 (1966); unpublished materials.

TABLE H.4

Deposit Money, 1966 Definition
(millions of dinars)

| | I | II | III | IV | V | VI | VII | VIII | IX | X | XI | XII |
|---|---|---|---|---|---|---|---|---|---|---|---|---|
| 1952 | | | | | | | | | | | | 2,771 |
| 1953 | | | | | | | | | | | | 2,620 |
| 1954 | | | | | | | | | | | | 3,665 |
| 1955 | | | | | | | | | | | | 3,581 |
| 1956 | | | | | | | | | | | | 4,341 |
| 1957 | | | | | | | | | | | | 4,705 |
| 1958 | | | 4,299 | | | 4,070 | | | 3,315 | | | 4,939 |
| 1959 | | | 4,066 | | | 4,366 | | | 4,573 | | | 5,720 |
| 1960 | | | 6,180 | | | 5,569 | | | 6,043 | | | 7,062 |
| 1961 | | | 6,844 | | | 7,690 | | | 7,194 | | | 8,118 |
| 1962 | | | 9,496 | | | 8,162 | | | 9,861 | | | 11,443 |
| 1963 | 12,236 | 11,625 | 12,669 | 12,794 | 13,594 | 13,776 | 14,063 | 14,358 | 14,778 | 14,553 | 14,685 | 14,825 |
| 1964 | 14,258 | 17,184 | 18,487 | 18,288 | 17,213 | 16,908 | 17,499 | 17,807 | 18,244 | 17,700 | 17,299 | 17,337 |
| 1965 | 16,929 | 17,378 | 18,495 | 17,547 | 17,446 | 16,991 | 16,260 | 16,928 | 15,972 | 15,808 | 16,244 | 17,710 |
| 1966 | 17,827 | 18,300 | 19,240 | 18,221 | 18,060 | 18,646 | 17,532 | 17,967 | 18,354 | 17,334 | 16,888 | 16,945 |
| 1967 | 17,416 | 17,722 | 16,192 | 15,972 | 16,734 | 15,702 | 15,814 | 16,139 | 15,994 | 15,919 | 15,327 | 15,529 |
| 1968 | 15,676 | 15,876 | 15,355 | 15,114 | 15,849 | 16,407 | 17,540 | 18,265 | 19,112 | 19,246 | 19,143 | 19,509 |
| 1969 | 19,871 | 20,028 | 20,267 | 20,120 | 20,334 | 19,590 | 19,755 | 20,160 | 19,846 | 20,020 | 19,938 | 20,673 |
| 1970 | 21,656 | 21,328 | 22,259 | 23,188 | 23,260 | 22,785 | 22,139 | 23,139 | 23,213 | 23,828 | 22,500 | 23,512 |
| 1971 | 24,116 | 24,488 | 23,645 | 24,311 | 25,858 | 23,563 | 24,212 | 25,138 | 24,370 | 25,081 | 25,096 | 25,533 |

Sources: Statisticki bilten Sluzbe drustvenog knjigovodsta, No. 2 (1967), Nos. 2, 6 (1969), No. 2 (1971), No. 2 (1972); unpublished materials.

## TABLE H.5

### Deposit Money, 1972 Definition
(millions of dinars)

| | I | II | III | IV | V | VI | VII | VIII | IX | X | XI | XII |
|---|---|---|---|---|---|---|---|---|---|---|---|---|
| 1966 | 15,659 | 15,355 | 16,177 | 15,554 | 15,366 | 15,638 | 14,997 | 15,398 | 15,990 | 15,341 | 15,056 | 14,953 |
| 1967 | 15,506 | 15,147 | 14,821 | 14,479 | 14,914 | 13,856 | 13,700 | 14,079 | 14,283 | 14,121 | 13,375 | 13,016 |
| 1968 | 14,242 | 14,282 | 14,600 | 14,015 | 14,668 | 13,789 | 14,533 | 15,284 | 15,825 | 15,837 | 15,164 | 15,701 |
| 1969 | 16,041 | 16,478 | 16,258 | 15,509 | 16,210 | 15,842 | 15,514 | 16,387 | 16,603 | 16,877 | 16,419 | 16,617 |
| 1970 | 18,403 | 18,788 | 18,715 | 18,257 | 19,507 | 19,208 | 19,054 | 20,530 | 20,495 | 20,725 | 19,990 | 19,813 |
| 1971 | 21,574 | 22,048 | 21,370 | 21,248 | 22,654 | 21,359 | 21,287 | 22,162 | 22,098 | 22,775 | 22,912 | 22,381 |
| 1972 | 24,885 | 26,060 | 26,830 | 25,795 | 27,237 | 26,220 | 28,353 | 29,904 | | | | |

Sources: Bilten Narodne banke Jugoslavije, No. 2 (1972); unpublished materials.

## TABLE H.6

Money Supply plus Quasi-Money ($M_2$), 1966 Definition

(millions of dinars)

| | I | II | III | IV | V | VI | VII | VIII | IX | X | XI | XII |
|---|---|---|---|---|---|---|---|---|---|---|---|---|
| 1952 | | | | | | | | | | | | 3,583 |
| 1953 | | | | | | | | | | | | 3,625 |
| 1954 | | | | | | | | | | | | 4,978 |
| 1955 | | | | | | | | | | | | 5,087 |
| 1956 | | | | | | | | | | | | 6,146 |
| 1957 | | | | | | | | | | | | 7,472 |
| 1958 | | | 7,034 | | | 7,106 | | | 6,769 | | | 8,416 |
| 1959 | | | 7,015 | | | 7,584 | | | 8,170 | | | 9,855 |
| 1960 | | | 10,025 | | | 9,770 | | | 10,335 | | | 11,459 |
| 1961 | | | 11,020 | | | 12,070 | | | 13,022 | | | 14,311 |
| 1962 | | | 15,416 | | | 15,066 | | | 16,275 | | | 19,666 |
| 1963 | 21,771 | 18,946 | 19,320 | 19,651 | 20,034 | 20,243 | 21,072 | 21,593 | 22,211 | 21,955 | 22,660 | 22,958 |
| 1964 | 22,591 | 24,412 | 25,569 | 25,976 | 26,964 | 27,395 | 27,419 | 26,739 | 27,631 | 27,527 | 27,560 | 27,955 |
| 1965 | 26,521 | 26,268 | 27,473 | 26,887 | 26,728 | 27,029 | 26,711 | 27,744 | 26,811 | 27,369 | 28,099 | 30,724 |
| 1966 | 30,004 | 29,830 | 30,853 | 30,655 | 31,433 | 32,359 | 32,304 | 32,913 | 33,422 | 33,481 | 33,733 | 35,088 |
| 1967 | 34,729 | 33,313 | 32,760 | 33,279 | 33,342 | 33,732 | 34,500 | 34,860 | 35,373 | 35,440 | 35,868 | 37,749 |
| 1968 | 36,797 | 36,502 | 36,167 | 36,679 | 38,454 | 39,093 | 40,751 | 41,483 | 42,334 | 43,115 | 43,719 | 45,449 |
| 1969 | 44,637 | 44,952 | 45,629 | 46,447 | 46,075 | 47,123 | 48,166 | 48,334 | 49,398 | 49,360 | 50,319 | 52,268 |
| 1970 | 52,746 | 52,329 | 54,218 | 56,704 | 56,379 | 57,846 | 58,000 | 58,951 | 60,139 | 60,536 | 60,426 | 62,311 |
| 1971 | 63,116 | 62,754 | 62,726 | 65,802 | 67,268 | 66,360 | 68,582 | 69,698 | 69,996 | 71,499 | 72,342 | 74,367 |

Sources: Statisticki bilten Sluzbe drustvenog knjigovodsta, No. 2 (1967), Nos. 2, 9 (1969), No. 2 (1971), and No. 2 (1972); unpublished materials.

248

## TABLE H.7

Money Supply plus Quasi-Money (M$_2$), 1972 Definition
(millions of dinars)

| | I | II | III | IV | V | VI | VII | VIII | IX | X | XI | XII |
|---|---|---|---|---|---|---|---|---|---|---|---|---|
| 1966 | 26,055 | 26,147 | 27,170 | 26,963 | 26,062 | 27,327 | 27,592 | 28,208 | 29,000 | 28,720 | 29,255 | 30,202 |
| 1967 | 30,174 | 28,955 | 28,178 | 28,675 | 28,492 | 27,923 | 28,425 | 29,009 | 29,102 | 29,188 | 29,251 | 29,421 |
| 1968 | 29,586 | 29,453 | 29,734 | 30,289 | 30,076 | 31,478 | 32,368 | 32,917 | 33,915 | 34,215 | 34,683 | 36,499 |
| 1969 | 35,792 | 36,291 | 36,420 | 36,975 | 36,783 | 36,853 | 37,432 | 38,382 | 38,880 | 39,496 | 40,420 | 42,022 |
| 1970 | 42,783 | 43,234 | 43,771 | 45,666 | 45,552 | 46,609 | 47,457 | 48,395 | 48,465 | 49,418 | 49,122 | 50,572 |
| 1971 | 50,854 | 51,524 | 50,535 | 52,883 | 53,619 | 52,694 | 54,832 | 56,205 | 55,121 | 56,332 | 57,297 | 58,872 |
| 1972 | 60,637 | 61,899 | 62,668 | 64,389 | 65,396 | 66,143 | 70,102 | 71,968 | | | | |

Sources: <u>Bilten Narodne banke Jugoslavije</u>, No. 2 (1972); unpublished materials.

## TABLE H.8

### Total Liquid Resources ($M_3$), 1966 Definition
### (millions of dinars)

| | I | II | III | IV | V | VI | VII | VIII | IX | X | XI | XII |
|---|---|---|---|---|---|---|---|---|---|---|---|---|
| 1952 | | | | | | | | | | | | 4,544 |
| 1953 | | | | | | | | | | | | 5,038 |
| 1954 | | | | | | | | | | | | 6,814 |
| 1955 | | | | | | | | | | | | 7,096 |
| 1956 | | | | | | | | | | | | 9,923 |
| 1957 | | | | | | | | | | | | 12,197 |
| 1958 | | | 12,312 | | | 12,538 | | | 12,181 | | | 13,567 |
| 1959 | | | 12,030 | | | 13,447 | | | 14,145 | | | 15,642 |
| 1960 | | | 15,228 | | | 15,015 | | | 15,931 | | | 17,786 |
| 1961 | | | 17,118 | | | 17,494 | | | 19,109 | | | 21,315 |
| 1962 | | | 21,707 | | | 22,630 | | | 24,609 | | | 28,131 |
| 1963 | 29,949 | 27,877 | 28,703 | 29,015 | 28,984 | 29,201 | 30,216 | 30,872 | 32,136 | 31,850 | 32,409 | 32,968 |
| 1964 | 31,365 | 33,425 | 34,526 | 34,886 | 35,867 | 36,236 | 36,258 | 35,763 | 36,493 | 36,378 | 36,200 | 37,118 |
| 1965 | 35,664 | 36,139 | 37,221 | 36,769 | 36,919 | 37,605 | 38,786 | 40,206 | 39,584 | 40,146 | 40,805 | 42,610 |
| 1966 | 41,243 | 41,362 | 43,621 | 43,083 | 43,568 | 44,358 | 44,480 | 44,726 | 45,057 | 44,995 | 45,073 | 46,596 |
| 1967 | 45,991 | 45,353 | 44,737 | 45,102 | 45,677 | 45,954 | 46,557 | 46,892 | 47,434 | 47,485 | 47,756 | 49,929 |
| 1968 | 38,774 | 49,056 | 48,981 | 48,947 | 50,255 | 51,254 | 52,881 | 53,584 | 54,601 | 55,597 | 56,289 | 58,333 |
| 1969 | 57,190 | 57,988 | 58,875 | 59,781 | 60,026 | 61,044 | 61,758 | 62,113 | 63,371 | 63,205 | 64,326 | 66,978 |
| 1970 | 66,495 | 66,632 | 68,356 | 70,620 | 70,652 | 72,307 | 72,132 | 73,292 | 74,575 | 75,071 | 75,153 | 78,222 |
| 1971 | 79,351 | 80,097 | 80,301 | 82,851 | 84,418 | 84,492 | 86,338 | 86,659 | 87,252 | 88,851 | 89,841 | 93,653 |

Total Liquid Resources ($M_3$), 1972 Definition
(millions of dollars)

| | I | II | III | IV | V | VI | VII | VIII | IX | X | XI | XII |
|------|--------|--------|--------|--------|--------|--------|--------|--------|--------|--------|--------|--------|
| 1966 | 35,669 | 36,168 | 37,706 | 37,114 | 36,020 | 37,144 | 37,015 | 37,922 | 38,670 | 38,396 | 38,745 | 39,793 |
| 1967 | 39,324 | 38,950 | 38,181 | 38,446 | 38,519 | 37,589 | 37,971 | 38,484 | 38,700 | 38,652 | 38,603 | 39,163 |
| 1968 | 39,471 | 39,885 | 40,517 | 40,472 | 39,742 | 41,284 | 42,235 | 42,994 | 44,247 | 44,904 | 45,711 | 48,216 |
| 1969 | 47,249 | 48,280 | 48,663 | 49,360 | 50,238 | 50,504 | 50,677 | 51,943 | 52,706 | 53,220 | 54,474 | 56,805 |
| 1970 | 56,662 | 57,422 | 58,063 | 60,002 | 60,432 | 61,831 | 62,622 | 63,926 | 64,237 | 65,472 | 65,689 | 67,927 |
| 1971 | 67,799 | 69,670 | 69,168 | 70,791 | 71,838 | 71,774 | 73,675 | 73,984 | 73,057 | 74,276 | 75,295 | 77,757 |
| 1972 | 79,980 | 80,528 | 80,590 | 82,865 | 84,387 | 85,900 | 89,910 | 91,950 | | | | |

Sources:  Bilten Narodne banke Jugoslavije, No. 2 (1972); unpublished materials.

## TABLE H.10

### Currency in Circulation
### (millions of dinars)

| | I | II | III | IV | V | VI | VII | VIII | IX | X | XI | XII |
|---|---|---|---|---|---|---|---|---|---|---|---|---|
| 1945 | | | | 360 | | 670 | | | | | | 178 |
| 1946 | | | 164 | | | 152 | | | 154 | | | 206 |
| 1947 | 196 | 193 | 193 | 198 | 195 | 200 | 209 | 232 | 256 | 280 | 286 | 301 |
| 1948 | 296 | 287 | 291 | 307 | 312 | 320 | 320 | 319 | 332 | 348 | 358 | 394 |
| 1949 | 395 | 403 | 407 | 435 | 407 | 406 | 411 | 416 | 430 | 444 | 447 | 454 |
| 1950 | 458 | 460 | 462 | 464 | 447 | 453 | 460 | 449 | 440 | 438 | 427 | 403 |
| 1951 | 385 | 379 | 367 | 383 | 373 | 473 | 383 | 389 | 399 | 385 | 398 | 389 |
| 1952 | 390 | 400 | 397 | 401 | 400 | 415 | 425 | 442 | 463 | 468 | 483 | 500 |
| 1953 | 519 | 544 | 531 | 578 | 572 | 592 | 616 | 632 | 644 | 668 | 679 | 680 |
| 1954 | 674 | 689 | 660 | 695 | 673 | 687 | 727 | 744 | 786 | 826 | 876 | 882 |
| 1955 | 863 | 868 | 857 | 901 | 838 | 856 | 877 | 869 | 871 | 862 | 883 | 876 |
| 1956 | 830 | 830 | 804 | 887 | 772 | 809 | 818 | 828 | 853 | 864 | 941 | 949 |
| 1957 | 904 | 911 | 896 | 992 | 934 | 967 | 1,010 | 1,073 | 1,107 | 1,169 | 1,279 | 1,262 |
| 1958 | 1,214 | 1,212 | 1,212 | 1,306 | 1,194 | 1,219 | 1,254 | 1,266 | 1,320 | 1,284 | 1,390 | 1,423 |
| 1959 | 1,374 | 1,363 | 1,324 | 1,459 | 1,371 | 1,410 | 1,505 | 1,538 | 1,542 | 1,596 | 1,727 | 1,760 |
| 1960 | 1,684 | 1,666 | 1,674 | 1,838 | 1,693 | 1,747 | 1,849 | 1,810 | 1,801 | 1,829 | 2,001 | 1,931 |
| 1961 | 1,835 | 1,851 | 1,825 | 2,096 | 1,879 | 1,971 | 2,076 | 2,073 | 2,118 | 2,157 | 2,319 | 2,459 |
| 1962 | 2,284 | 2,327 | 2,350 | 2,608 | 2,290 | 2,343 | 2,436 | 2,413 | 2,471 | 2,536 | 2,751 | 2,838 |
| 1963 | 2,783 | 2,828 | 2,803 | 3,023 | 2,796 | 2,938 | 3,087 | 3,091 | 3,138 | 3,210 | 3,498 | 3,596 |
| 1964 | 3,514 | 3,549 | 3,535 | 3,851 | 3,618 | 3,713 | 3,935 | 3,965 | 3,971 | 4,131 | 4,506 | 4,599 |
| 1965 | 4,392 | 4,509 | 4,403 | 4,833 | 4,550 | 4,598 | 4,618 | 4,732 | 4,776 | 4,971 | 5,337 | 5,144 |
| 1966 | 4,988 | 5,303 | 5,260 | 5,861 | 5,365 | 5,727 | 6,309 | 6,166 | 6,254 | 6,549 | 7,279 | 6,948 |
| 1967 | 6,632 | 6,856 | 6,796 | 7,541 | 6,832 | 7,485 | 7,805 | 7,686 | 7,673 | 7,635 | 8,189 | 7,954 |
| 1968 | 7,658 | 7,829 | 7,783 | 8,427 | 7,965 | 8,435 | 8,928 | 9,261 | 9,568 | 9,554 | 10,093 | 9,584 |
| 1969 | 9,284 | 9,770 | 9,674 | 10,592 | 10,070 | 10,572 | 11,169 | 11,144 | 11,031 | 11,306 | 12,023 | 11,935 |
| 1970 | 11,663 | 12,081 | 12,095 | 13,374 | 12,900 | 13,415 | 14,356 | 14,188 | 14,065 | 14,414 | 15,267 | 14,942 |
| 1971 | 14,241 | 14,219 | 14,321 | 15,825 | 15,263 | 16,164 | 17,507 | 17,279 | 17,053 | 17,257 | 18,303 | 18,350 |

Sources: Statisticki bilten Sluzbe drustvenog knjigovodsta; unpublished materials.

## TABLE H.11

### Money in Hands of Socialist Enterprises (M$_1$), 1966 Definition
### (millions of dinars)

| | I | II | III | IV | V | VI | VII | VIII | IX | X | XI | XII |
|---|---|---|---|---|---|---|---|---|---|---|---|---|
| 1952 | | | | | | | | | | | | 1,888 |
| 1953 | | | | | | | | | | | | 1,455 |
| 1954 | | | | | | | | | | | | 2,347 |
| 1955 | | | | | | | | | | | | 2,100 |
| 1956 | | | | | | | | | | | | 2,398 |
| 1957 | | | | | | | | | | | | 2,469 |
| 1958 | | | 2,234 | | | 2,291 | | | 2,211 | | | 2,482 |
| 1959 | | | 2,439 | | | 2,523 | | | 2,676 | | | 2,855 |
| 1960 | | | 3,015 | | | 2,930 | | | 2,958 | | | 3,066 |
| 1961 | | | 3,134 | | | 3,261 | | | 3,086 | | | 3,379 |
| 1962 | | | 3,655 | | | 3,706 | | | 4,179 | | | 5,127 |
| 1963 | 4,714 | 4,308 | 4,322 | 4,096 | 4,420 | 4,700 | 4,384 | 4,563 | 4,939 | 4,702 | 4,515 | 5,581 |
| 1964 | 5,159 | 4,700 | 5,042 | 4,656 | 5,047 | 5,509 | 5,111 | 5,524 | 5,814 | 5,579 | 5,267 | 6,583 |
| 1965 | 5,846 | 5,943 | 6,170 | 5,313 | 5,750 | 6,157 | 5,888 | 6,055 | 6,771 | 6,574 | 6,562 | 8,006 |
| 1966 | 7,860 | 7,536 | 8,130 | 7,427 | 7,457 | 7,876 | 6,931 | 7,194 | 7,784 | 7,247 | 6,870 | 7,474 |
| 1967 | 6,144 | 5,455 | 5,295 | 5,107 | 5,516 | 5,276 | 5,100 | 5,289 | 5,275 | 5,140 | 4,514 | 5,358 |
| 1968 | 5,359 | 4,790 | 4,966 | 4,515 | 4,943 | 5,522 | 5,963 | 6,304 | 6,636 | 6,567 | 5,982 | 7,077 |
| 1969 | 6,581 | 5,885 | 6,131 | 5,778 | 6,227 | 5,976 | 5,886 | 6,177 | 6,255 | 6,045 | 5,759 | 6,745 |
| 1970 | 6,853 | 6,681 | 6,768 | 6,616 | 7,238 | 7,263 | 6,821 | 7,303 | 7,256 | 7,304 | 6,502 | 7,462 |
| 1971 | 7,000 | 7,441 | 7,337 | 7,198 | 8,007 | 7,440 | 7,639 | 7,985 | 7,778 | 7,675 | 7,555 | 8,117 |

Note: Deposit money only. The holdings of currency are estimated to amount to around 10 percent of the deposit money holdings.

Sources: Bilten Narodne ⁻nke Jugoslavije, No. 2 (1972); unpublished materials.

## TABLE H.12

Money plus Quasi-Money (M$_2$) in Hands of Socialist Enterprises, 1966 Definition
(millions of dinars)

| | I | II | III | IV | V | VI | VII | VIII | IX | X | XI | XII |
|---|---|---|---|---|---|---|---|---|---|---|---|---|
| 1952 | | | | | | | | | | | | 1,952 |
| 1953 | | | | | | | | | | | | 1,541 |
| 1954 | | | | | | | | | | | | 2,481 |
| 1955 | | | | | | | | | | | | 2,389 |
| 1956 | | | | | | | | | | | | 2,771 |
| 1957 | | | | | | | | | | | | 2,967 |
| 1958 | | | 2,941 | | | 2,951 | | | 2,777 | | | 2,959 |
| 1959 | | | 2,994 | | | 3,036 | | | 3,289 | | | 3,546 |
| 1960 | | | 3,696 | | | 3,546 | | | 3,506 | | | 3,625 |
| 1961 | | | 3,702 | | | 3,757 | | | 4,738 | | | 4,746 |
| 1962 | | | 4,501 | | | 4,206 | | | 5,336 | | | 7,202 |
| 1963 | 6,700 | 5,429 | 4,974 | 4,697 | 5,002 | 5,252 | 5,125 | 5,584 | 6,023 | 5,798 | 5,725 | 6,767 |
| 1964 | 6,231 | 5,305 | 5,526 | 5,177 | 5,557 | 6,101 | 5,896 | 6,364 | 6,993 | 6,983 | 6,734 | 7,766 |
| 1965 | 7,033 | 6,568 | 6,636 | 5,804 | 6,266 | 6,656 | 7,142 | 7,328 | 8,073 | 8,283 | 8,277 | 9,727 |
| 1966 | 9,585 | 8,487 | 9,020 | 8,311 | 8,310 | 8,700 | 8,292 | 8,705 | 9,371 | 9,271 | 8,867 | 9,528 |
| 1967 | 8,662 | 7,452 | 7,261 | 6,896 | 7,216 | 7,042 | 7,175 | 7,401 | 7,618 | 7,644 | 7,127 | 8,328 |
| 1968 | 8,464 | 7,386 | 7,616 | 7,279 | 7,763 | 9,412 | 10,043 | 10,204 | 10,320 | 10,361 | 9,752 | 10,862 |
| 1969 | 10,490 | 9,509 | 9,630 | 9,075 | 9,327 | 8,981 | 9,169 | 9,385 | 9,525 | 9,432 | 9,088 | 10,043 |
| 1970 | 10,468 | 9,890 | 10,187 | 9,919 | 10,590 | 10,670 | 10,245 | 10,713 | 10,681 | 10,814 | 9,989 | 11,148 |
| 1971 | 11,549 | 11,650 | 11,489 | 11,309 | 12,409 | 11,717 | 11,669 | 12,206 | 12,464 | 12,722 | 12,602 | 13,999 |

Note: Deposit money only. The holdings of currency are estimated to amount to around 10 percent of the deposit money holdings.

Sources: Statisticki bilten Sluzbe drustvenog knjigovodsta, No. 2 (1967), Nos. 2, 9 (1969), No. 2 (1971), and No. 2 (1972); unpublished materials.

**TABLE H.13**

Total Liquid Resources (M$_3$) in Hands of Socialist Enterprises, 1966 Definition

(millions of dinars)

| | I | II | III | IV | V | VI | VII | VIII | IX | X | XI | XII |
|---|---|---|---|---|---|---|---|---|---|---|---|---|
| 1952 | | | | | | | | | | | | 2,079 |
| 1953 | | | | | | | | | | | | 1,697 |
| 1954 | | | | | | | | | | | | 2,844 |
| 1955 | | | | | | | | | | | | 3,005 |
| 1956 | | | | | | | | | | | | 4,170 |
| 1957 | | | | | | | | | | | | 4,922 |
| 1958 | | | 5,130 | | | 4,961 | | | 4,820 | | | 5,075 |
| 1959 | | | 5,091 | | | 5,207 | | | 5,662 | | | 6,122 |
| 1960 | | | 6,333 | | | 6,145 | | | 6,273 | | | 6,545 |
| 1961 | | | 6,575 | | | 5,255 | | | 6,386 | | | 6,645 |
| 1962 | | | 6,632 | | | 6,874 | | | 8,278 | | | 10,639 |
| 1963 | 10,173 | 9,598 | 9,540 | 9,236 | 9,021 | 9,146 | 9,032 | 9,602 | 10,390 | 9,912 | 9,861 | 11,098 |
| 1964 | 9,623 | 8,985 | 9,302 | 8,844 | 9,176 | 9,532 | 9,265 | 9,597 | 10,062 | 9,983 | 9,771 | 11,212 |
| 1965 | 10,416 | 10,550 | 11,012 | 10,110 | 10,634 | 11,352 | 12,681 | 12,721 | 13,497 | 13,900 | 13,996 | 15,570 |
| 1966 | 14,851 | 14,243 | 15,065 | 14,369 | 14,318 | 14,511 | 14,068 | 14,452 | 15,177 | 15,040 | 14,614 | 15,505 |
| 1967 | 14,544 | 13,835 | 13,807 | 13,271 | 13,729 | 13,482 | 13,257 | 13,378 | 13,784 | 13,622 | 12,993 | 14,249 |
| 1968 | 14,675 | 14,056 | 14,460 | 13,735 | 14,197 | 15,629 | 16,317 | 16,757 | 16,999 | 17,368 | 16,704 | 18,303 |
| 1969 | 17,635 | 17,094 | 17,491 | 17,129 | 17,983 | 17,843 | 17,904 | 18,323 | 18,680 | 18,630 | 18,444 | 19,760 |
| 1970 | 19,861 | 19,496 | 19,787 | 19,695 | 20,484 | 20,877 | 20,285 | 70,766 | 20,658 | 20,721 | 20,047 | 22,021 |
| 1971 | 22,484 | 22,977 | 22,823 | 22,849 | 24,849 | 23,746 | 23,227 | 22,595 | 22,853 | 22,893 | 22,901 | 24,733 |

Note: Deposit money only. The holdings of currency are estimated to amount to around 10 percent of the deposit money holdings.

Sources: Bilten Narodne banke Jugoslavije, No. 2 (1972); unpublished materials.

TABLE H.14

Money in Hands of Individuals ($M_1$), 1966 Definition
(millions of dinars)

| | I | II | III | IV | V | VI | VII | VIII | IX | X | XI | XII |
|---|---|---|---|---|---|---|---|---|---|---|---|---|
| 1958 | | | 1,294 | | | 1,297 | | | 1,349 | | | 1,529 |
| 1959 | | | 1,438 | | | 1,535 | | | 1,677 | | | 1,893 |
| 1960 | | | 1,826 | | | 1,882 | | | 1,943 | | | 1,962 |
| 1961 | | | 1,874 | | | 2,028 | | | 2,177 | | | 2,526 |
| 1962 | | | 2,414 | | | 2,422 | | | 2,549 | | | 2,918 |
| 1963 | 2,842 | 2,910 | 2,889 | 3,132 | 2,885 | 3,095 | 3,406 | 3,217 | 3,258 | 3,327 | 3,562 | 3,827 |
| 1964 | 3,689 | 3,709 | 3,678 | 3,996 | 3,788 | 3,927 | 4,119 | 4,129 | 4,166 | 4,424 | 4,689 | 4,780 |
| 1965 | 4,536 | 4,635 | 4,538 | 4,983 | 4,718 | 4,772 | 4,747 | 4,848 | 4,905 | 5,097 | 5,480 | 5,285 |
| 1966 | 5,099 | 5,430 | 5,424 | 6,045 | 5,517 | 5,882 | 6,456 | 6,301 | 6,393 | 6,689 | 7,429 | 7,099 |
| 1967 | 6,758 | 6,980 | 6,923 | 7,682 | 6,975 | 7,623 | 7,945 | 7,814 | 7,811 | 7,778 | 8,337 | 8,125 |
| 1968 | 7,793 | 7,967 | 7,931 | 8,590 | 8,143 | 8,666 | 9,139 | 9,450 | 9,769 | 9,739 | 10,277 | 9,791 |
| 1969 | 9,454 | 9,970 | 9,876 | 10,798 | 10,277 | 10,780 | 11,371 | 11,335 | 11,239 | 11,517 | 12,377 | 12,262 |
| 1970 | 11,908 | 12,319 | 12,364 | 13,689 | 13,224 | 13,754 | 14,647 | 14,498 | 14,429 | 14,866 | 15,724 | 15,409 |
| 1971 | 14,634 | 14,542 | 14,610 | 16,109 | 15,571 | 16,481 | 17,828 | 17,558 | 17,328 | 17,546 | 18,612 | 18,704 |

Sources: Statisticki bilten Sluzbe drustvenog knjigovodsta, No. 2 (1967), No. 2 (1969), No. 2 (1971), and No. 2 (1972); unpublished materials.

256

## TABLE H.15

Money plus Quasi-Money (M$_2$) in Hands of Individuals, 1966 Definition
(millions of dinars)

| | I | II | III | IV | V | VI | VII | VIII | IX | X | XI | XII |
|---|---|---|---|---|---|---|---|---|---|---|---|---|
| 1958 | | | 1,605 | | | 1,625 | | | 1,686 | | | 1,985 |
| 1959 | | | 1,942 | | | 2,064 | | | 2,246 | | | 2,544 |
| 1960 | | | 2,567 | | | 2,679 | | | 2,758 | | | 2,860 |
| 1961 | | | 2,883 | | | 3,096 | | | 3,279 | | | 3,725 |
| 1962 | | | 3,769 | | | 3,784 | | | 3,914 | | | 4,394 |
| 1963 | 4,398 | 4,531 | 4,559 | 4,837 | 4,598 | 4,823 | 4,940 | 4,914 | 4,975 | 5,070 | 5,349 | 5,729 |
| 1964 | 5,713 | 5,838 | 5,858 | 6,205 | 6,030 | 6,186 | 6,395 | 6,426 | 6,482 | 6,756 | 7,084 | 7,299 |
| 1965 | 7,219 | 7,385 | 7,324 | 7,784 | 7,526 | 7,507 | 7,483 | 7,558 | 7,603 | 7,802 | 8,214 | 8,169 |
| 1966 | 8,130 | 8,827 | 9,034 | 9,752 | 9,290 | 9,925 | 10,592 | 10,536 | 10,691 | 11,073 | 11,926 | 11,857 |
| 1967 | 11,832 | 12,175 | 12,165 | 12,950 | 12,237 | 12,736 | 13,095 | 13,049 | 13,089 | 13,169 | 13,810 | 13,332 |
| 1968 | 13,984 | 14,322 | 14,367 | 15,051 | 14,614 | 15,168 | 15,723 | 15,942 | 16,027 | 16,109 | 16,868 | 16,939 |
| 1969 | 17,121 | 17,886 | 17,964 | 18,394 | 18,546 | 19,162 | 19,865 | 19,931 | 19,868 | 20,233 | 21,236 | 21,578 |
| 1970 | 21,781 | 22,475 | 22,733 | 24,206 | 23,827 | 24,463 | 25,501 | 25,431 | 25,437 | 25,924 | 26,937 | 27,092 |
| 1971 | 27,095 | 27,332 | 27,640 | 29,046 | 28,527 | 29,526 | 30,975 | 30,838 | 30,467 | 30,761 | 31,947 | 32,750 |

Sources: Statisticki bilten slubze drustvenog knjigovodsta, No. 2 (1967), Nos. 2, 9 (1969), No. 2 (1971), and No. 2 (1972); unpublished materials.

257

**TABLE H.16**

Total Liquid Resources (M$_3$) in Hands of Individuals, 1966 Definition
(millions of dinars)

| | I | II | III | IV | V | VI | VII | VIII | IX | X | XI | XII |
|---|---|---|---|---|---|---|---|---|---|---|---|---|
| 1958 | | | 1,605 | | | 1,625 | | | 1,686 | | | 1,985 |
| 1959 | | | 1,942 | | | 2,064 | | | 2,246 | | | 2,544 |
| 1960 | | | 2,591 | | | 2,744 | | | 2,862 | | | 3,002 |
| 1961 | | | 3,052 | | | 3,303 | | | 3,524 | | | 4,009 |
| 1962 | | | 4,036 | | | 4,040 | | | 4,162 | | | 4,634 |
| 1963 | 4,579 | 4,682 | 4,700 | 4,974 | 4,733 | 4,955 | 5,071 | 5,093 | 5,103 | 5,196 | 5,474 | 5,852 |
| 1964 | 5,761 | 5,863 | 5,877 | 6,221 | 6,045 | 6,200 | 6,408 | 6,439 | 6,495 | 6,768 | 7,096 | 7,310 |
| 1965 | 7,230 | 7,396 | 7,335 | 7,794 | 7,537 | 7,518 | 7,494 | 7,569 | 7,806 | 8,011 | 8,395 | 8,267 |
| 1966 | 8,212 | 8,922 | 9,123 | 9,825 | 9,362 | 9,994 | 10,660 | 10,601 | 10,754 | 11,135 | 11,985 | 11,915 |
| 1967 | 11,891 | 12,227 | 12,212 | 12,995 | 12,281 | 12,777 | 13,133 | 13,086 | 13,124 | 13,204 | 13,845 | 13,971 |
| 1968 | 14,021 | 14,353 | 14,397 | 15,081 | 14,695 | 15,199 | 15,751 | 15,972 | 16,067 | 16,148 | 16,909 | 16,984 |
| 1969 | 17,168 | 17,935 | 18,019 | 19,062 | 18,623 | 19,223 | 19,932 | 19,999 | 19,941 | 20,314 | 21,325 | 21,668 |
| 1970 | 21,872 | 22,559 | 22,822 | 24,256 | 23,865 | 24,494 | 25,531 | 25,461 | 25,467 | 25,952 | 26,965 | 27,116 |
| 1971 | 27,118 | 27,354 | 27,662 | 29,065 | 28,546 | 29,545 | 30,995 | 30,857 | 30,485 | 30,779 | 31,965 | 32,771 |

Sources: Bilten Narodne banke Jugoslavije, No. 2 (1972); unpublished materials.

TABLE I.1

Interest Rates in Yugoslavia

| | Discount Rate | Ceiling Rate for Credits | Savings Deposits | | Other Deposits | |
|---|---|---|---|---|---|---|
| | | | Sight | Time | Sight | Time |
| 1945 | -- | -- | 2.0 | 4.0 | 1.0 | -- |
| 1946 | -- | 7.0 | 2.0 | 4.0 | 1.0 | -- |
| 1947 | -- | 7.0 | 2.0 | 4.0 | 1.0 | -- |
| 1948 | -- | 6.0 | 5.0 | 5.0 | 1.0 | 1.0 |
| 1949 | -- | 6.0 | 5.0 | 5.0 | 1.0 | 1.0 |
| 1950 | -- | 6.0 | 5.0 | 5.0 | 1.0 | 1.0 |
| 1951 | -- | 6.0 | 5.0 | 5.0 | 1.0 | 1.0 |
| 1952 | -- | 7.0 | 5.0 | 5.0 | 1.0 | 4.0 |
| 1953 | -- | 7.0 | 5.0 | 5.0 | 1.0 | 4.0 |
| 1954 | 5.0 | -- | 5.0 | 5.0 | 1.0 | 3.0 |
| 1955 | 5.0 | -- | 5.0 | 6.0 | 1.0 | 5.0 |
| 1956 | 5.0 | -- | 5.0 | 6.0 | 1.0 | 5.0 |
| 1957 | -- | 9.0 | 5.0 | 6.0 | 1.0 | 5.0 |
| 1958 | -- | 9.0 | 5.0 | 6.0 | 1.0 | 5.0 |
| 1959 | -- | 9.0 | 5.0 | 6.0 | 1.0 | 5.0 |
| 1960 | -- | 9.0 | 5.0 | 6.0 | 1.0 | 5.0 |
| 1961 | -- | 10.0 | 5.0 | 6.0 | 2.0 | 5.0 |
| 1962 | -- | 7.5 | 5.0 | 6.0 | 1.0 | 5.0 |
| 1963 | 6.0 | 7.5 | 5.0 | 6.0 | 1.0 | 5.0 |
| 1964 | 6.0 | 7.5 | 5.0 | 6.0 | 1.0 | 5.0 |
| 1965 | 6.0 | 8.0 | 5.0 | 6.0 | 1.0 | 5.0 |
| 1966 | 6.0 | 8.0 | 5.0 | 6.0 | 1.0 | 5.0 |
| 1967 | 6.0-7.0 | 10.0 | 6.0 | 7.0 | 2.8 | 5.0 |
| 1968 | 6.0 | 8.0 | 6.0 | 7.0 | 3.0 | 6.0 |
| 1969 | 6.0 | 8.0 | 6.0 | 7.5 | 3.0 | 6.0 |
| 1970 | 6.0 | 8.0 | 6.0 | 7.5 | 3.0 | 6.0 |
| 1971 | 6.0 | 8.0 | 6.0 | 7.5 | 3.0 | 6.0 |

Sources: "Kamata u nasem privrednom sistemu" (Interest in our economic system) (Belgrade: Yugoslav Banking Association, 1969), pp. 250-52; our own rough estimates.

Annual Report of the National Bank of Yugoslavia.

Bancni vestnik, monthly publication of business banks in
    Slovenia, Ljubljana, Subiceva 2/V.

Banka, monthly publication of the Credit Bank, Zagreb,
    Paromlinska, bb.

Bilten Jugoslovenske banke za spoljnu trgovinu, monthly
    publication of the Yugoslav Bank for Foreign Trade,
    Belgrade, 7 Jula 19-21.

Bilten Narodne banke Jugoslavije, quarterly publication of
    the National Bank of Yugoslavia, Belgrade, Bulevar
    revolucije 15.

Finansije, monthly publication, "Sluzbeni list SFRJ," Jovana
    Ristica 1.

Index, monthly publication of the Federal Institute of
    Statistics.

Jugoslovensko bankarstvo, monthly publication of the Yugo-
    slav Banking Association, Belgrade, Zmaj Jovina 12.

Poduzece-banka, monthly publication, "Stanbiro," Zagreb,
    Brace Kavurica 22.

Statisticki bilten Sluzbe drustvenog knjigovodsta (Statis-
    tical Bulletin of the Social Accounting Service),
    monthly publication of the Social Accounting Service,
    Belgrade, Pop Lukina 7-9.

Statisticki godisnjak Saveznog zavoda za statistiku (Sta-
    tistical Yearbook of the Federal Institute of Statis-
    tics), annual publication of the Federal Institute of
    Statistics, Belgrade, Milosa Velikog 8.

Vesnik Jugoslovenske investicione banke, monthly publica-
    tion of the Yugoslav Investment Bank, Belgrade, Tera-
    zije 7-9.

YUGOSLAVIA'S FOREIGN TRADE
A Study of State Trade Discrimination

Ryan Amacher


THE POTENTIAL FOR JOINT VENTURES IN EASTERN EUROPE

Robert S. Kretschmar, Jr. and Robin Foor
Foreword by Donald A. Webster and Christopher S. Stowell


ECONOMIC REFORMS IN EASTERN EUROPE

Radoslav Selucky
Translated by Zdenek Elias


OPINION-MAKING ELITES IN YUGOSLAVIA

Edited by Allen H. Barton, Bogdan Denitch,
and Charles Kadushkin